The New Zealand ADVENTURE GUIDE

SHANE BOOCOCK

NEW
HOLLAND

Contents

Acknowledgements

Putting together a guidebook like this one means being swamped with a huge array of image CDs, leaflets, brochures, press releases, website addresses, telephone calls and letters. There are many organisations that unreservedly passed on information that was sourced from national, regional and local tourism bureaux and historical societies: TravMedia, the Ski Tourism Marketing Network, the New Zealand Speleological Society (caving), along with national and regional parks and wildlife services. Some historical facts were collated using Department of Conservation (DoC) information.

Reviewing all the activities this diverse island nation has to offer took me to many corners of our magnificent country – a rare opportunity to discover for myself what a wonderful slice of the world we live in. But without the help of others it wouldn't have been possible. Therefore I would really like to thank Penny Gardiner who on numerous occasions over many months finely tuned and edited my text, as well as Stephen Lunn who proofread the copy. Frequent visits around the country meant invading the spare bedrooms of good friends like Leanne McMillan and Peter McNally, Geoff Holland and David and Mandy Kennedy in Queenstown, as well as trips to Anna Thompson's beachside home. I would also like to thank my friend Mark Gibson for all his advice on surfing, Murray Pilcher for his advice on sailing and surfing in New Zealand, Jack Benson for his bluewater sailing advice, and input and assistance from my good friend Mark Sheehan in Sydney. Lastly, I would like to thank Belinda

Cooke and Christine Thomson at New Holland Publishers for all their wonderful help in bringing this adventurous project to fruition.
I would also like to thank the following organisations: Christchurch and Canterbury Tourism, Destination Fiordland, Destination Lake Taupo, Destination Manawatu, Destination Marlborough, Destination Northland, Destination Queenstown, Destination Wairarapa, Destination Wanganui, Hawke's Bay Tourism, Lake Wanaka Tourism, Nelson & Tasman Tourism, New Zealand Tourism, Positively Wellington Tourism, Tourism Auckland, Tourism Central Otago, Tourism Coromandel, Tourism Dunedin, Tourism Eastland, Tourism Rotorua, Tourism West Coast, Venture Southland, and Visit Ruapehu.

It is now over to you to discover some of the most amazing adventures in New Zealand.

Author Shane Boocock, high above Lake Waikaremoana.

Foreword

As Minister of Tourism and Prime Minister, it's my great pleasure to welcome you to New Zealand — the world's greatest adventure playground. Our islands are blessed with clear skies, a benign climate, an abundance of lakes and rivers, an outdoor sports-loving culture, innovative tourism operators, and some of the most breathtaking scenery on earth. In other words, they are an adrenalin-seeker's paradise. The 100% Pure New Zealand experience offers thousands of opportunities for adventure seekers to get up in the air, out on the water, and into our beautiful countryside. There's kayaking, paragliding, rafting, swimming with dolphins, snowboarding, jetboating, mountain biking, rock climbing, diving, windsurfing, bungy jumping, and hundreds of other exciting activities from one end of the country to the other.

And when your feet are back on the ground, and you need a break, there's plenty of other ways to explore New Zealand. From visiting a marae, and learning the stories and traditions of Maori, to enjoying the cafés and bar culture of Wellington. From sampling our delicious food and wine in restaurants and wineries, to relaxing in hot pools, pampering yourself in a spa or eco resort, or enjoying the sparkling beaches of our summer hot-spots.

Whatever your thrill, and whatever your itinerary, New Zealand is waiting for you to explore and enjoy.

Best wishes

John Key
Minister of Tourism
Prime Minister

Sailing *Arcturus* on the Auckland harbour.

'Twenty years from now, you will be more disappointed by the things you didn't do than by the things you did. So, throw off the bowlines; sail away from the safe harbour. Catch the trade winds in your sails. Explore. Dream. Discover.'

MARK TWAIN

Introduction

New Zealand is a land of enormous contrast, with a geography that includes both magnificent beaches and calm, pristine lakes next to craggy mountain ranges, fiords, wild rivers and world-famous wilderness parks. The potential for adventure is limited only by personal preference. This book provides adventure activities of every variety, right across the country, ensuring that you will experience the very best of whichever region you decide to visit.

Adventure in New Zealand is not something that just happened when bungy jumping first leapt to prominence some 20-odd years ago. It started way back when in the Southern Alps — a place where Victorian-era mountaineers like Alex and Peter Graham and Jack Clarke began guiding tourists as long ago as 1903. In fact, Jack Clarke was a former chief guide at Mt Cook, and on Christmas Day in 1894, in a group of three, made the first ascent of that peak. By November 1909, mountain guides Jack Clarke and Alex Graham and their client Bernard Head had stepped onto the 3027m summit of Mt Aspiring — known figuratively as the 'Matterhorn of the South'. From their starting point in Wanaka the expedition took them two weeks to complete. Today a fit group can hike it there and back in three days from the road end.

New Zealand is one of the most adventure-flavoured countries on the planet — in fact, some folk even refer to it as the adventure capital of the world. What we do know is that active adventures are an integral part of the New Zealand landscape, a place so diverse and changeable that it demands respect whatever undertaking or exploit you may attempt. Our country is 268,680sqkm in size, it has over 4.4 million inhabitants (as of 2010), and per capita more people own boats here than in any other country in the world — so it's no wonder sailing is one of our most instantly recognisable outdoor sporting activities. Yet this little country can supply an insight into almost every exhilarating adventure imaginable and then some.

This guide is intended for adventurers of all ages who like to dive over wrecks, horse trek in high-country stations, raft whitewater rapids, explore some of the best surf beaches in the Pacific, or ice climb in snow-capped mountains. For real adrenalin junkies there are spine-tingling adventures ranging from high-wire swings to high-altitude bungy jumps as well. In fact, in 2008 over 681,000 international visitors — nearly a third of all overseas travellers to this country — undertook some form of adventure tourism activity, which is today seen as the cornerstone of overseas tourism marketing by the New Zealand government.

This guidebook is also aimed at those who want to escape to enjoy adventure-filled holidays, to actively participate in what our geographically blessed country has to offer. Adventures can be undertaken at any age or stage — from hiking a rainforest track or cross-country skiing to sailing in the Marlborough Sounds. Life is about exploring different paths that suit different individuals, and as such your choice of adventure will differ from your neighbour's or your spouse's. The idea is to just venture outdoors and do it.

As Ed Grenby, the travel editor for Britain's *Sunday Times*, is so aptly quoted as saying about New Zealand: *'[It is] the ruggedest, prettiest, friendliest, most cultured, least crowded, most adrenaline-burning, most serenely peaceful, best-value-booze-and-foodiest, most just-plain-wonderful holiday destination in the world . . . the once-in-a-lifetime trip you should aim to do every few years.'*

Whether you spend half a day, a week or a lifetime in our great country, my wish is that you'll find this book a valuable and user-friendly tool for making the most of your activity time here. I do hope you enjoy making use of the guide as much as I've enjoyed putting it all together.

NOTE: There is nothing worse than reading guidebooks only to find a company's details are outdated just a few months after publication, so I have purposely refrained from quoting prices, timetables, physical and email addresses, telephone numbers and so forth. However, I have included well over 300 website addresses that will allow the reader to make their own qualified judgement of the operator, enquire about tours, days of operation and prices, or check current facts and figures.

Outdoor Safety

Every year there are reports of people getting into serious trouble after encountering difficulties when tackling adventures in our breathtakingly beautiful country. People are lost at sea because they are not wearing lifejackets, or someone is swept away in a flooded river, 4-wheel-drive vehicles roll down embankments, glaciers crush unsuspecting visitors who step out of bounds, skiers sustain injuries, mountaineers make mistakes and vanish, and hikers are lost in the bush or during snowstorms. It happens all too often.

Staying out of the statistics

While adventure inevitably presents dangers, minimising those dangers is not only sensible, it just may save your life. So there are some general survival skills that you will need to take on board before venturing forth on your own or in groups. These all have been expanded in each individual chapter, but here a few starters:

- Always read the rules if they are posted and wear suitable clothing for the conditions you're in.
- Keep an eye on the weather and listen to weather reports.
- Carry a small radio and a mobile phone whenever possible — this has saved countless lives over the last few years.
- A first-aid kit is something everyone should carry when venturing outdoors on land or at sea.
- Leave a message about your destination and how long you expect to be gone with the police or wherever you last stayed before setting off.
- Use common sense and be keenly aware of your surroundings to maximise your chances of making it back safely.

Adventure holidays are the fastest growth market in the world — just make sure you don't become a tourism accident statistic on the nightly news or the front page of our newspapers.

Staying in one piece

Whether it's snorkelling in the Bay of Islands, climbing glaciers in the Southern Alps, paragliding in Queenstown, skiing on Mt Ruapehu or biking through Rotorua forests — be careful, it's a dangerous world out there. The following tips can help prevent accidents, minimise the risk, and ensure that your adventure is a healthy one:

- Consult with a health professional before attempting any big adventure.
- Adjust to your environment and respect it.
- Protect yourself from the sun and from biting bugs.
- Wear good boots and protective clothing when in extreme locations.
- Try to ensure your water is purified if you have to use outdoor sources. Carry additional water in reserve.
- Always carry some freeze-dried supplies for emergencies.
- Wash it, peel it or forget it.
- Consider carefully your means of transportation.
- Always have a contingency plan in place.

CHAPTER 1

TOP ADVENTURES

We all have a favourite adventure that puts a smile on our faces and an ache into our muscles. Yet some experienced New Zealand adventurers take up the challenge in a multitude of pursuits, in various regions and in all seasons. The **Best of the Best Adventure Activities** offers a diverse range of adventures from the top of the North Island to the bottom of the South Island, in which the whole family can participate.

For those who like to go to extremes, **The Best of the Best Multi-combos** are adrenalin-fuelled activities that can be completed in either one day or over numerous days — a bundle of adventures gathered together to extend the fun.

THE BEST OF THE BEST – ADVENTURE ACTIVITIES

THE BEST OF THE BEST – MULTI-COMBO ADVENTURES

Early morning flight over the Canterbury Plains.

'Life is NOT a journey to the grave with the intention of arriving safely in a pretty and well-preserved body, but rather to skid in broadside, thoroughly used up, totally worn out, and loudly proclaiming — WOW, what a ride!' **Anonymous.**

This book in fact offers all sorts of adventures; some of a more leisurely kind, such as ballooning or whale watching, as well as those that are quite physically challenging like mountaineering or caving.

Somehow, invention and adventure is the lifeblood of New Zealanders when it involves active outdoor pursuits. Aotearoa (the Maori name for New Zealand) is full of unusual and unexpected surprises, and given its diverse terrain — oceans, gulfs, inlets, estuaries, lakes, rivers, even fiords, thermal hot pools, active volcanoes, spectacular hiking trails, mountain-biking tracks, desert-like plateaus, high-country stations and glacier-covered mountain ranges — it is undeniably one of the world's great adventure playgrounds. With so many escapades waiting in this country, the task of picking what to do and where to do it can be challenging.

To smooth the path for you, I have selected some of the best must-do adventures that are really worth experiencing — the ones that should at the very least be ticked off your 'must do list'. To this end, I've put together an inventory of some of the best places to enjoy in New Zealand. From rough 4-wheel-drive tracks to serene ballooning at sunrise, breathtaking hikes, underground caves, marine encounters and costal surfing spots, as well New Zealand's natural wonders and attractions ranging from rivers and mountains to aerial adventures such as bungy jumping and parapenting — it's a veritable smorgasbord just waiting to be discovered and savoured.

Of course, such a selection is always subjective, so let's just agree to use it as a starting point, a source from which to simply pick and choose from among some of the best spots in New Zealand to explore and venture into — perhaps somewhere to put one foot forward, or hang your hat, or wet your feet, or even float on air . . .

Jumping between boulders on the Tongariro Crossing.

Biking the Otago Rail Trail.

THE BEST OF THE BEST
— Adventure Activities

■ Balloon Flights — Canterbury

It's not exactly the adrenalin rush you'd expect, but an early-morning ascent into the clear air of a new day in a hot-air balloon is one of the greatest pleasures in life. There is a tranquil grace associated with such an adventure that is heightened by the feeling of stillness because you are moving with the wind. There is no sensation of movement, no sensation of rising into the heavens — rather, the earth just seems to drop away. Hot-air ballooning has to be one of the most romantic ways to fly — just add some champagne and you'll know what I mean. Few can resist the attraction as up to 5,000 cubic metres of nylon majestically rises with the dragon burners. Flights typically take place early morning, just after sunrise when the wind conditions are the calmest. As the pilot never knows where he or she might land, each trip is unique and it's always a one-way ticket. **For a round-up of the best balloon flight locations go to page 37.**

■ Bungy Jumping — Queenstown

It's what New Zealand has built its adventure adrenalin-fuelled reputation on and it's what most active adventure seekers still put as a priority on their list of things to do. When you consider that more than 200,000 people have jumped off the Kawarau Bridge near Queenstown attached to latex rubber, it's clearly a phenomenon that continues to be addictive. From bridges in Auckland and platforms in Taupo to a crane-inspired jump in Rotorua, it is still Queenstown that's the place most people are willing to spend their money for 10 seconds of hanging upside down and dipping their head in the water. Add the t-shirt, DVD and still pictures and you'll come away with a lifetime of memories and a slightly lighter wallet. **For a round-up of the best bungy jumping locations go to page 21.**

■ Cycle Journey — Otago Rail Trail

Technically not a serious mountain-bike route — but hey, who cares? This little gem has become the blueprint for the future of cycle paths in New Zealand. So dust off the bike shorts, buy a new pair of gloves and hire a bike and gear for the trip's 3-day duration. With 150km of trail and 618m being the highest point, you can go as fast or as slow as you please. The trail follows, as you might have guessed, the old Central Otago branch railway line from Clyde to Middlemarch. The Rail Trail is a public reserve, and so cars are off limits. Thus cyclists, hikers and horse riders have the route all to themselves. The spectacular scenery is never far from the trail, ranging from mountains, hills and gorges through to old gold-mining towns, and ending among the fruit-growing areas of Central Otago. The heritage of the old railway line has been preserved, with the retention of viaducts and bridges, and some of the old railway stations. There is even a free booking service that will coordinate your bike hire, accommodation, luggage and shuttle transfers. **For a round-up of the best bike-riding locations go to page 61.**

◼ 4-Wheel-Drive Trip — Macetown, Near Queenstown

For visitors who want to explore 4-wheel-drive tracks, this is certainly one of the most historical and technically difficult routes under certain conditions. Located approximately 16km up the Arrow River from Arrowtown, access to Macetown is via a 4-wheel-drive track which fords the river 25 times — the river can rise rapidly when it rains and shouldn't be attempted in winter months. Vehicles should not go in alone. First settled in the early 1860s, Macetown is one of the most intact and accessible historic goldfield towns managed by DoC in Otago and attracts over 7500 visitors annually either on foot, by mountain bike or 4-wheel drive. Alternatively, you can go there with one of several guided tour operations. There are many historical points of interest along the way, with a tale around almost every bend. There are also plenty of day walks around the township or up the valleys as well as picnicking spots and mountain-bike trails. It's worthwhile purchasing a small booklet titled *Macetown and the Arrow Gorge* from the Lakes District Museum which locates and describes the historic features along the way. **For a round-up of the best 4-wheel-drive tracks go to page 51.**

◼ Franz Josef Glacier Hiking — West Coast, South Island

Roll these words off your tongue: séracs, terminal face, moraines, blue ice and crevasses — glacier terminology! Impressive glaciers always look stunning from a distance, but up close and under foot they take on quite another aspect. Hiking a glacier is certainly one of the types of adventure you can have bragging rights to for years to come. Unlike the regular hiking trails around our country, the shifting terminus of an ice glacier presents a whole new set of challenges. For one thing, there are no trail signs so it's not something you can do alone — especially as the route can change overnight. It pays to go on a trip with a commercial outfitter who employs knowledgeable guides who are also fully trained in ice hiking, weather patterns and what to do in an emergency. **For a round-up of the best glacier hiking locations go to page 111.**

Glacier hiking on Franz Josef Glacier.

■ Hiking The Hollyford Track, Fiordland — Multi-Day

Of all the famous tracks in New Zealand, this is one of the least travelled and the only one that goes from the inland valleys to the sea. It also offers a combo: hiking, jetboating and a scenic flight over awe-inspiring Fiordland. This track can be done without guides staying in DoC huts or via a guided trip staying in lodges with all meals included.

The first day of the trip is a spectacular 17km hike through the Hollyford Valley as it undulates gently through native beech forest and alongside tumbling waterfalls. Day 2 begins with a short hike to Lake Alabaster followed by a jetboat ride across Lake McKerrow. Additional hiking takes you through an ancient podocarp forest and on to a seal colony — only 12km. The last day is a mere 8km guided tour of the foreshore sand dunes, lagoon and beach. The final part of the trip is a spectacular scenic flight out of Martins Bay and into Milford Sound. **For a round-up of the best hiking tracks go to page 73.**

■ River or Lake Jetboating Trip — North Island

If there's one thing that will put a grin on your face like a kid collecting free candy it's the day you take your first jetboat trip. This New Zealand invention and worldwide tourism attraction has the ability to send shivers down your spine, pump blood to the brain and set your heart racing. There are plenty of operators and a range of rivers and lakes around our beautiful country that cater to the public with a whole range of different options when taking a jetboat trip: heli-jetboating is one way to do it, or a 4-wheel drive in and jetboat out combo; you can even combine a vineyard tour with a jetboat ride home, or simply do a triple combo trip with helicopter start, followed by a whitewater rafting excursion and jetboat finish. **For a round-up of the best jetboating locations go to page 164.**

■ Marine Encounter — East Coast, South Island

Seeing whales and dolphins up close in the wild is certainly high on the list for many visitors to New Zealand, and there are places on both the North and South Island where operators put to sea. However, one of the best locations to spot marine life is off Kaikoura on the east coast of the South Island. Every whale watch tour is a unique experience and Kaikoura Whale Watch say they guarantee a 95 per cent chance of spotting them. Giant sperm whales

Hiking on the Hollyford Track.

Late autumn kayaking at McLaren Falls Park.

are the stars of the show and year-round residents. A typical whale watch tour may encounter New Zealand fur seals, pods of dusky dolphins and the endangered wandering albatross. Depending on the season, you may also see migrating humpback whales, pilot whales, blue whales and southern right whales. In addition, Kaikoura often hosts the world's largest dolphin — the orca — and is home to its smallest and rarest — the Hector's dolphin. **For a round-up of the best marine encounter locations go to page 131.**

◼ River or Lake Canoe Trip — North Island

With hundreds of rivers and lakes in the North Island it is going to be hard for you to choose which one is best suited for that kayak or canoe trip where there are no roads, no phones, no television and very few other people. Aside from the idyllic Whanganui River, other similarly enticing places to dip your kayak in the water include Lake Taupo, Lake Rotoiti, the Puhoi River, the Mohaka River and the Rangitikei River. You can hire canoes and kayaks independently or book with outfitters who offer day-long excursions through to 5-day canoe expeditions. This is your chance to leave urban life behind and explore the great stretch of wilderness in some of the wilds of New Zealand's interior heartland. It's the ultimate way to take your family on an adventurous vacation.

For a round-up of the best kayaking and canoeing locations go to page 153.

◼ Sailing America's Cup Yachts — Auckland

Very few of us will ever partake in an America's Cup yacht race, the world's oldest sporting event, but the next best thing is available in downtown Auckland. NZL 40 and NZL 41, former America's Cup yachts, now offer the unique opportunity for everyone to participate in sailing in one of these 'grand prix' racing machines. Here is your chance to become part of the crew. You are also encouraged to take the helm, work your arm muscles on the grinders, or simply sit back and enjoy the action as both yachts tack against each other down the Auckland Harbour. There are 2 trip types: a regular 2-hour sailing experience or a 3-hour match-racing experience when both boats go bow to bow. These trips suit people of all abilities including 'landlubbers' with no previous sailing experience. **For a round-up of the best sailing locations go to page 122.**

◼ Sea Kayaking Abel Tasman National Park — South Island

Almost anywhere there is a good coastline you'll find kayakers preparing for a day's journey out to sea. The truth is, even a person with limited experience can be kayaking around bays, inlets and up estuary systems that most other craft find hard to reach. Of course, guided trips are recommended for true beginners. It's the view of the land from a different perspective that sets this adventure apart and nowhere is it more popular than the protected coastline of Abel Tasman National Park. Here you'll find deserted, forest-fringed, golden-sandy beaches, hidden coves and sculpted granite headlands. For additional enjoyment most people venture out in double kayaks as stability is enhanced and there is also the added advantage of having 2 people sharing the paddling effort. **For a round-up of the best kayaking locations go to page 153.**

Ski a Volcano — North Island

Where else in the world can you ski a volcano — and an active one at that? Mt Ruapehu is one of the most active volcanoes in the world and last had a hydrothermal eruption as recently as 25 September 2007. The volcano is the highest mountain in the North Island at 2797m and is also home to 2 ski resorts known as Turoa and Whakapapa, together making up the largest skiing and snowboard skifields in New Zealand. Mt Ruapehu offers something for everyone: fantastic learners' facilities, terrain parks for snowboarders and sensational runs for skiers of all abilities, and some say the best spring skiing in the country. There are huge snow-filled basins, steep chutes, drop-offs and enough soft powder to keep off-piste skiers very happy. On a good day the hike to Mt Ruapehu's Crater Lake is well worth it for the 1000m vertical rip-roaring ride back down. **For a round-up of the best skiing locations go to page 99.**

Surfing — Great Barrier Island

Lying 90km northeast of Auckland, Great Barrier Island offers some of the best surfing and boogie boarding in New Zealand. Although there are certainly more famous surf locations with coveted spots that locals call their own, New Zealand's better-known beaches are often crowded, especially on weekends and over summer. Yet travelling out to the rugged isolation of Great Barrier Island is an adventure in itself, and the bonus is the beautiful deserted beaches on the island's eastern side, combined with the huge waves that roll in off the Pacific — at times big enough to test most surfers to the limit. The 4 best-known spots are: Medlands Beach with its famous Shark Alley; Kaitoke, the largest beach on the island, which boasts a number of good surf breaks

down at the south end; Awana Beach which is noted for its good all-year-round surfing conditions and its variety of waves; and lastly Whangapoua where good sets of surf waves break over sandbanks across the mouth of the Whangapoua Estuary producing barrels in a northeasterly swell. **For a round-up of the best surfing locations go to page 143.**

Tandem Paragliding — Queenstown

Being strapped to another person who is strapped to a large kite is now big business and one of the most exciting adventures to experience in New Zealand. So if falling from the sky is right up your alley, there are a number of opportunities in the Queenstown region including skydiving, hang-gliding or paragliding. Paragliding from above the Queenstown Gondola involves the use of a light, rectangular, manoeuvrable parachute (called a parapente) which acts like a large wing. You don't need any special skill to go tandem paragliding, which is where the thrill comes in — no licence or years of practice is required. It's simple — paragliding involves jumping off a mountainside with a certified instructor and floating gently to earth, or alternatively you can spiral downwards in a head-spinning washing-machine-like ride. Either way it's a thrill-surging rush that will stay with you forever. **For a round-up of the best paragliding locations go to page 45.**

Tongariro Alpine Crossing — 1-Day Hiking Trip

The travel bible *Lonely Planet* calls it 'life-changing' and rates it as the world's finest day hike. If there is one North Island 1-day hike that encompasses all that is perfect about our landscape it has to be this traverse across Mt Tongariro. The Tongariro Alpine Crossing passes over varied and spectacular volcanic terrain. In the presence of active volcanoes you can experience some of Tongariro National Park's extraordinary natural surroundings. A cold mountain spring, rare plants, lava flows, glacial valleys, an active crater, steam vents, emerald-coloured lakes and magnificent views combine to make this one of the most enjoyable and memorable trips on earth. Start early as at peak times foot traffic can rise to 2500 people. The Crossing is a challenging hike taking 7 to 8 hours, covering a distance of 18km one-way. Winter crossings are considerably more challenging and require expert guidance or at least some technical expertise. **For a round-up of the best hiking tracks go to page 73.**

THE BEST OF THE BEST
— Multi-combo Adventures

Multi-combos are adventure companies and operators that combine a multitude of adventures into one ticket — a way of revving up the adrenalin and pushing the boundaries for thrill seekers. The result is usually so good you'll have bragging rights over your friends for years. In turn, it also reduces the price so that you'll get a discount off each attraction. There is an array of choices on offer, ranging from jetboating, rafting, helicopter, gondola, bungy jumping, canyon swings, mountain biking, skydiving, quad biking, 4-wheel driving, kayaking to horse trekking. But here is a list that might whet your appetite when it comes to making up your mind on which adventures you can do in just 1 day.

Bungy jumping towards the Waikato River.

◼ Abel Tasman Combo: Kayaking + Boat Ride + Mountain Biking

Half a day kayaking, a water-taxi ride, sumptuous lunch and half a day mountain-bike riding — sounds too good to be true, right? This company have put together one of the best packages in the region. Your morning begins with a half-day guided kayak trip in sheltered seas from Marahau to Watering Cove. This is a cruisey paddle through beautiful blue waters, past white-sand beaches and idyllic islands. After lunch, hop on your bike up on Takaka Hill overlooking the Abel Tasman National Park. From here you can retrace and map out the morning's journey along Tasman Bay. Begin your mountain-bike descent through some historic private farmland which the company has exclusive consent to access. You can expect some fun and fast sections where you can jump that little kicker or just cruise at your own pace.
Go to: **www.abeltasmanmountainbiking.co.nz**

◼ Air3 Combo — Taupo: Bungy Jump + Tandem Skydive + Flying Fox

This is a combo to put the wind up you! Combine 3 experienced operators and you'll have the ultimate thrill in first-class air travel. To start with you'll bungy jump from the world's first cantilevered platform 47m above the Waikato River. Then you'll be flown to 4500m above Taupo for your tandem skydive with the help of gravity to bring you back to planet Earth. Lastly you'll travel a kilometre at 160kph on Mokai Gravity Canyon's extreme flying fox. Now if that doesn't put some velocity into your system you need to become an F1 race car driver.
Go to: **www.airextreme.co.nz**

■ Hassle Free Tours Ltd — Canterbury: Coach Tour + Jetboating + 4-Wheel Drive + Scenic Train

This has got to be one of those combos that fits the bill for the whole family. The Alpine Safari Tour combines a coach ride, jetboat ride, 4-wheel drive and scenic train ride back to Christchurch. Okay, getting there and getting back isn't all that adventurous but it certainly bookends 2 great outdoor activities in the middle. The 45-minute jetboat ride is through the 'Waimak' Gorge on the sensational Waimakariri River. On the return leg the adrenalin kicks in again as you board a 4-wheel-drive vehicle for a trip across Torlesse Station, a 10,000-acre working sheep and cattle farm. This combo has it all: breathtaking mountain, river and lake scenery as well as a glass of wine on the train journey home. Go to: **www.hasslefree.co.nz**

■ Queenstown Combos: Bungy Jump + 4-Wheel Drive + Jetboat + Rafting

This company works with all the leading adventure operators in the Queenstown region to offer over 20 different combos that will literally take your breath away. Here is just one combo to whet your appetite. The 'Awesome Foursome' is a full day of adrenalin rush that includes an AJ Hackett Bungy, Nevis Bungy jump of 134m (including the 4-wheel drive to get you there), and then a jetboat ride with Shotover Jet in the Shotover river canyons. Throw in a whitewater rafting trip on the Shotover River and as an add-on option you can also have a Kawarau Bungy or Nevis Arc Swing. Now if that doesn't do it for you, nothing will. Go to: **www.combos.co.nz/bungycombos.asp**

■ Rap, Raft And Rock — Waitomo: Abseiling + Rafting + Caving + Climbing

If you are looking for value for money and want 5 adventures all rolled into one then this is for you. ABSEILING: your adventure starts with a 27m abseil into a huge chasm in the earth. Experience the refracted light highlighting the amazing plant and rock formations — a truly awesome descent. GLOW WORMS: you will cave upstream to the cathedral-style 400sqm cavern where you will witness a glow-worm display that will absolutely light up your life. BLACKWATER RAFTING: next, blackwater raft downstream floating through caverns filled with more glow worms. CAVING: squeeze through passages until you reach the exit. ROCK CLIMBING: the final challenge is a breathtaking 20m climb back to the

Jetboating on the Shotover River.

rest of the world where a well-deserved hot shower awaits. Everything you need is provided including full wetsuit, boots, helmet and all safety equipment. You just need your swimsuit, towel and a spare pair of socks. Allow 5 hours to complete your adventure. The main caves in the area are Waitomo Cave, Ruakuri Cave, Aranui Cave and Gardners Gut.
Go to: **www.caveraft.com/blackwater-rafting**

■ Simply Wild Combo — Nelson: Heli-Biking + Heli-Hiking + Heli-Rafting + Sea Kayaking + Sailing

This might well be the ultimate New Zealand combo adventure. Called 'Journeys at the Edge', this is a continuous 4-day adventure featuring heli-biking, heli-hiking, heli-rafting, sea kayaking and sailing through Richmond Forest Park, Kahurangi National Park and Abel Tasman National Park. The trip offers 5 soft adventure activities plus 5 scenic plane and helicopter flights, through a stunning landscape of golden beaches, natural native bush, wilderness rivers and rugged mountain landscapes at the northwestern tip of the South Island. Consider it a 'once in a lifetime' shared experience for active families and small groups of friends. Two nights are in lodges and 1 aboard the 15m yacht *Simply Wild*.
Go to: **www.simplywild.co.nz**

■ Skiing Combo — Queenstown: Ski 4 Skifields In 1 Day

For those who are undecided on which skifield to choose in the Southern Lakes region you'll relish this once-in-a-lifetime experience. Over the Top Helicopter Company have come up with something truly remarkable by arranging for you to ski 4 mountain skifields — Coronet Peak, The Remarkables, Cardrona and Treble Cone — all in 1 day. Yes, it is achievable but only with your own helicopter and personal guide. So you'll enjoy lift queue priority and the best routes on each field with your instructor and guide leading the way. The trip includes all helicopter transfers, guides, lift passes and an alpine luncheon. It does come with a price tag — but then how often do you get to tell your friends of such an adventure? Go to: **www.flynz.co.nz**

■ Triple Tremble Combo — Te Puke: Jetboating + Rafting + Helicopter

What happens when you put jetboating, river rafting and a helicopter into a North Island adventure mix? The Triple Tremble. The jetboat ride is pure action and adventure rolled into one as you spin and flash up and down the Kaituna River. Next up is whitewater rafting on the Kaituna which has the world's highest commercially rafted waterfall. At 7m,

Okere Falls offers an unparalleled rafting challenge that's enough to give you a bad hair day. Lastly, go for a buzz over the treetops, cliffs, hills and lakes that surround Rotorua with an aerobatic chopper ride. Go to: **www.longridgepark.co.nz**

■ Ultimate Descents — West Coast: Heli-Rafting 3 Rivers In 3 Days

This is your chance to raft 3 serious whitewater rivers in 3 days. The first day's raft is on the Buller River, a full Grade 3 to 4 whitewater in the Upper Buller Gorge. At the end of the day you'll continue your journey by road back to the West Coast to your base where the river flows into the sea. The second day commences with a spectacular flight up the Mokihinui River, a prized Grade 4 whitewater run. This river is a rafter's paradise with unique native forest cascading down to the sandy beaches. After a full day of excitement head to camp to enjoy an evening spent around an open fire with a sumptuous barbecue in true Kiwi style. On the last day enjoy a scenic drive up to Karamea where you'll meet the helicopter for your flight to the final descent. This is an unrivalled Grade 5 rafting run, with technical sections that will set your adrenalin surging. Trips are limited departures or on request.
Go to: **www.rivers.co.nz**

River rafting on the West Coast.

 **CHAPTER 2**

HANGING ABOUT
ADVENTURES ON LINE

From the humble origins of the flying fox has sprung an abundance of different ways to excite adventure seekers throughout our country. Operators nowadays continue to invent and introduce bigger and better ways to jump off things attached by wires or ropes from a multitude of places such as buildings, cliffs, bridges or aircraft. Strapped into a harness, you can swing across a canyon, skim through the tree line or dive headfirst towards earth attached by wire or long lengths of elastic. One thing is certain, if there's a way to become airborne, you'll find it somewhere in New Zealand — and certainly somewhere within this chapter.

ELASTIC FANTASTIC – BUNGY JUMPING

WIRED IN – FLY BY WIRE, FLYING FOX, ROPE AND CANYON SWINGS

The Nevis Bungy.

Flying like an eagle at the Kawarau Bridge.

Elastic Fantastic — Bungy Jumping

It's easy to trace the origins of how New Zealand became the world's most inventive outdoor adventure country — just search the name of the Kiwi who first threw himself off fixed structures. Alan John (AJ) Hackett is a New Zealand entrepreneur who popularised the extreme sport of bungy jumping. Inspired by the Vanuatu ritual and the Oxford University Dangerous Sports Club experimental jumps in the 1970s, Hackett is said to have made his first bungy (the New Zealand spelling) jump from Auckland's Greenhithe Bridge in 1986. A few years later, Hackett performed a number of additional jumps from bridges and other structures after developing a super-stretchy elastic bungy cord. The famous 'Champagne' jump down the centre of the Eiffel Tower in 1987 — a stunt that was filmed and later televised — attracted the public's wider interest in the sport.

As the 'Father of Bungy Jumping', he launched his own company, AJ Hackett Bungy, and created a site on the Kawarau Bridge, Queenstown in 1988, making it the world's first commercial public bungy jump. He later expanded his enterprise by founding bungy sites across the world. Hackett is widely known for his bungy stunts that have earned him numerous Guinness World Records and personal milestones including:

- **1988**: Jumping off the Auckland Stock Exchange Tower, establishing the record for the world's first bungy off a building
- **1990**: Jumping 380m out of a helicopter for the first time
- **2000**: Jumping off the highest suspension bridge in the world, the Royal Gorge Bridge in the USA
- **2006**: Jumping out of the Macau Tower in China measuring 233m above ground for the title of highest commercial sky jump
- **2007**: Doubling the previous record of 700m out of a helicopter with 1499.6m in Malaysia, with his new bungy technology allowing bungy stretches of over 1km.

Hackett, along with his pioneering co-founder Henry van Asch, eventually garnered international acclaim for transforming bungy jumping from a distinctly New Zealand tourism icon into a world leader. In fact, the bungy phenomenon acted as a catalyst for the creation of New Zealand's adventure tourism industry. Kawarau Bridge in Queenstown is now the most popular New Zealand bungy site, a place where 350,000 people visit each year and around 25,000 people make the jump.

Bungy jumping nowadays is one of the most popular adventure thrill-seeking sports around the world, with an 'elastic fantastic' attached to suspension bridges, dams, platforms, cranes, buildings and towers almost everywhere. For the purposes of concentrating on one type of bungy jump, however, just gravity-based operators and not 'reverse bungy' outfits are covered here.

BUNGY JUMPS — NORTH ISLAND

■ AJ Hackett Bungy — Auckland Bridge Bungy

It's true that Hackett rules the airwaves when it comes to bungy jumps in New Zealand, with 4 locations across the country. There is a 40m-high jump from the Auckland Harbour Bridge that includes a walk beneath the traffic to reach the bungy pod. If you are limited for time, then this is the fastest way to see the Waitemata Harbour. There are options of staying dry or touching the water as well as a unique retrieval system. This is an all-weather operation. Note: Age minimum 10 years, Weight minimum 35kg, maximum 150kg, Height minimum 120cm. Go to: **www.bungy.co.nz**

Letting go at the Auckland Harbour Bridge.

Mokai Gravity Canyon Bungy — Taihape, Manawatu

This little adventure playground offers a flying fox, wired swing, wired chair and of course a bungy jump all from the Mokai Bridge. Like all bungy jumping, there is usually no turning back, especially once you are airborne. This is the highest bungy jump in the North Island with an 80m freefall. Options are to go solo or jump with a good mate. The fun part is the retrieval as they winch you back up to the bridge in their water-powered chairlift.

Go to: **www.gravitycanyon.co.nz**

Rotorua Bungy — Rotorua

From a purpose-built 43m-high platform located on the outskirts of Rotorua at Agroventures, there's enough space between you and the ground to give you a few tummy wobbles. There are also great views of rolling farmland, Lake Rotorua and out to Mokoia Island, and far below the trout-filled Ngongotaha Stream. You need to be 10 years of age and over (the legal age limit in NZ), and those 15 years and under must have parental or guardian consent. Yes, it is safe. No, they won't push you if you chicken out. Single or tandem jumps are available. Go to: **www.rotoruabungy.co.nz**

Action and adrenalin at the Rotorua Bungy.

■ Taupo Bungy — Taupo

Fly like a bird! This particular bungy jump boasts the world's first cantilever platform, jutting out 47m above the clear waters of the Waikato River, making it the highest water-touch bungy in New Zealand. Your solo jump will reach speeds of 60km an hour — enough to make your eyes water. The minimum weight for all jumps is 45kg and the minimum age is 10 years old. The tandem jump option is also possible with a maximum combined weight of 180kg. Go to: **www.taupobungy.com**

BUNGY JUMPS — SOUTH ISLAND

■ AJ Hackett Bungy, Kawarau Bridge Bungy — Queenstown

The one and only original bungy is still hard to beat even though at times it has the look of a congested railway platform in India. As most Kiwis already know, this phenomenon kick-started the whole extreme adventure genre in New Zealand after it opened in 1988. The bridge is 43m high so you'll get an extra few seconds to freefall and bounce in space before being lowered to the waiting boat below. Tens of thousands of people make the leap of faith from here every year as it is the only bungy jump in Queenstown where you can choose to bob above the water, touch it, or be fully immersed.
Go to: **www.bungy.co.nz**

■ AJ Hackett Bungy, Nevis Bungy — Queenstown

If you were nervous or apprehensive about jumping off the Kawarau Bridge, then you'll need to drum up nerves of steel to make a Nevis Bungy jump. At 134m this is the highest bungy jump in New Zealand, so the take-your-breath-away ground rush lasting longer at 8.5 seconds will more than surpass your expectations. For many people, this could be one of the greatest personal challenges of their life. Just getting to the platform is pure adventure, starting with a 35-minute 4-wheel-drive trip to reach the canyon. Then you're harnessed into a shuttle to whisk you across to the suspended bungy pod. The rest is all up to you. Note: Age minimum 13 years, Weight minimum 45kg, maximum 127kg.
Go to: **www.bungy.co.nz**

It is 47m to the crystal clear waters of Lake Taupo.

Dive head first off the Ledge Bungy in Queenstown.

AJ Hackett, The Ledge Bungy — Queenstown

Yes, this is another AJ Hackett bungy, but once again there are a few different aspects to your leap into space. The first obvious difference is that it is located in Queenstown itself and is just a Skyline Gondola ride up Bobs Peak to reach the specially designed platform with the bonus of sensational views over Queenstown and Lake Wakatipu. Here they have included a runway, a sort of launch pad that allows you to dive out into the universe and plummet towards Queenstown. There are over 10 ways to jump at The Ledge including the infamous Flying Squirrel, The Matrix, Daywalker, The Elevator and the aptly named The Darkside. Note: Age minimum 10 years, Weight minimum 35kg, maximum 130kg. Go to: **www.bungy.co.nz**

Thrillseekers — Hanmer Springs

This is one not to miss and will give you the thrill of a lifetime! The Waiau Gorge Bridge, built in 1864, is the site of this bungy jump. At 35m high it allows jumpers enough time to encounter the full power of gravity as emotions of sheer terror turn to pure elation in the few seconds it takes you to see the water close up. Like most operators, certificates are issued to everyone who jumps as well as souvenir photos and t-shirts to those wanting that little extra reminder of their experience.
Go to: **www.thrillseekerscanyon.co.nz**

SAFETY AND SURVIVAL SKILLS

All operators consider safety considerations as fundamental to every aspect of their operations. The key to safety is to perceive the risks and to ensure that the experience is as safe and as fun-filled as possible.

■ Companies have to have a number of checks and balances in place, including very thorough and comprehensive task analysis and inspection routines which ensure they are operating at or above the very high standards that have been set. With just a few serious accidents over the past 20 years, it can't be said bungy jumping has a 100 per cent safety record. Most accidents have occurred when people have slipped their ankles from the bungy harness. In the case of an accident, operators immediately suspend operations until the police and Department of Labour personel investigate the circumstances fully.

■ As pioneers of the sport, AJ Hackett Bungy quickly recognised the need for a Code of Practice for bungy jumping. This was then established as a written set of standards — namely, the 'Australian and New Zealand Standards Authority Guidelines for commercial operations in Bungy Jumping'. This document was written in conjunction with several other interested industry partners. In particular, advice was sought from the construction, adventure tourism and alpine industries. This standard is reviewed biannually and is altered or updated as new innovations and situations arise.

■ In addition, regular external audits of the standard are carried out by two organisations — Bureau Veritas, an internationally recognised auditing company, and the New Zealand government's Accident Compensation Corporation (ACC).

Zipping across the Mokai Canyon.

Wired in — Fly by Wire, Flying Fox, Rope and Canyon Swings

As opposed to the flying fox you find in children's playgrounds, the adventure-based versions often run hundreds of metres across canyons at considerable heights in the air. A flying fox (sometimes known here as a zip-line) is a simple device consisting of a taut stainless-steel wire strung between trees, structures or across canyons with a pulley system attached to a harness, basket seat or multi-chair-like contraption that is fed by gravity. Besides being able to access remote regions, this vacation activity has grown in popularity and can now be found at obstacle courses, in forest canopies and adventure camps, and at certain resorts. These commercial operators give the thrill seeker a very fast ride reaching speeds from 60 to 160kph very high above the ground. So strap yourself in and plunge into this category for the ride of your life.

WIRE DESCENTS — NORTH ISLAND

■ Adventure Waikato — Matira, Northwest Waikato

Adventure Waikato offer a wide range of adventure activities such as abseiling, caving and orienteering which are all conveniently available on their property. At 220m long, they have one of the longest flying-fox rides in the North Island. The fox can reach speeds of over 60km an hour at 40m above the ground. If you're looking for a fast adrenalin rush, it's guaranteed.

Go to: **www.adventurewaikato.co.nz**

■ Mokai Gravity Canyon Flying Fox — Taihape, Manawatu

Beware of flying insects — goggles provided. Yes, you'll need to wear some pretty funky goggles as you are launched off a ledge more than 175m above the river canyon. You'll gather speed rather quickly before reaching about 160kph over the 1km length of wire. Remember, even when screaming you'll probably eat a few bugs, so it's probably a good idea to keep your mouth shut!

Go to: **www.gravitycanyon.co.nz**

■ Mokai Gravity Canyon Swing — Taihape, Manawatu

This is one of those adventures that draws forth big smiles and a few screams from people who are swinging like Tarzan. The swing is suspended from the Mokai Bridge and begins with a 50m freefall that is enough to push the heart rate skywards. Swingers (as these adventurous devils are known) can swing solo or as a tandem pair.

Go to: **www.gravitycanyon.co.nz**

■ Rotorua Swoop — Rotorua

It isn't surprising to find yet another exhilarating way to be attached by wire and experience the thrill of speed. With the Swoop, up to 3 people are cocooned in a special harness and then hoisted 40m into the air. One of them then has to pull the ripcord triggering a headfirst freefall towards the ground at 130kph, pulling 3Gs on the way. Expect to scream, laugh and be scared. Located in the Agroventures 'thrill factory' grounds on the outskirts of Rotorua.

Go to: **www.agroventures.co.nz**

Eye-watering times at the Rotorua Swoop.

SkyJump — Auckland

If you take the plunge and leap off Auckland's famous Sky Tower it's 192m straight down! Strictly speaking this is not a bungy jump, but is instead what is referred to as a 'decelerator descent' jump, using a steel cable and decelerator system rather than an elastic rope. It can be likened to freefalling while attached to a wire — just like a movie stuntman. SkyJump is one of New Zealand's best-known and thrilling tourist attractions and one of Auckland City's 'don't miss!' experiences. You'll fall extremely fast (approximately 85kph) for around 11 seconds and then come to a very smooth landing in the plaza below. It is estimated that 10,000 people a year jump from Sky Tower.

Go to: **www.skyjump.co.nz**

Views across Auckland from the SkyJump at the Sky Tower.

WIRE DESCENTS — SOUTH ISLAND

■ AJ Hackett Bungy, Nevis Arc — Queenstown

One of Queenstown's numerous extreme adventure activities is called the Nevis Arc, said to be the world's highest swing and launched by bungy pioneers AJ Hackett Bungy. Now all you thrill-seeking specialists can swing down through a 500m-wide gorge. Located at the Nevis Gorge, you can choose your maximum fear level in a 300m arc down through the valley, followed by the choice to continue solo or in tandem. Release yourself and your fear factor and you'll then accelerate to 125kph! Go to: **www.bungy.co.nz**

■ Shotover Canyon Swing — Queenstown

For fans of cliff-edge diving this is a classic. First there is the 60m freefall until the ropes pendulum you out smoothly over the river at 150km an hour in a giant 200m arc. The purpose-built, cliff-mounted platform is the starting point at 109m high. There are no speed bumps here. At the platform you are fitted into a seat and chest harness and connected to the jump ropes. Being secured in a full body harness leaves your arms and legs free to do what they want as you head off the platform in any conceivable position. There are over 10 ways of jumping or being released ranging from mild to mind-blowing. If you can't jump yourself, there's a specially designed launch system to release you. Good old gravity does the rest in one of the most spectacular valleys in the Southern Alps region. Go to: **www.canyonswing.co.nz**

TOP All Black Dan Carter trying out the Nevis Arc.

BOTTOM Mahe Drysdale and Olaf Tufte heading into the canyon on the Nevis Arc Tandem.

The world's longest flying fox at Cable Bay, Nelson.

■ Skywire — Cable Bay, Nelson

Sunny Nelson lays claim to the world's longest flying-fox adventure with this specially designed 4-seater flying-fox contraption called the Skywire — a first of its kind and a one-off invention. The ride takes place at a height of 130m above native forest and you'll fly like a bird for 3km. Once you're in motion, expect the first 800m of freewheeling drop to reach speeds of 100kph, as the chair goes both forward and backwards — and expect a weird feeling in reverse as well. You'll experience high speeds mixed with absolute quiet as you swing in the harnessed comfort of your racing-car seats for all of 10 minutes.

Go to: **www.happyvalleyadventures.co.nz**

Old and young will enjoy Queenstown's Ziptrek tours.

■ Ziptrek — Bobs Peak, Queenstown

The newest adventure attraction in Queenstown opened in December 2009. Fully guided Ziptrek Ecotours take you on an inspiring 2-hour journey through the forest via a series of observation platforms and flying foxes. The foxes operate on cables anchored between treetop platforms. (The Douglas fir trees are not at all damaged in their 'tower' role.) Intrepid zip-liners are outfitted with a climbing harness and then attached to the cable with a pulley. At each aerial launch platform, you'll step off to soar down the cable. While attached, you can move around freely and position yourself in various ways (even upside down) to take in the view from any angle you choose. Between flying foxes, Ziptrek guides offer an interpretive adventure with a strong ecological focus.

Go to: **www.queenstown-nz.co.nz**

SAFETY AND SURVIVAL SKILLS

It would be fair to say that many of the 'wired in' adventure activities outlined above seem dangerous, but as New Zealand authorities certify extreme adventures with a comprehensive range of regulations, there have been only a handful of injuries sustained from taking part in wire-related sports. These are more likely to be of the pulled muscle or backache variety, so otherwise you should just go out and enjoy the different options on offer and feel perfectly safe.

CHAPTER 3

Ever since humans first observed birds fly they have tried to emulate this achievement. Leonardo da Vinci certainly sketched out a few ideas and gave the Italians the first look at what a man-made contraption might be capable of, should anyone have been stupid enough to test it. In reality it took centuries to finally come up with a way to lift those flimsy wings into the air for any length of time, notably when the Wright brothers first managed to become airborne at the turn of the last century, albeit with an engine. It is also inconclusive whether Richard Pearse, a New Zealander in the South Island, managed mechanically powered flight before the Wright brothers, yet it can be confirmed that at least one of his powered flights took place on 31 March 1903. Nowadays there are so many ways to fly without an engine and sometimes without instruments that it's hard to keep a wing count. If you intend taking an airborne adventure that requires you to be in a sling alongside or attached by a harness to an instructor, such as hang-gliding, paragliding or sky diving, then it is known as a tandem ride. So when checking out websites always look for the 'tandem' tag to click you immediately through to their options. For those of you amping to fly through the air or fall from the sky, you're sure to come across it one way or another in this chapter.

SOARING
ADVENTURES ON HIGH

ON A WING AND A PRAYER – SKYDIVING

ON CLOUD NINE – HOT-AIR BALLOONS

THERMAL GLIDE – GLIDING, HANG-GLIDING, PARAGLIDING

WINGING IT – AQUA AIR, FREEFALL EXTREME, MICROLIGHT FLYING, RED CAT BIPLANE

Skydiving in tandem is a true leap of faith.

On a Wing and a Prayer — Skydiving

How many people, I wonder, have jumped out of a plane shouting 'Geronimo!'? Undoubtedly skydiving will always be edgy, adrenalin fuelled and a personally challenging adventure. As you'd expect, virtually any town that has an airport probably has some skydiving enthusiasts and tandem skydiving operators. From the top of the North Island to the bottom of the South, small planes in summer and winter will be taking off and letting adventure junkies strap themselves to an instructor for the once-in-a-lifetime leap of faith.

Discovering the adrenalin rush and overcoming your fears is what skydiving is all about. The planes you'll fly in will vary in size and usually be small, allowing for between 5 tandem jumpers (10 slots) and 8 tandem jumpers (16 slots). Most companies fly daily but always check first as they need the sky above the airports to be clear with few clouds and the wind must be less than 25 knots on the ground. New Zealand itself is a dream place to skydive due to such a variety of sensational scenery that it's a marvel our skies aren't even more crowded. If you want to freefall at 200kph then get a jump start on everyone else and pull the ripcord and check out some of the top operators in our heavenly skies.

Note: Expect to pay additional dollars for digital images and the DVDs on top of the price of jumping out of a plane. It's all part of the marketing that goes with many adventure-based activities. Your own cameras are sometimes allowed in the planes (check the website's FAQs first as some operators ban them) but they are NOT allowed to be used on any parachute descents for safety reasons.

SKYDIVING — NORTH ISLAND

■ Freefall Skydive — Taupo Airport
They say Taupo is the Mecca of freefall gravity adventures in New Zealand and they may well be right. Lake Taupo, if you didn't already know it, is the gateway to Tongariro National Park and some of the most stunning scenery to be found anywhere in the world. So all you have to do now is decide whether to jump from 3650m for a 45-second freefall or step out at 4500m for a 60-second freefall. The rest is up to you, your instructor and gravity. Expect about 5 minutes under the parachute before landing. Go to: **www.freefall.net.nz**

■ NZone Skydive Rotorua — Rotorua Airport
They say one skydive is the same as the next but instructors know differently. Rotorua has geothermic geysers, mud pools and lakes surrounded by volcanic mountains and huge forests making jumping out of a plane at 4500m a unique achievement and one that will last in your memory a lifetime. With NZone you have the choice of a 25-second freefall from 2750m, a 45-second freefall from 3650m, or a 60-second freefall from 4500m. Whatever the choice, it will be mind-blowing. Go to: **www.nzone.biz**

■ NZ Skydive — Mercer Skydiving Centre, Auckland
Located just 40 minutes from Auckland, the Mercer Skydiving Centre is the nearest place to our biggest city to find tandem skydiving. Once you have gone through a 10-minute briefing it's time for a 20-minute scenic flight before exiting the plane at either 2100m or 4500m. Expect a freefall of 45 to 55 seconds at up to 200kph with a 5-minute parachute descent. Maximum passenger weight 100kg. They offer a free daily Auckland return door-to-door shuttle service. Go to: **www.nzskydive.com**

■ NZ Skydive — Paihia, Bay Of Islands
This is the same company that handles the Auckland skydiving reins. The Bay of Islands is again one of those places that begs to be seen from above to appreciate just how stunning the region is below. This 45 to 55 second freefall will give you a 100 per cent adrenalin rush. Exit altitudes are 1800m and 3600m, giving you a terminal velocity of 200kph. Go to: **www.nzskydive.com**

Tandem skydiving in the South Island.

An aerial view of Lake Taupo.

Soaring above the Southern Alps in Queenstown.

▨ Skydive Ballistic Blondes — Whangarei, Northland

If you're having a blonde moment, then it may well be your lucky day. Ballistic Blondes are serious about the art of skydiving and they are now operating out of Whangarei (as well as Auckland and the Bay of Islands). You'll be strapped to one of their big air junkies and drop out of the plane at 3650m to experience freefall down to 1500m, before suddenly all goes nice and quiet as you glide above Whangarei Harbour before landing at Onerahi Airport. Go to: **www.skydiveballisticblondes.co.nz**

▨ Skydive Lake Taupo — Taupo Airport

Welcome to the Central Plateau and some of the most breathtaking landscapes on the planet. For an unrestricted view of the earth below try their 3600m shortfall or their 4500m exit strategy. This outfit's motto is 'Fear is Temporary — Achievement is Permanent'. Like all skydiving companies, they supply you with a jumpsuit, gloves, a hat and goggles. Go to: **www.skydivetaupo.co.nz**

▨ Skydive Waikato — Matamata

Strapped into a dual harness is one way to make sure you're going to jump above the beautiful Waikato region. There's no turning back at 2700m, 3000m or 3600m. The parachute ride can be a wild descent with exciting spiral turns or a gentle scenic flight — the choice is yours. You'll be in freefall for about 35 to 45 seconds until your chute is deployed at 1500m. Go to: **www.freefall.co.nz**

▨ Skydive Zone — Kerikeri, Northland

For the highest skydive north of Auckland make your way up to Kerikeri. Here you can float back to earth for 60 seconds at 200kph from 4500m. The plane's exit door is not a good place to experience vertigo as you will be about 3km in altitude above Kiwi-land. They offer a free pick-up service from Kerikeri or Paihia. Go to: **www.gojump.co.nz**

▨ Taupo Tandem Skydiving — Taupo Airport

Adrenalin rises as you ascend in altitude for this sensational skydive. Up to 8 tandem jumpers can fit into their planes so it's a great opportunity for you to jump with mates or family. The guy jumping ahead of you with the head-mounted camera is there to record the occasion, so don't worry, be happy and smile. Choose a 3600m or 4500m jump and gently drift back to earth with views of the towering summit of Mt Ruapehu and Tongariro National Park. Go to: **www.tts.net.nz**

SKYDIVING — SOUTH ISLAND

■ NZone Skydive Queenstown — Queenstown Airport

Plummeting to earth at 200kph sounds exhilarating and it will have the heart pounding in the adventure capital of Aotearoa. This pure alpine scenery should be seen from above not below. The drop zone is just 15 minutes from town so you'll be able to brag about it faster than you freefall. They offer exits of a 25-second freefall from 2750m, a 45-second freefall from 3650m, or a 60-second freefall at 4500m.
Go to: **www.nzone.biz**

■ Skydive Abel Tasman — Motueka Airport

If this is your first ever parachute jump, don't worry, one of the instructors here has jumped over 15,000 times so he knows the ropes. You'll have stunning views as you climb to altitude over snow-capped mountains, golden beaches and turquoise seas.

Then you'll have 50 seconds of adrenalin-fuelled freefall over the Tasman District, taking in views of both the North and South Islands of New Zealand. Skydive Abel Tasman is a skydive company owned and operated by a skydiver who has a passion for the sport. They offer 2 jumps: 3600m and 3960m.
Go to: **www.skydive.co.nz**

■ Skydive Kaikoura — Kaikoura Airport

If you want to go whale watching then do it in style, gliding to earth for 5 minutes under a parachute. They don't actually guarantee you'll spot any cetacean mammals, but then the backdrop of alpine and east coast scenery all but makes up for it. This is a more one-on-one personal skydiving service providing instruction in English, Dutch, German and with the odd Kiwi slang word thrown in. Try a 2700m, 3350m or a 50-second freefall from 3960m.
Go to: **www.skydivekaikoura.co.nz**

Floating over Kaikoura on a tandem skydive.

Enjoying the ride above Wanaka.

■ Skydive Wanaka — Wanaka Airport

Skydiving with a difference is what they offer in Wanaka. As much as the flight to altitude and the experience of freefall is the same, it's the location that sometimes defines the overall experience. The hard-to-match scenery including Aoraki/Mt Cook and Mt Aspiring makes this drop zone very special. This experienced and highly qualified skydive team are dedicated to giving you a personalised experience and helping you take adventure tourism to its most extreme level with minimum risk and maximum adrenalin return — jumps are from 3600m and 4500m. Go to: **www.skydivewanaka.com**

■ Skydive New Zealand — Fox Glacier Airport

Combine awesome coastal, rainforest, alpine and glacier scenery with a tandem skydive and you get a totally exhilarating activity. If you have already hiked over it and climbed up it, now's the time to skydive above Fox Glacier. Before you take that leap of faith, you'll fly around mighty Aoraki/Mt Cook and over the top of the Fox and Franz Josef glaciers taking in panoramic views of the most spectacular parts of the Southern Alps. The company is based at Fox Glacier and jumps from 2700m and 3600m give you 30 to 45 seconds of freefall. Go to: **www. skydivingnz.co.nz**

SAFETY AND SURVIVAL SKILLS

Watch the DVD, listen to your instructor, don't panic, breathe normally and remember it's compulsory to wear a parachute attached to your instructor. Skydiving is always weather dependent, so operators will not fly in strong winds, in rainy conditions or snowstorms, especially in alpine regions. There is usually a minimum age limit and height size, plus a maximum weight limit, and closed footwear is required to ensure your safety. All operators are certified and regulated under New Zealand Civil Aviation Authority rules.

On Cloud Nine — Hot-air Balloons

HOT-AIR BALLOONING — NORTH ISLAND

■ Balloon Expedition Company — Auckland

This well-known Auckland operator has been successfully launching balloons for over 17 years, with the same pilot who has logged over 1500+ hours. They handle bookings by appointment for individuals and groups of up to 8 people. Balloon flights are by nature dependent on wind speed and direction. Therefore their flights take place over Auckland's northwest and/or the upper reaches of the harbour, although they do on occasion fly over Auckland City. While flight duration is approximately 1 hour, the availability of suitable landing sites will determine actual time in the air.
Go to: **www.balloonexpeditions.co.nz**

■ Early Morning Balloons — Hawke's Bay

What better place to go ballooning than over Hawke's Bay wine country? Your sunrise rendezvous is on the outskirts of Hastings where the launch sites are decided to get the best advantage of wind direction. The group is small with just 6 passengers and the pilot. Rising majestically, the balloon drifts over a patchwork of farmland, vineyards, orchards and Hastings, all with a picturesque mountain backdrop. After packing up, share a traditional ballooning picnic before returning to the meeting place and perhaps fitting in a vineyard visit afterwards to celebrate. Like all balloon companies, their chase vehicle will return you to your vehicle at the launch site. Expect a 1-hour flight and a 4-hour total excursion.
Go to: **www.early-am-balloons.co.nz**

■ Early Morning Balloons — Wairarapa

This is another part of the country where an early-morning balloon flight makes you thirst for a glass of bubbles afterwards. Join a group of 10 passengers and the pilot. It's warm inside the basket so dress as though you're going for a stroll outside. Part of the magic of ballooning is that the pilot never knows in advance where you will land. However, the wide open landscape of the Wairarapa makes for ideal landing sites that could include anything from a school playground to a vineyard — now that would be appropriate! Flight time is approximately 1 hour out of a 4-hour total excursion.
Go to: **www.early-am-balloons.co.nz**

■ Kiwi Balloon Company — Hamilton, Waikato

This company operates flights daily depending on the weather over the Waikato. The balloon was built in the Czech Republic and is 10 storeys high with a basket that holds 9 to 10 passengers, making it one of the biggest in New Zealand. Like all balloons, it can go up and down but cannot be steered. Normally, the balloon takes off in the early morning somewhere around sunrise. It takes 30 minutes for the team to assemble it and the flight lasts 1 hour. As usual, you'll land somewhere in the direction the breeze has taken your basket. The total excursion lasts about 4 hours.
Go to: **www.kiwiballooncompany.co.nz**

■ Let's Go Ballooning — Whangarei, Northland

Wafting over gentle landscapes of rolling green hills and numerous streams, this Northland adventure will fulfil your passion for ballooning. Based in Whangarei, the gateway to the North, Let's Go Ballooning offer sunrise flights in their gentle giant from the first day of November to the last day of February. As with all ballooning, you'll assist with preparing the balloon beforehand and packing it away again at the end of the flight. From start to finish it usually takes 4 hours with 35 to 40 minutes in the air. Expect to fly about 10km from the takeoff point and gain altitude of anywhere between 150m and 1200m. Go to: **www.letsgoballooning.co.nz**

HOT-AIR BALLOONING — SOUTH ISLAND

▓ Aoraki (Hot-Air) Balloon Safaris — Methven, Canterbury

Aoraki Balloon Safaris has been operating since 1992, with its main base at Methven (by Mt Hutt) on the Central Canterbury Plains. They have a total of 6 balloons of which 5 are Aerostar Internationals. The company claims to have taken aloft the oldest known person to have ever flown in a hot-air balloon. On 25 September 1996, Florence Laine, at 102 years and three months, made her very special flight. Nestled well inland, the Canterbury Plains are what you'll be flying over, the prevailing breeze from the Southern Alps gently ushering your flight out across the plains with views up to 300km. The Methven location also allows your balloon to be flown to higher altitudes for a portion of the flight without any restrictions. Flight times are 1 hour approximately — followed by a champagne breakfast, of course.

Go to: **www.nzballooning.com**

▓ Sunrise Balloons — Queenstown

This is one special place to wake up early and watch the sunrise surrounded by a truly majestic landscape. From your wicker basket you'll have views of Coronet Peak and The Remarkables skifields, Mt Aspiring in the Southern Alps and Mt Tutoko in Fiordland National Park. A bonus is Lake Wakatipu, Lake Hayes and the Shotover and Kawarau rivers. Some locations used in *The Lord of the Rings* movie trilogy can also be seen, including Mt Earnslaw, one of the great mountains seen in Isengard. Balloon capacities vary from 6 to 7 adults, 10 to 12 adults, and 12 to 14 adults.

Go to: **www.ballooningnz.com**

Dawn take-off in Queenstown.

BALLOON FESTIVALS

Balloons Over Waikato

This is an annual ballooning event that takes place over 5 days in March. In 2009 an estimated crowd of 80,000 attended the 'Nightglow' alone, with many other tens of thousands enjoying the balloons as they fly from Innes Common or simply float over Hamilton City bringing traffic to a standstill. The event is spectacular, with wonderful special-shaped balloons, lots of entertainment and a week of fun-filled activities.

Go to: **www.balloonsoverwaikato.co.nz**

Balloons Over Wairarapa

This is another annual event held in March/April. Balloons Over Wairarapa has been held since 1999 in this premier wine-growing and farming region just an hour's drive from the capital city of Wellington. The region's landscape of large open paddocks, good roads and welcoming landowners helps make life easy for the balloonists, crews and spectators. Uncontrolled airspace and absence of a major airport in the Wairarapa gives balloon pilots more freedom than at comparable events. Here you are able to enjoy flights up to 3000m, with stunning views of New Zealand's snow-capped Southern Alps to the south and the Pacific Ocean to the east.

Go to: **www.wairarapanz.com**

Lift Off Levin — Horowhenua, Manawatu-Whanganui

Whereas similar balloon festivals in the Wairarapa and Hamilton take place in March, Lift Off Levin is usually held in early April. The event has grown in stature each year since its inception in 2005, joining the other 2 great ballooning events on the annual calendar. The people of the Horowhenua have really taken to hot-air balloons and love to see them drifting by. This 4-day festival located on the west coast north of Wellington and Kapiti has developed a distinct identity and nowadays attracts a huge following, especially the 'Nightglow' evening flights.

Go to: **www.lift-off-levin.co.nz**

Balloon reflections in a Queenstown pond.

SAFETY AND SURVIVAL SKILLS

Safety is of paramount importance to New Zealand's hot-air ballooning operators, so all pilots and equipment are maintained to the highest standards approved by the New Zealand Civil Aviation Authority. All pilots need a Commercial Balloon Pilot's Licence. Private balloonists will soon also have to sit a pilot's licence test as part of moves to bring ballooning further under the aviation safety umbrella.

Gliding over the Manukau harbour in Auckland.

Thermal Glide — Gliding, Hang-gliding, Paragliding

'A gliding club has been formed at Dannevirke, Hawke's Bay, New Zealand. Mr I. L. Knight has accepted the presidency and Mr E. R. Perkins is the secretary. At a recent meeting in November, after the election of all the other officers, it was proposed to start work on the club's first glider and since many of the members were trained in the R.A.F., this should be ready by now. Another club which has been formed is the Palmerston North club, so that it would seem that the wave of gliding enthusiasm which was recently started in England has now reached all our Dominions. Those who are interested in the former club should apply to the honorary secretary, 6 Barraud Street, Dannevirke, Hawke's Bay, New Zealand.'
Printed in *Flight*, **23 January 1931**

Not everyone knows it, but one famous face in New Zealand is also an accomplished glider pilot — Richie McCaw, captain of the All Blacks rugby team. He has been quoted in *Canvas* magazine as saying, *'Gliding is about being aware of where things are, the conditions, and being able to process all that, just like in rugby. You're using the atmosphere, the wind, and whatever the sun is doing, and you have to learn to use those elements to stay up in the air.'*

New Zealand, and especially the South Island, is considered one of the finest locations on the planet to go gliding. The well-known American aviator Steve Fossett thought so in 2002 when he spent three weeks there with plans to break the world altitude record for gliding. However, light winds prevented Fossett's specially modified German glider from soaring higher than 9000m.

In the South Island, the backbone of the Southern Alps creates almost perfect conditions for gliding, as the Tasman Sea lies to the west of the mountain ranges and the Pacific Ocean is off to the east. As hot air rises in the mountains, colder sea air is drawn in and converges, which creates long bands of lift. In the basins of Canterbury, and especially Otago, the hot summer climate creates these vertical updraughts of warm thermal air, and pilots then circle within the thermals much like hawks, gaining lift and soaring to altitude before flying onwards.

Due to the strong gliding conditions and spectacular scenery in the Omarama area, as well as the entire Mackenzie Basin, this world-class gliding location gained fame among sailplane pilots around the world after hosting the 1995 World Gliding Championships. Pilots go to Omarama to experience strong lee wave conditions, ridge soaring and thermal flying. It is common for Omarama-based gliders to soar hundreds of kilometres along the Southern Alps each day. In ideal conditions, it is possible for gliders to reach distances in excess of 1000km. Several national and world gliding records have been achieved from here.

There are 27 gliding clubs in New Zealand with many of them providing glider training, towing and trial flights to club members, visiting sailplane pilots and the public. Go to: **www.gliding.co.nz/clubs/list**

Gliding over the Southern Alps near Lake Station.

■ Southern Soaring — Omarama, South Island

If you have ever considered taking the controls of a glider, then this is your chance. Southern Soaring offers scenic flights to the public from their base in Omarama. Their speciality is to provide you with the ultimate introductory flight in one of their dual-seat, high-performance gliders. Once the safety briefing is complete, you'll be towed aloft by a towplane, the glider will be released at around 600m above the airfield and your pilot will begin to search for thermals. This involves finding updraughts of rising air (thermals) as you soar along or above the nearby mountain ridges. It doesn't get any better than this as the views are breathtaking. Before landing, you will be given the opportunity to control the glider yourself under the guidance of your pilot. Choose from a 20- or 30-minute flight or go for an epic experience lasting 1 or 2 hours. The soaring season is October to March. Go to: **www.soaring.co.nz**

SAFETY AND SURVIVAL SKILLS

Gliders, unlike hang-gliders and paragliders, surround the pilot with a strong structure, so most accidents cause no injuries, but there are some occasional hazards. Though training and safe procedures are central to the ethos of the sport, a few fatal accidents occur every year, almost all caused by pilot error. In particular there is a risk of mid-air collisions between gliders, because two pilots might choose to fly to the same area of lift and therefore might collide. Because of this risk, pilots usually wear parachutes. To avoid other gliders and general aviation traffic, pilots must comply with Civil Aviation Authority regulations and rules of the air.

HANG-GLIDING IN NEW ZEALAND

Launch techniques include foot-launching from a hill, tow-launching from a ground-based tow system, aerotowing (behind a powered aircraft), powered harnesses and being towed upwards by a boat. Modern winch tows typically utilise hydraulic systems designed to regulate line tension. This reduces lockout as strong winds result in additional lengths of rope spooling out rather than direct tension on the towline. Other more exotic launch techniques have also been used successfully, such as hot-air balloon drops for very high altitude. Flights in non-soarable conditions are referred to as 'sled runs'.

You cannot teach yourself to fly hang-gliders safely but a club instructor or commercial school with modern equipment can bring you up to speed quickly. Initial training is usually from flat ground to low slopes, followed by higher flights as your ability and confidence increases. Training to a stage that allows pilots to fly unsupervised can take from 7 days to a couple of months or more depending on available time and weather conditions. As well as the practical skills needed to fly the hang-glider, schools teach meteorology, flight theory, piloting skills and air law. So join a club or team up with a certified pilot on a tandem trip with one of the operators listed below.

TANDEM HANG-GLIDING — NORTH ISLAND

■ Active Sky Hang-Gliding Ltd — Auckland

If you want to reach new heights, then get to grips with an instructor and join a tandem hang-gliding ascent with these two blokes. Active Sky Hang-Gliding was formed by owners Sebastian Katz and Carlos Palmer to introduce people to the experience of free flight, and bring new members into the sport of hang-gliding. Most of their introductory tandem flights and training are carried out at Karioitahi Beach — southwest of Auckland, about 50 minutes from the city. You don't need any prior knowledge of hang-gliding as your pilot will brief you before takeoff. There is a weight limit of 100kg for the passenger. If you're interested in taking up the sport, they offer structured lessons for those who would like to soar like a bird.
Go to: **www.activeskyhanggliding.co.nz**

■ Aqua Air Adventure — Auckland

This is a spectacular way to become airborne as your glider is towed behind a jeep and you are catapulted into the sky, high above some breathtaking west coast scenery. The instructor releases the cable and you both then fly however you wish, from a nice relaxing float to adrenalin-surging aerobatic swoops. Aqua Air Adventure is run by Paddy Monro, a master tandem pilot, test pilot and designer, with 28 years' experience flying all sorts of crazy contraptions but mostly hang-gliders. Aqua Air are based in Auckland but fly where the conditions are best, often on the west coast from Muriwai to Karioitahi, or out on Auckland's Waitemata Harbour. Go to: **www.gethigh.co.nz**

TANDEM HANG-GLIDING — SOUTH ISLAND

■ Extreme Air Hang-Gliding — Queenstown

Is it a bird or is it a plane? No, it's just another tandem hang-glider taking off again. Way up at 1200m on Coronet Peak is where this young company operates. After a brief introduction to the basics of hang-gliding, you'll take off for an unforgettable flight experience that allows you to skim quiet and free over some of the most sensational countryside around Queenstown. They also offer paragliding as well — so if you want to have a double dose of air adventures, you won't be disappointed. Extreme Air operate year-round, weather permitting.
Go to: **www.extremeair.co.nz**

■ Hang-Gliding New Zealand — Upper Moutere

This operator uses a tow-launched tandem flight offering participants the most intense means of experiencing hang-gliding at its most spectacular. Tasman Bay offers some of New Zealand's best soaring sites with heights greater than 650m and above. These flights offer the greatest opportunity for sustained soaring flight and maximum flying time. Approximate time in the air is from 15 to 20 minutes. Soaring conditions will extend time aloft depending on time availability and passenger comfort. Go to: **www.hanggliding.co.nz**

Tandem hang-gliding at Queenstown.

◼ Nelson Hang-Gliding Adventures — Nelson

At the top of the South Island, less than 10km from Nelson, is Barnicoat, a 660m hill that is ideal for hang-gliding. Expect the flight to last from 15 to 20 minutes, which includes soaring high and then gliding across to their landing zone about 3.5km away. You may even be lucky if the pilot gives you a chance to take control (even on your first tandem) and instructs you on how to operate the hang-glider. There is always the option of some in-flight aerobatics and then an effortless landing on soft rubber wheels. Go to: **www.flynelson.co.nz**

◼ Tasman Sky Adventures — Motueka

Forget the noise of a microlight — stick to a hang-glider and soar on rising thermals above forests and mountains. There are 2 types of launches: off hills and mountains or via aerotowing. Tasman Sky Adventures use the latest tandem aerotowing techniques. The tandem hang-glider is towed into the air by a specially designed towplane called a 'tug'. Unlike hill launching, aerotowing allows the glider to take you as high as 750m and then release you anywhere. The weight limit for passengers is 100kg. They are located at Motueka Airport and operate year-round. Go to: **www.skyadventures.co.nz**

◼ Skytrek — Queenstown

Of all the activities you can possibly undertake in Queenstown, tandem hang-gliding would have to be right up there as one of the most exhilarating you can experience. Skytrek provide scenic flights as well as instructional flights from both Coronet Peak and The Remarkables mountains which are located just 20 minutes' drive from Queenstown. Launch areas range between 900 to 1150m high. Tandem professional pilots are highly experienced and tailor the flight to suit your requirements, whether it be a gentle glide over pristine 'Middle-earth' or a more adventurous ride that involves dips and dives much like an out-of-control pigeon. Established in 1992, the company has so far flown over 40,000 passengers and is the only one to have access to The Remarkables mountain range.
Go to: **www.skytrek.co.nz**

SAFETY AND SURVIVAL SKILLS

Despite the perception of hang-gliding being an extremely dangerous adventure sport, it is in fact a relatively safe and exciting activity with rarely any injuries or fatalities. The NZHGPA (New Zealand Hang-Gliding and Paragliding Association) acts as a governing body and exists to develop, protect and promote the sport of hang-gliding and paragliding in New Zealand. On the website you can find information about paragliding schools, hang-gliding schools, tandem flight operators, local paragliding and hang-gliding clubs, paragliding and hang-gliding competitions and national distance records. Go to: www.nzhgpa.org.nz

PARAGLIDING IN NEW ZEALAND

For most people, the fastest way to feel the thrill of paragliding (sometimes known as parapenting) is to ride a tandem paraglider. It's both easy and cost-effective to fly with a commercial company in the capable hands of a professional paragliding pilot. It lets you experience the thrill of free flying without going through a lengthy learning process. In mere minutes you can be soaring on thermals and taking in the view.

The top of the Skyline Gondola in Queenstown is considered one of the premier flying sites in New Zealand. Besides the very impressive lake and mountain views, 750m below you lies downtown Queenstown. Your flight can be a smooth scenic sightseeing experience or a gut-twisting rotating rollercoaster-type ride — the choice is yours. Besides Queenstown, paragliding experiences can be found in and around Nelson, Hawke's Bay, Christchurch and Auckland. So pick the region and operator that suits your needs — whether it's a 30-minute flight or a full day's instruction, you'll be in safe airborne hands riding tandem. Go to: New Zealand Hang-Gliding and Paragliding Association: **www.nzhgpa.org.nz**

Paragliding above the waves at Muriwai Beach, Auckland.

PARAGLIDING — NORTH ISLAND

■ Airplay Paragliding School — Hawke's Bay

Tandem paragliding is the quickest and easiest way to experience flight in its purest form. Airplay offer 2 types of tandem experience: 1. The Peak Experience is a foot takeoff from above the cliffs of Te Mata Peak, Havelock North. You'll enjoy the panoramic views of the Tukituki river valley below and the views across the Heretaunga Plains to the Ruahine and Kaweka ranges. The flight time will be 15 minutes. 2. The Cross Country Experience is for those with an adventure in mind. If it's airtime you're after, this cross-country flight is all about flying as far away as possible from Te Mata Peak over some spectacular Hawke's Bay countryside — distance is what it's all about. To do this the sky needs to be full of cumulus clouds and plenty of thermals. Bookings for this experience are essential. Flight time may be up to 4 hours.
Go to: **www.airplay.co.nz**

■ Levitate Paragliding — Bay of Plenty

Whether you are age 10 or 100, there's no reason you can't do a tandem paraglide. In the Bay of Plenty you can sit back and relax and take in the view as your pilot guides the parachute over the Kaimai Range and the Greater Bay of Plenty. There are numerous coastal flying sites at your doorstep including both the Kaimai and Paeroa ranges. These 2 sites are renowned for their thermal flight capabilities. Sometimes you're flying and sometimes you're floating — no matter, paragliding will probably change the way you view the earth forever. Go to: **www.levitate.co.nz**

■ Sky Wings Paragliding and Paramotoring — Panmure, Auckland

This South Auckland group offer a huge range of options, whether it's tandem paragliding or instructor courses. Once you have gone through your instructions, you'll soon be soaring — that's the art of catching the updraughts: an invisible wave or lift allowing you to surf in the sky. You will be soaring on the updraughts with the instructor for about 20 to 30 minutes without the need of any experience or skill and regardless of fitness level. The venues they operate from are inland cross-country and coastal Auckland.

Go to: **www.skywings.co.nz**

■ Wings and Waves Paragliding and Kitesurfing — Bayswater, Auckland

This company, as the name implies, offer both airborne and waterborne adventures. This is your chance to fly with a champion as the New Zealand distance record of 147km was set by Wings and Waves pilot Grant Middendorf. The last three NZ Champions also teach for Wings and Waves. Without any training or experience, you'll be smoothly soaring for 20 to 30 minutes in a tandem flight. Their introductory 1-day course has the aim of having you achieve several solo flights by the end of the day. There is also a Big Day introductory course that includes a long tandem paraglide. Finally, there's a 3 to 4-day course that helps you gain a learner's rating (PG1) issued by the New Zealand Hang-Gliding and Paragliding Association.

Go to: **www.wingsandwaves.co.nz**

PARAGLIDING — SOUTH ISLAND

■ Adventure Paragliding and Kite Boarding — Nelson

As you can see by the number of operators in the Nelson region, this is a stunning place to try paragliding as there are at least 7 locations ranging in height from 50 to 1600m. This is the easy way to spread your wings and try paragliding over the Richmond Range either on a gentle glide or indulging in more extreme acrobatics as this company will tailor the flight to your wishes.

Go to: **www.skyout.co.nz**

Tandem paragliding off Coronet Peak.

■ Coronet Peak Tandems Paragliding and Hang-Gliding — Queenstown

Once you've made the decision to strap yourself alongside your pilot, there really is no turning back. Coronet Peak is the highest of the 3 main sites in the region. On this little adventure you'll experience Queenstown from a hawk's-eye view. The exhilaration of paragliding with one of their experienced tandem pilots is a never-to-be-forgotten 20- to 30-minute adventure. Whether you want a relaxing scenic flight or an adrenalin-pumping joyride, let the pilot know and he will tailor the flight to your needs. After all, it's your flight! In summer, Coronet Peak Tandems use an 1150m launch point. In winter, the chairlifts allow access to the 1650m snow takeoff. Go to: **www.tandemparagliding.com**

■ Cumulus Paragliding — Nelson

No exam, no test, means no hassle — tandem flights are simply the best way to get airborne. Besides gliding from Barnicoat Hill, you should try Cumulus Paragliding's all-day tandem option which takes off from the top of Takaka Hill, at 800m high. This is where with favourable conditions you'll journey about 14km out and back across the Takaka Valley to land at the base of the mountain. This all-day trip is for 2 to 4 people.

Go to: **www.cumulus-tandems.co.nz**

A paragliding descent over Christchurch.

▥ Extreme Air Hang-Gliding & Paragliding School — Queenstown

This is the same company that offers hang-gliding off Coronet Peak. Being strapped in front of the pilot instead of by his side on a tandem hang-glider seems a little strange at first but the separate harness allows him to control the paraglider very effectively. Your flight off Coronet Peak will steal the show as the surrounding mountains display their incredible beauty. If you are there in winter take the opportunity to descend from the very top of the highest chairlift at 1645m.
Go to: **www.extremeair.co.nz**

▥ Nelson Paragliding — Nelson

With 5 cross-country flying sites, excellent training hills and some of the best year-round weather in the country, Nelson is a great place to take to the skies. Being strapped into the harness will feel like armchair flying as you glide in quiet solitude above the region's 3 national parks: Abel Tasman, Nelson Lakes and Kahurangi. If this doesn't set your heart ticking and your camera clicking, nothing will.
Go to: **www.nelsonparagliding.co.nz**

▥ Nimbus Paragliding — Christchurch

Christchurch is another sweet spot that draws plenty of paragliders and not surprisingly some professional outfits. These guys fly from places like Taylors Mistake that's about 25 minutes from town, Scarborough Cliffs or Castle Rock, so you'll get awesome views of Christchurch City, the Canterbury Plains and Pegasus Bay. The average flight time gives you about 20 minutes in the air and enough free flying thrills to shake a witch's broomstick at.
Go to: **www.nimbusparagliding.co.nz**

▥ Parapro — Christchurch

As the old adage goes — if people were meant to fly, they'd have wings! Well nowadays people have a variety of wings. Likewise, Parapro choose a variety of sites to launch from including Taylors Mistake, Whitewash Head, Castle Rock, Upper Cass and Allandale. So what do you need to do and wear? On a windy day you should be able to slowly walk, but on a windless day you'll need to jog 10m before liftoff. Wear a windbreaker and some warm clothing as down in this neck of the country it can get quite chilly, but the views and experience will be worth it. Your flight suit will of course be provided.
Go to: **www.parapro.co.nz**

Paragliding above Lake Wakatipu.

■ Wanaka Paragliding — Lake Wanaka

Located at Treble Cone with a top launch altitude of 1100m or alternatively 800m from takeoff to landing in the Matukituki Valley, Wanaka Paragliding offer one of this country's highest tandem flights. Big is best when you're choosing where to fly! You'll be airborne for about 15 to 25 minutes, so relax back in the comfortable harness — it's smooth, quiet and pure flying. You'll cruise along the valley walls and right beside 2 massive waterfalls. Choose a gentle descent or wingovers and spirals to land softly down. The entire trip takes 2 hours from Wanaka back to Wanaka or 1 hour from Treble Cone.
Go to: **www.wanakaparagliding.co.nz**

SAFETY AND SURVIVAL SKILLS

Downdraughts are the Achilles' heel of paragliding enthusiasts who sometimes suffer injuries, especially when taking off from coastal cliffs as the winds can force you directly into steep jagged rocks. Every year some people still take off alone and if they get in trouble find out that help is not readily at hand. Ensure you start off by flying tandems, and if you are flying alone let someone know the time you are due back and if possible make sure you head out with mates. For emergencies carry a mobile phone and a first-aid kit.

Despite the perception of paragliding being an extremely dangerous adventure sport, it is in fact a relatively safe and exciting activity with rarely any injuries or fatalities. The NZHGPA (New Zealand Hang-Gliding and Paragliding Association) acts as a governing body and exists to develop, protect and promote the sport of hang-gliding and paragliding in New Zealand. On their website you can find information about paragliding schools, hang-gliding schools, tandem flight operators, local paragliding and hang-gliding clubs, paragliding and hang-gliding competitions and national distance records.
Go to: www.nzhgpa.org.nz

Winging It — Aqua Air, Freefall Extreme, Microlight Flying, Red Cat Biplane

■ Aqua Air Adventures — Auckland

These guys are different — tandem hang-gliding with a twist. The twist is that the specially designed gliders have wheels attached (or floats), so there is no running involved as you fly off flat beaches (or water) to get airborne. The glider is attached to a 4-wheel-drive vehicle or a boat that pulls the glider as it rises to an altitude of 30m. The instructor, who is lying in a harness beside you, releases the tether and you fly like a seagull until you land either on the black-sand beaches or on the water with a splash. Each flight lasts 3 to 5 minutes. It's best to wear clothes that you don't mind getting wet or dirty! Either way, it's literally a thrill a second.
Go to: **www.gethigh.co.nz**

■ Freefall Extreme, Body Flying — Rotorua

Have you ever wanted to fly — or better still, parachute from a plane — but the altitude thing puts you off? Well, now you can experience the thrill of body flying in a one-of-a-kind Southern Hemisphere adventure without really leaving the ground. You'll just step out into the flight zone and be suspended about 4m high above a wind tunnel. Actually, you're suspended in the flight zone by the power of a V12 diesel engine, which turns a DC-3 aircraft propeller creating winds of 180kph. Learn how to rotate sideways and back, or do flips just like the extreme skydiving boys. As the engine slows down, you'll land on a soft air cushion as you come out of your flight. Allow about 10 minutes in flight. Full training is provided as well as the flight suit. Minimum weight is 35kg.
Go to: **www.agroventures.co.nz**

Liftoff at Freefall Extreme in Rotorua.

Hang-gliding
with a difference
in Auckland.

■ Tasman Sky Adventures, Motueka — Microlight Flying

This is really an adventure sport like no other with an avid club-based following in New Zealand. For enthusiasts, microlights are about simpler, cheaper, more personal recreational flying. The microlight aircraft was a transition from hang-gliders (and powered hand-gliders) and started life as a very low performance aircraft with a limited range. However, there's been a huge growth in the sport over the last 25 years, especially in the area of advanced technology. Microlights are still considered low-momentum aircraft even though they've developed models with a cruise speed in excess of 140 knots. The beauty of these small aircraft is that they have 2-seater versions, so for some lucky souls you don't need a licence to fly tandem.

This operator offers the only place in New Zealand where you can experience the thrill of open-air flight and in one of the South Island's most beautiful areas — Abel Tasman National Park. You'll be flying in a purpose-built state-of-the-art tandem microlight where you'll feel the winds of change in your face. These aircraft feature a hang-gliding wing and weight-shift operation, very much like a traditional hang-glider but powered by a Rotax aircraft engine. There are 3 alternative flight options: 1. A Sand Flats introductory flight that lasts for 15 minutes. 2. An Abel Tasman cross-country flight that lasts for 30 minutes. 3. A Grand Tour that you can customise to plan your own flight based on an hourly rate. Go to: **www.skyadventures.co.nz/microlight.html**

■ Red Cat Scenic Biplane Flights — Omarama

This one must be special as it's the only scenic flight (other than skydiving and heli combos) included in the guide. The beauty of this flight is that it's an open-cockpit biplane that has room for 2 passengers and the pilot, so mum-and-dad or father-and-son families can enjoy the flight together. The really cool thing is wearing an old-fashioned style leather jacket and leather helmet (kitted with headphones to hear pilot commentary). Try one of 4 flight options: 1. The 20-minute Dam Buster. 2. The 35-minute Waitaki Heights. 3. The 35-minute Lake Pukaki Highlights. 4. The 1 hour 20-minute Mt Cook Spectacular. Based at Omarama in the Mackenzie Basin just south of Mt Cook. Go to: **www.redcat.co.nz**

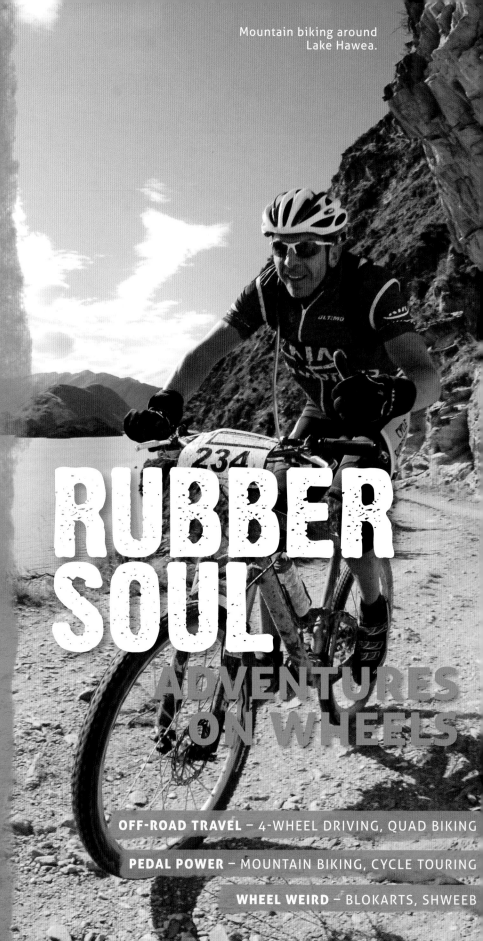

CHAPTER 4

Mountain biking around Lake Hawea.

You are either an enthusiastic off-road, 4-wheel-drive, mud-on-your-wheels type person or you're not. The same goes for cycling — you're either into biking or you're not. This category deals with both activities and highlights the options for people to explore the country using either 2 or 4 wheels. Unlike tens of thousands of Kiwis who own 4-wheel-drive vehicles but never ever intend to use them for going off-road (just look how many mums drop their kids off at school in the big beasts), this chapter is where you can find hands-on knowledge to go it alone or find the right operator in the right part of the country to take you places you might only see in the cinema.

The same thing applies to cycling — whether it's mountain biking or touring, the options available are endless in a land full of adventurous routes waiting to be explored. This country is bigger than the United Kingdom. The cycle touring option is therefore going to need both energy and planning. However, the mountain-biking trails are mostly doable in a day. So now it's time to put the pedal to the metal and find out what New Zealand has to offer both on and off the road.

RUBBER SOUL
ADVENTURES ON WHEELS

OFF-ROAD TRAVEL – 4-WHEEL DRIVING, QUAD BIKING

PEDAL POWER – MOUNTAIN BIKING, CYCLE TOURING

WHEEL WEIRD – BLOKARTS, SHWEEB

Off-Road Travel — 4-Wheel Driving, Quad Biking

Preparation

If your plan is to go off-road by yourself, take the time to prepare your vehicle first and always have safety in mind. Driving off-road through forests, across ranges and sheep stations and on beaches, over logging roads and bush tracks in a 4-wheel drive or on a quad bike, you can be sure it's going to be a big adventure. But if you get into trouble by being unprepared it can also lead to more trouble. So here's some advice before engaging the gear stick in a place where no gear stick has gone before.

There are literally thousands of 4-wheel-drive tracks across the country ranging from firebreak roads, alpine ski routes, gold-mining trails and shingle riverbeds to remote coastal beaches, old mining and timber tracks, and cattle and sheep stations in New Zealand's beautiful natural bush. However, whether you go it alone or join a commercial operation, of which there are many throughout the country, we'd recommend you first get some instruction and then buy a definitive guide to 4-wheel driving before you turn on the ignition.

Technique

Respect the environment once you're driving through it. Keep to the track and don't blaze new trails — quad bikes are not regarded as eco-friendly to dunes and native plants, so be warned. It's in everybody's interest to protect our wonderful landscape for the next generation to enjoy.

When driving off-road there are some important rules to bear in mind:

- Drive slowly and your vehicle will stay the course — otherwise you are bound to do damage to your tyres, suspension or transmission.
- If it's sand dunes you're crossing, keep your speed up, use higher gears and don't stop until you are clear of the dunes. Spinning your tyres will just dig them in further if you do become stuck. First try letting the air out of the tyres, then clear out any built-up sand (a fold-up army spade is a useful tool to carry) and lay down whatever may be at hand to find traction: wood, brush, towels etc. In flat sand, try to stay on packed surfaces if at all possible.
- When off-road on forest tracks always try to ride on the ruts not in them. Engage 4-wheel drive before an obstacle, not once you're stuck in it, and use the low-ratio gears to take some of the extra strain off the engine. When crossing streams, get out first, check the depth and speed of the water, and then pick the best line to cross.
- Hills are another problem. Approach them with caution and maybe walk up partway to gain a feel for the size and difficulty before making an attempt — don't just rush in blindly. If you decide to drive up a hill, first make sure you can do the descent. Then engage low ratio and let the natural speed of the vehicle take you down the other side. And whatever you do, don't go down unless there is another clear and obvious trail out.
- Last but not least, all trips look shorter on a map, and 4-wheel driving is always much slower than you'd expect. All journeys change with the seasons and present completely different conditions to the last time someone else made it through. Just allow enough time to complete the trip.

4-WHEEL DRIVE — SELF-DRIVE ROUTES

■ Akatarawa Forest, Wellington — 41km

This is a great location to test your quad-bike skills. Here you'll find an extensive network of roads and old logging tracks through the regenerating bush and pine trees of the Akatarawa Forest. The main 4-wheel-drive roads through the forest are open to the public for quad and trail biking. Ride 8km up Karapoti Gorge past McGhies Bridge to the clearing. Cross the Akatarawa River, climb over the Pram Track (530m) and down to Dopers Creek. Turn left and climb steadily up Rimu Road. At Toi Toi Road turn right down Hydro Road to Orange Hut. From Orange Hut the return route is downstream to Dopers Creek

and back over the Pram Track to Karapoti. Be aware that Karapoti can get quite busy and the tracks are all two-way, so always keep left. All casual bikers must have individual permits. Greater Wellington issues these permits at no charge. Contact the Upper Hutt office for yours.
Go to: **www.gw.govt.nz/office-contact-details**

◼ Arrowtown to Macetown — 16km

It's only 16km long, but this 4-wheel-drive track from Arrowtown to the old gold-mining camp known as Macetown is a cracker. It fords the Arrow River a total of 25 times en route, so make sure the river isn't in flood mode. Macetown started life in the 1860s when gold was discovered and the village owes its existence to the rugged men who worked there until the 1930s. It is one of the most intact and accessible historic goldfield towns managed by DoC in Otago. It attracts about 7500 visitors a year, either independently (by foot, mountain bike or 4-wheel drive) or along with a couple of operators who now lead guided 4-wheel-drive tours.

◼ Clarence Reserve, Kaikoura — 30km

This route is only open about 6 times a year on weekends between October and early April. Participating in these selected weekend trips and travelling into the Clarence is at the driver's own risk. The section between the Kahutara gate and Quail Flat is 30km and will take a minimum of 2 hours. The road is steep, rough and narrow in places, with several fords. Slips and floods are common; there can be no guarantee of a safe vehicle passage. The road is suited to people with 4-wheel-drive experience, and drivers need to be fully aware of their surroundings. Located in the Clarence River Valley inland from Kaikoura, the conservation area straddles the Seaward Kaikoura Range.

◼ Lake Mavora, Te Anau — 17 to 20+km

This area is a very beautiful scenic location that is a popular camping area during summer with opportunities for trout fishing, water sports, horse trekking, tramping, mountain biking and 4-wheel driving. It's 17km to the fork when you can either veer right to the Mavora Hut or left up to the Forks Hut. The track is very rough and is not recommended for vehicle access although it is suitable for mountain biking. From the fork it is 7km to either hut. The track from the camping area to Boundary Hut is suitable for mountain biking and 4-wheel-drive vehicles. Be prepared for mountain ranges,

Through the sand in a forest near Auckland.

Heading off on an excursion through Skippers Canyon.

and shingle road — rocky, pea gravel, boggy. The Mavora Lakes are located on State Highway 94 between Mossburn and Te Anau.

■ Skippers Canyon, Queenstown — 22km

A trip to Skippers has all the hallmarks of an adventure. This road was hacked by hand into the sheer cliff sides of the Shotover river valley. Once you've crossed the historic suspension bridge built in the 1900s, you'll start twisting and turning through spectacular mountain scenery and rugged canyons where gold panning was the main source of income for many pioneering families from the 1860s onwards. There is still some excitement to be had 4-wheel driving between the Queenstown end and what's known as the Branches, so keep your wits about you. However, the road is better maintained nowadays with the rise in river rafting and some guided tours — all in all, it's worth a day's adventure exploring this scenic region. Allow 4 hours minimum.

■ Thompsons Track, Kaimai Range, Tauranga — 10km

Thompsons Track runs across the Kaimai Range from Te Aroha to Katikati. Don't be deceived because it's only about 10km long. The Te Aroha side is maintained, yet the Katikati side is a series of bog holes and steep drop-offs. This route is renowned for solo vehicles becoming bogged down. The first side of the track is fairly uneventful, a gentle climb, muddy in places, but no problems for anyone with experience. The rest of the track can easily be defined as a series of at least half a dozen big bog holes and a whole lot more that can be driven if you are game. However, beware as there are big rutted ditches that need manpower and sometimes picks and shovels before attempting. Measure the water and mud levels first and the steepness of your exit. Expect mud up to bumper level and more when negotiating huge ruts and massive washouts. This route requires technical driving skills, some bush bashing, with very little rip, shoot and bust as you slowly progress along the track.

Winding above Wellington with picturesque views.

■ Woodhill Forest, Auckland — 20+km

This forest is a commercial Crown forest located to the northwest of Auckland. The forest covers approximately 12,500ha of land from Muriwai to South Head in the north. It is Auckland's weekend playground and a popular location for a number of recreation activities including Woodhill 4WD Adventure Park. Simply turn up on any Saturday or Sunday, bring your lunch, a full tank of gas in your 4-wheel drive and enjoy! They have a number of different grades of difficulty in their tracks/routes on flat to steep forested sand hills with areas of clay for you to drive (from beginner to advanced). The park caters to all skill levels from first-time off-road users and factory-standard 4-wheel-drive vehicles to club-level 4-wheel-drives. There are options such as Night Adventures, 4WD Club Member Days, Tag-along-Trips and Driver Training.
Go to: **www.jeep4wdpark.co.nz**

■ 4 Track Adventures — Kumeu, Auckland

This is a quick and easy way to get into the bush on a quad bike. After just 15 minutes' training you'll be zipping along on a 1, 2 or 3-hour quad-bike safari. These bike safaris range through the 12,500ha Woodhill Forest and along the wild, black-sand beaches of the west coast just outside of Auckland. No experience is necessary, all you need to do is park your bum over a 300cc bike engine and follow your leader, as all tours are guided. On the 3-hour journey you'll ride 45 to 55km. They can cater to all levels of quad riding — novice, experienced and experts. Go to: **www.4trackadventures.co.nz**

■ Capital Adventure (CAT) Tours — Wellington

This is a unique opportunity to venture beyond Wellington city centre and see some of the rugged landscapes and coastlines surrounding this beautiful region. CAT Adventures is a family business with a custom-built, 12-passenger Mercedes Unimog. Tours are tailored to suit the differing needs of each group. The time of pick-up, departure and drop-off points and the addition of picnic or activity options are all planned to be convenient for you. The final cost is dependent on what you have selected. However, tour options include the South Coast, *Lord of the Rings*, Pencarrow Station, Orongorongo Station and an Ultimate Nature Tour in conjunction with Karori Wildlife Sanctuary. Go to: **www.cattours.co.nz**

■ Wairere Valley Quad Bike Tours — Wairere, Northland

If you have yet to discover a bit of Northland, this would be a good place to start. These quad 4-wheel-drive tours guide you deep into the Wairere Boulder Valley with the bonus of panoramic views of Northern Hokianga Harbour and mountain ranges. They specialise in customised guided quad-bike safaris riding on powerful 500cc quad bikes that take you through farmland, native bush and into deep rainforest. The tours last about 90 minutes and they are located near Hokianga Harbour. Go to: **www.wairerevalley.com**

■ Wilderness Safaris — Hawke's Bay

Experience a full-day wilderness safari on an exciting 6-hour 4-wheel-drive trip. Wilderness Safaris Hawke's Bay has exclusive access to never-before-reached areas of the Cape Kidnappers peninsula and Ocean Beach Wildlife Preserve. You'll see ancient moa bone sites and a dramatic Maori pa site including ancient kumara pits and old Maori walking tracks. A short walk takes you to the little blue penguin box areas which have been installed to encourage nesting and breeding. The trip continues along a 180ha high-country basin and home of the endangered North Island brown kiwi release area. Lunch includes a view of the largest mainland gannet colony in the world at Cape Kidnappers. Set high on the cliffs above the Pacific Ocean, this dramatic landscape plays host to some 20,000 gannets in the September to April season. The afternoon safari traverses riverbeds, broad rolling pastures, stands of native bush, steep gullies and breathtaking inclines.
Go to: **www.kidnapperssafaris.co.nz**

4-WHEEL DRIVE — GUIDED TRIPS SOUTH ISLAND

■ 4x4 Adventures New Zealand Limited — Canterbury

If you want to get away from the crowds, take a 4-wheel-drive tour with 4x4 Adventures into the Canterbury high country. You'll see glistening lakes, glacier-fed streams, alpine valleys and magnificent mountains, travelling through privately owned high-country stations not accessible to the public. Following old gold-miners' routes, packhorse trails and musterers' tracks, you will take in at leisure the breathtaking scenery. With no strict timetable, the day is exclusively yours — you're welcome to stop for photos as often as you like, walk alongside a river, take a swim in a lake, or fish for a big trout or land-locked salmon. Choose from 5 set tours of either 1 or 2 days' duration or help design a 'custom-made' tour from 1 day to 6 weeks around the South Island. These can be either chauffeured or on a tag-along basis (or both), with everything arranged to suit your personal interests.
Go to: **www.4x4adventures.co.nz**

■ 4x4 New Zealand — Canterbury

Located in the town of Geraldine, this is a small family-run company which provides safe, individualised access deep into the alpine wilderness of the Southern Alps. Their tours meander along a valley with mountains towering 2100m above, using a 4-wheel-drive Mitsubishi van and a 12-passenger specially designed Mercedes Unimog. Exclusive access allows you to enjoy being the only people travelling through this incredible landscape. Tours include half- and full-day *Lord of the Rings* Tours, a Mesopotamia Station Tour, an Algidus Station Tour and a 2-day Wilderness Experience Tour. Geraldine is only 2 hours' drive south of Christchurch and a similar drive to Dunedin. The region is the ideal base from which to explore Aoraki/Mt Cook and the Waitaki Lakes.
Go to: **www.4x4newzealand.co.nz**

■ Adventure Trailrides NZ — Christchurch

If you are looking to go off-road into country that is hardly ever seen, then the best way to do it down in Canterbury is by joining one of these Adventure Trailrides tours. They have access to private land on high-country farms and forests where you can enjoy the thrills of riding ATV quad bikes.

Out in the back country there are single-track forest trails, rivers to cross, tussock-covered high country with views to the coast, braided rivers and untouched beaches. They offer an ATV Introduction Tour, a Half Day Novice Tour and a Two Day Hillrun Tour. No motorcycle licence is required.
Go to: **www.adventureride.co.nz**

■ BackTrax Quad Bike Tours — Hanmer Springs

This is a good way to combine a tour of the Hanmer Springs back country and then enjoy a hot thermal soak afterwards. BackTrax operate 5 different quad-bike tours including River Express, Hanmer River Ride, a Half Day Tour, Twilight Trip and their delicious Big Breakfast Trip. If you enjoy fording rivers, splashing in mud holes with the chance to view wildlife, this could be the way to go. Trips vary from 2 to 4 hours including safety instruction, splash gear and gumboots. They will shuttle you to and from Hanmer Springs. For the extreme quad-bike adventure, try their 3-day trip in the Kaikoura Ranges. The only way to experience this rugged terrain properly is with BackTrax.
Go to: **www.backtrax.co.nz**

■ Buller Adventure Tours — Westport

If you fancy a scenic safari or a challenging, adventurous quad-bike ride, the terrain around Buller will provide turf to suit everybody: beaches, rivers, bush tracks, creek crossings, steep trails and hairy, twisting descents. This is ideal West Coast countryside for learning the basics or going full throttle on their latest Suzuki 'All Terrain Vehicles' with easy-to-drive 5-speed transmission and automatic clutch. Allow about 2 hours.
Go to: **www.adventuretours.co.nz**

■ Cardrona Adventure Park — Cardrona Valley

This is another one of those places that is hard to define. As the name implies, these guys offer a range of activities that the whole family can enjoy, but especially this is a place that kids can ride quad bikes from age 6 and upwards while the adults have the chance to ride monster trucks. You can also take a 2.5-hour quad-bike safari over 1300m up into the mountains to discover some of New Zealand's pioneering history. Expect some thrilling hill climbs, water, mud, and snow in winter.
Go to: **www.adventurepark.co.nz**

■ Maniototo 4WD Safaris — Ranfurly

If you weave together rugged wilderness, craggy ranges, fertile farmland, flowing rivers and the scars of the 1860s gold-mining era you'll get yourself one great Otago 4-wheel-drive adventure: 1. The Goldfield Tour takes in Naseby, the Kyeburn diggings, the old Hamilton site and cemetery, the Styx Gaol, Paerau Valley and the Serpentine Church and onward through *Lord of the Rings*, Rohan country. 2. The High Country Tour takes you over and beyond the Mt Ida Range, visiting the old Mt Buster goldfields (at 1200m) and following the Tailings Creek before looping back to cross spectacular open tussocks. Go to: **www.maniototo4wdsafaris.co.nz**

■ Molesworth Tour Company — Blenheim, Marlborough

This Tag-along Tour (following a lead vehicle in your own 4-wheel-drive vehicle) is quite special. Bring your own 4-wheel-drive vehicle to drive through Molesworth Station in the South Island high country. You'll be one of the few to visit and drive to areas only the company can access. Tours depart from Blenheim and are only available on certain dates from January through to the end of March each year. Tour highlights include access to 5 private farms, 1 day touring round a 35,000-acre high-country station in the upper reaches of the Awatere Valley, homestead visits with great meals, fabulous local wine, genuine back-country shearer's-style accommodation and a lodge in Hanmer Springs, plus guaranteed access with expansive panoramic scenery through the iconic Molesworth and Rainbow stations. Go to: **www.molesworthtours.co.nz**

■ Nomad Safaris — Queenstown

This outfit offers small, personalised tours into the South Island back country, exploring historic gold-mining areas, some *Lord of the Rings* filming locations and an exclusive high-country farm. They use fully equipped Land Rover Defenders for their 4-wheel-drive safaris. Their quad-bike tours use Honda 400cc ATV quads which are all automatic. All tours include pick-up and drop-off at Queenstown accommodations or from their central Queenstown store on Shotover Street. Included in the price are light refreshments on all tours and gold panning on some trips. Tours are year-round, morning and afternoon (subject to road, weather, trail and river conditions). Go to: **www.nomadsafaris.co.nz**

Fording streams near Queenstown.

■ Pure Glenorchy Overland Tours — Glenorchy

This operator specialises in the Glenorchy and Dart River valleys, so you'll travel with locals who have a real passion and knowledge of the area. This is a chance to uncover for yourself the sheer beauty of this untouched, paradise-like region. You will come away with images of breathtaking scenery, extending from diverse landscapes of ancient beech forest to braided rivers and glacier-carved valleys. You'll also visit film locations from *The Lord of the Rings*, *Wolverine* and *Narnia*. Allow about 4 hours.
Go to: **www.pureglenorchy.com**

■ Time Out Tussock Tours — Ranfurly

If you embark on a journey with this company, you'll be travelling over a forgotten land, once hot enough to buckle railway iron, cold enough to freeze a steam engine's whistle, and nestled under snow-tipped mountains in Central Otago. It's an outdoor adventure experience off the beaten track, full of history and fun and guided by true-blue local characters! They include half-day tours for 3 to 4 hours, or a 1-day tour lasting 7 hours with an overnight at a musterers' hut. This tour includes all

food and some drinks and accommodation — all you need is a sleeping bag as everything else is supplied. A minimum of 2 people are required.
Go to: **www.highcountrytours.co.nz**

■ Wilderness Safaris — Te Anau

Like many smaller tour operators in New Zealand, this is a family-run business. On their small group tours they use trusty Land Rovers to bounce you around many inspiring locations even locals don't know about. Their 4-wheel-drive safari tours are half or whole days with knowledgeable local guides who will keep you informed as they ford rivers and traverse mountain passes, taking in the beauty of alpine lakes and glacier-carved mountains in 4-wheel-drive air-conditioned comfort. This is a unique, uncrowded, personalised back-country adventure. Tours include Mavora Lakes, Mt Nicholas Station, Southern Lakes, and the Overlander which starts in Queenstown and uses the TSS *Earnslaw* to ferry you to Walter Peak Station.
Go to: **www.wildernesssafaris.co.nz**

SAFETY AND SURVIVAL SKILLS

Sadly, even on 4-wheel-drive guided tours accidents sometimes happen. Most 4-wheel-drive tracks are in rural settings where there is little room for error — don't expect crash barriers, fences or warning signs or even tracks that are maintained. What you should expect is mud, ruts, steep hills and steeper drop-offs and no safety net. Operators might be running a safety-conscious tour, but in the end it is usually driver error that causes accidents. If you are driving quad bikes remember to follow the rules, regroup often, proceed slowly in rough sections and be alert to your surroundings. After all, you are on an adventure in rugged countryside and you can't expect the owner or operator to swaddle you in bubble wrap. These trips are excitement-based experiences and the last thing you'd expect is for them to remove all aspects of risk — it's what you take the tours for in the first place!

A note of warning: Quad biking is more likely to cause injuries than an enclosed 4-wheel-drive vehicle. Quad bikes can roll easily and are often ridden too fast by inexperienced drivers. If you are going with a tour and it's your first time, do your research and pick a reputable company who give full instructions and details of what the trail is like before you climb aboard.

If you are not going with a guided tour, being prepared is the first rule of the track. You do not want to break down en route in some lonely forest or find that the stream you're crossing is actually a river! So work on your requirements at home first. With a little internet research, you will soon have an idea of what you should take along.

If you are going solo, no matter what your vehicle preference, you must make sure it's off-road ready and in good condition. Check the vehicle fully from top to bottom before you leave — this is your lifeline. If you're not mechanically minded, have your local garage carry out a full service before you leave — and check the spare tyre has air in it too!

Travellers should be prepared for all weathers: snow, rain, sun. It is important to carry water and be equipped with warm, waterproof clothing, adequate food and accurate maps. Remember, your safety is your responsibility. Let relatives, friends or the authorities know where you are going, and how long you plan on being away. When you return, don't forget to call them to say you're back safely tucked up in your hotel or lodge — unless you want to receive a rescue bill in the mail. Don't rely on your mobile phone to get you out of trouble either, as many off-road tracks are out-of-service areas. If you get stuck in treacherous conditions, especially snow and freezing temperatures, stay with your vehicle until help arrives or the conditions get better — your chances of survival will be infinitely greater.

If you are going it alone, you should also have plenty of maps of the area you're driving through, and for further assistance consider installing a GPS to keep track of your position. Guidebooks are another good way to learn what lies ahead. A boxful of survival gear is also vital. Carry enough equipment to keep you alive and relatively comfortable for several days in adverse conditions and you will survive.

In the event of a breakdown, consider the following advice:

- Stay with your vehicle and make yourself visible with a brightly coloured tarp or something similar.
- Find some open ground and be prepared to start a smoky signal fire without burning down the forest.
- Above all, keep calm — panicking will not help your situation.
- Spend your time constructively: think through your options and take stock of your supplies.
- If you choose to leave your vehicle to hike out, wait until the early morning as you will have a better chance of finding civilisation than at night.
- Lastly, leave a note on the windscreen detailing your direction of travel, your destination, and the date and time you left.

For further information, go to the NZ Four Wheel Drive Association website: www.nzfwda.org.nz

Pedal Power — Mountain Biking, Cycle Touring

Steeped in History

New Zealand has a rich background in cycling. In August 1869, under the headline 'The First Bicycle In Auckland', the *Southern Cross* newspaper reported that coachbuilders test-rode a 'velocipede' that they had just built on commission. New Zealanders were awestruck by the new contraption and it swiftly rivalled horses or walking as a preferred form of transportation. But these early models were also dangerous — perhaps that was part of their attraction, as well as their downfall — and were seldom used for anything more than sport and recreation.

Believe it or not, the first bicycle race in Christchurch was held in 1869 near Hagley Park, and in 1879 the Pioneer Cycle Club became the first of its kind in New Zealand. In 1928 the great Christchurch bike rider Harry Watson won a professional 'Round The Harbour Race', shortly before departing for Europe where he became the first New Zealander to ride in the famous Tour de France — quite a feat in those days. Eventually, Tino Tabak riding for New Zealand finished 18th in the 1972 Tour de France — the best result ever for a New Zealand bike rider.

In the 1970s there was a resurgence in cycling as both recreation and sport as New Zealanders' love affair with bikes steadily grew — first 10-speeds, then BMXs, and finally mountain bikes which were first introduced in 1981. By 1990, a survey showed cycling to be our second most popular participation sport. Since then, cycle sales have remained high, averaging over 150,000 per annum, as Kiwis pursue fun, fitness, competition and back-country adrenalin rides. However, it was a Kiwi lady who did New Zealanders proud and single-handedly elevated the profile of cycling in our country. Sarah Ulmer was a cyclist of true world-class standing. She has been a World and Olympic Champion and is the current holder of the world record for the showcase track cycling event, the 3000m Women's Individual Pursuit. Sarah was also a back-to-back Commonwealth Games Champion (1998, 2002), Commonwealth Games record holder and New Zealand Sportsperson of the Year.

In a land blessed with some of the best biking countryside in the world, it's not surprising that today all forms of biking are very popular — road biking, mountain biking and touring. There will be even more incentive to get out there on 2 wheels in 2010 once the government-funded New Zealand Cycleway starts being implemented.

So clip in your pedals and check out a list of the best-known bike trails and tours in this chapter — some are must do 'bucket list' entries. For any truly serious bike enthusiasts, we recommend you buy a specific biking guidebook for your individual needs.

Choice of Bicycles

There are 4 main choices of bike — if you discount the clunkers that have hung around the backyard since you were a kid — as follows:

Touring bikes are the type of bike favoured by people who have the time to wander back roads and byways without a care in the world — mainly long-distance cyclists. The bikes have drop handlebars and front and rear panniers typically overloaded with camping gear and all their worldly goods. These bikes usually offer 21 gears to help you ascend high passes and steep hills even with all the excess baggage. Touring bikes can also be used for multi-day or week-long adventures. They are built for reliability, strength, comfort and for taking in the scenery — something that is supplied in ample quantities in this fair land.

Hybrid bikes are simply a mixture of mountain bike and road bike. The newest versions are best described as 'an all-round bike', since they combine the best features of both types. They are fast, very sturdy, and handle well on tarmac or light trails. You can ride them leisurely around town, comfortably on longer rides, and on non-extreme mountain trails. Usually, they have shock-absorbing forks, maybe a wider saddle, but still include many of the features you'll find on street versions such as

Bike touring on
State Highway 48
at Whakapapa.

fenders, a chain guard, kickstands and safety lights. The hybrid is the one to choose if you're looking for a versatile bike that you can use safely in the city, around town, for longer rides in the country, and even for light, off-road paths. It's an excellent choice for beginners.

Mountain bikes, as the term implies, are suitable for all types of rugged trails. These bikes are designed with one thing in mind — taking you across inhospitable terrain no matter what the weather forecast predicts on a mountain or forest trail, over boulders, tree roots, or pretty much whatever else nature throws at you. They are lightweight and have front and rear suspension to absorb shock. Mountain bikes typically have 21 but up to 27 gears. In recent years, disc brakes have surpassed rim brakes as the preferred choice because of superior stopping and the ability to stay dry and clean. Wheels come in different styles and width diameter

depending on where you want to traverse and your style of riding. Knobbly tyres are a vital component of increased traction and determine where and for how long you can venture.

Racing bikes are the sports cars of cycling. There are no frills, no reflectors, no kickstand, no fenders — in other words, the type opted for by Lance Armstrong and the other Tour de France bikers. These bikes are built for speed, so are definitely not for a beginner or for those getting back into biking after last riding a bike to school decades earlier. They feature very thin tyres (at very high pressure, which make them fast but bumpy and hard on the bum), aerodynamically shaped, drop handlebars, carbon or titanium saddles, and many gears close together that allow the rider to match the gear precisely to the conditions. Oh, and I almost forgot to tell you — they also cost a lot of money!

CYCLE TOURING SELF-GUIDED ROUTES

Self-guided cycle routes can encompass anything from a 1-day family fun-ride around Waiheke Island or along the Auckland waterfront through to a month-long tour of the South Island. These types of trips can be done on an old clunker, a fancy mountain bike, or a specially equipped road bike fitted out with panniers for carrying all your gear. The great thing about New Zealand is that no matter where you are, you'll soon find yourself out on the open road and away from the crowds pedalling through some world-class scenery. The beauty is that here there is less road traffic, less pollution, a temperate climate and friendly locals — what more could a cyclist ask? Whether you want a coastal route, alpine passes, heritage trails, lakeside jaunts, island adventures or natural countryside — one of these shorter 1 to 3-day routes will probably suit you.

■ Auckland City — Busy and Bursting with Heritage

People don't usually think of New Zealand's largest city as a Mecca for cycle touring, but if Cycle Action Auckland has their way they'll hitch their back wheels onto the government's $50 million national cycleway with their proposal for 3 cycle routes taking in the best of Auckland's urban cityscape. The 3 routes will showcase the city and include a 13.6km ride from the Harbour Bridge through Westhaven, along the waterfront, up to Parnell and around the Domain into Newmarket, across onto Ponsonby ridge and back to the start. The Heritage Route is 8.8km long from Ponsonby ridge, through Herne Bay and into Westmere, skirting Western Springs back along Great North Road and into Ponsonby again. The Volcanic Route will start in Newmarket and take in Mt Hobson, Mt St John and Mt Eden on the 12.4km journey. Go to: **www.caa.org.nz**

■ Christchurch — Round The Harbour

For local riders, the area around Lyttelton's spectacular but challenging harbour bays has been the benchmark for cyclists dating back to the very first time a bicycle was seen on these shores. You can take on this challenging 80km ride at any time of year, but for 1 day every December, the Armstrong Festival of Cycling sees more than 1500 riders snaking their way alongside the spectacular harbours and bays. The route is basically from McCormacks Bay around the base of the Port Hills, over Gebbies Pass

Biking through Wairarapa vineyards.

to Lyttelton Harbour, before one final fling over Evans Pass and Sumner to finish back at McCormacks Bay — an iconic trip with roots that hark right back to the earliest settlers and cyclists alike.

■ Queenstown to Wanaka — Lake Wakatipu to Lake Wanaka

To say this ride is more than challenging is putting it lightly. From the shores of Queenstown's Lake Wakatipu to Lake Wanaka via the Crown Range is truly a route that will not be easily forgotten. For one thing, this is the highest main road in New Zealand — twisting, steep and muscle fatiguing, but offering some unbelievable panoramic views. It is about 70km in distance and worth the considerable pedalling effort. The clearly marked turnoff to the Crown Range is just past Lake Hayes on State Highway 6, about 18km from Queenstown. The road zigzags back and forth steeply up to the Crown Terrace and from there you can look down to Arrowtown in the Arrow Valley and back across to the road up to The Remarkables skifield. The road then climbs very steeply to the summit at 1119m. It is all downhill thereafter as the road descends steadily through the steep-sided Cardrona Valley beside the Little Cardrona River. Remember to stop for a beer at the Cardona Hotel built in 1870. From here to Wanaka is mainly farmland shaded by willows and poplar trees. This is a superb ride that will leave you gasping for more.

■ Taupo to Napier — Lake to Ocean via State Highway 5

This is another great route, taking in some of the best scenery in the middle of the North Island. Starting at Taupo, which sits about 400m above sea level, the route follows State Highway 5 rising to heights of nearly 800m at places like Rangitaiki and Titiokura with some big valleys in between such as the Mohaka River Gorge. The distance covered is approximately 140km. For serious riders it can be completed in 1 day, but for enjoyment and pleasure it's better to take it in 2 stages.

MOUNTAIN BIKING — NORTH ISLAND TRAILS

■ Eskdale Mountain Bike Park, Hawke's Bay — Grades 2 to 4, 50km

Located on the east of the North Island, this is a humdinger of a mountain-bike location with over 50 named trails, most averaging 1km in length. Once again, this is a commercial forest, so you must have a permit to access this 600ha privately owned area. You can buy a 3-week pass for a nominal fee.

Newbie bikers in the forest are best to begin with the Barley Trail that runs for 7km, and if it feels good you can link this up with a cluster of other twisting, winding, downhill and stump-jumping trails such as Twoman, Upper Magog, Luge, Lower Magog, Drop, Boulder, Burden Road, Mervs and Pace before finally coming back to Burden Road — this should keep you happy for a good hour or more on a great single-track route.

DIRECTIONS: North of Napier on State Highway 2, left on State Highway 5 to Esk Valley, 18.5km from Napier, turn right onto Waipunga Road where the signpost clearly indicates the Eskdale Mountain Bike Park. Go to: www.hawkesbaymtb.co.nz

■ Great Barrier Island — Ungraded

This is way off the beaten track, but unbeknown to most people Great Barrier Island offers a wide-ranging choice of mountain-bike trails. You'll experience the stunning scenery of the Barrier if you take up the challenge in this wild and rugged landscape. Expect panoramic views of steep, craggy, forest-covered peaks and white sandy beaches and the opportunity to see some of New Zealand's most endangered flora and fauna. The mountain-bike trails range from easy to very difficult, encompassing fast downhills and technical climbs as well as easy ascents through bush and farmland. The best-known trail is the Forestry Road from Whangaparapara to Port FitzRoy. Great Barrier Island lies 90km from Auckland. SeaLink Ferries is your best option for getting all your gear over there. For a winter or summer schedule go to www.sealink.co.nz

■ Karapoti Forest — Grade 4+, Length 45km Loop

This is the course for New Zealand's longest-running mountain-bike race. The renowned Karapoti Classic is a rugged 45km ride which can be enjoyed at a leisurely pace or you can rip it up at any time of year. The route starts from a 4-wheel-drive track that leads you into the Karapoti Gorge. About 6km from the parking lot there is a fork branching off to the right which is the start of the 32km loop track.

Mountain biking at Whakarewarewa near Rotorua.

The challenging Karapoti Classic mountain biking race.

DIRECTIONS: From 3km north of Upper Hutt at Brown Owl head up the Akatarawa Road for 6km until you reach Karapoti Road. Turn left and follow Karapoti Road for 2km to the car park and the start of the route which is 30 per cent gravel, 55 per cent 4-wheel drive, 10 per cent single track, 5 per cent unrideable — watch out for motorbikes, forestry vehicles, hunters and horses.
Go to: **www.karapoti.co.nz**

■ Makara Peak Mountain Bike Park — Ungraded

This is considered Wellington's number one playground especially for mountain bikers. The fact that it is just 15 minutes from downtown makes it a perfect location for city people as it boasts 8km of 4-wheel-drive track and 24km of custom-built single mountain-bike track. The tracks have been developed for a variety of bikers from beginners through to expert. All the single tracks can be soft and slushy during and after rain, so it's best to wait 2 or 3 days after a soaking before hitting the routes. The car-park entrance to the park is 1km down South Karori Road. Go to: **www.makarapeak.org**

■ The 42 Traverse, Tongariro Forest Park — Ungraded

As the name implies, this route is in State Forest 42 in the Tongariro Forest Park. Billed as one of New Zealand's best mountain-bike rides, it has plenty of downhills yet enough climbs to give even good mountain bikers a few cramps. This is a one-way adventure lasting about 5 to 7 hours depending on your level of fitness as you will traverse around 47km of native bush, with extensive views of volcanic mountains. There are also streams to cross and canyons to explore. This is a remote trail with plenty of mud and gravel sections, so take extra rations, a good repair kit, additional weather-related clothing, a map and compass. A good base for this adventure is National Park where you can hire bikes and obtain a good forest trail map. For guided tours go to: **www.planetbike.co.nz**

■ Whakarewarewa, Rotorua — Grades 2 to 5, Length 6km+

This is a specifically designed dual-use mountain-biking/tramping trail through native bush that both riders and walkers can enjoy. Named after the respected and feared Tuhourangi tohunga (priest) who predicted the Mt Tarawera eruption of 1886, the Tuhoto Ariki Trail starts at the highest point in the Whakarewarewa Forest Conservation Park and provides native forest surroundings not otherwise seen on the rest of the trail network. Being Grade 4 in difficulty means that the trail has some excellent long downhill segments, but don't be put off by the height gain at the start as this is a true cross-country track with some technical climbs. If an outback adventure is what you're looking for, this is the trail for you. Built by the Rotorua Mountain Bike Club and named in honour of the legendary warrior who hunted in this area, Hatupatu is an alternative end to the Tuhoto Ariki Trail bringing you back towards the main network of Whakarewarewa Forest trails. It is a Grade 5 mountain-bike trail running through mature forest containing tawa, mahoe, puahou (five-finger), with mistletoe and juvenile rata. The surroundings mean that Hatupatu provides an experience unlike other trails in the area. While it is generally undulating, it descends a total of 160m over its 1km distance. This is a challenging ride for those who like technical trails.

DIRECTIONS: Head south on State Highway 5 from Rotorua. About 1km from the city limit on the left you'll find the Waipa Mill, the entrance to the Whakarewarewa Forest. From the Waipa Mill car park, ride up the Waipa State Mill Road which will turn into Hill Road. Follow this for 5.5km until Moerangi Road appears on your right; go 1km further on this and turn left onto Tawa Road — after 2.5km you'll be at the highest point in the forest and then you're at the start of the track.
Go to: **www.redwoods.co.nz**

■ Woodhill Forest, Auckland — Grades 1 to 6, Length 1 to 30km

This is a commercial Crown forest located to the northwest of Auckland covering approximately 12,500ha of land extending from Muriwai in the south to South Head in the north. The forest is Auckland's weekend playground and a popular location for a number of recreation activities, including horse riding, 4-wheel driving, trail biking, mountain biking, hiking, tree-climbing adventures and orienteering.

Woodhill Forest is a sand-based pine forest, providing all-weather trails and recreation. The Woodhill Mountain Bike Park operated by Bike Parks Ltd has become renowned throughout New Zealand's riding community as an exceptional and unique mountain-biking destination. This biking trail offers over 50 named trails providing 100km of single-track riding and over 100 purpose-built, council-compliant jumps and stunts including their huge and pretty scary 'North Shore'. They offer year-round riding, but all riders must register first.

DIRECTIONS: Access is via Rimmer Road, 3km south of Helensville, 30km northwest of Auckland. Go to: **www.bikepark.co.nz**

MOUNTAIN BIKING — SOUTH ISLAND TRAILS

■ Naseby Forest, Otago — Grades 2 to 5, Length up to 50km

Once again, this region is a forest production area with ongoing logging operations. Here walkers and forest trucks have right of way but beyond that the tracks are all yours. The holiday township of Naseby is an ideal base for adventurous holidaymakers intent on exploring the area. The local bike tracks provide a neat range of scenic and easy trails suitable for all ages. This region is close to Naseby village and is festooned with great single tracks — locals rave about the Rollercoaster, Skatebowl and Ejector Seat. Catch a shuttle bus up to Clarks Junction or ride the train which runs from Dunedin to Pukerangi during summer. Go to: **www.mountainbikingotago.co.nz**

■ Port Hills Tracks — Grade 3 to 4, Length up to 50km

Good on Christchurch City Council for working so hard on bike tracks! Put together 10 suburban tracks with a very impressive mountain-bike track that has been completed by the city and you have a trail to rival the best in the country. Putting it in plain terms, this is a continuous single track that floats along the Port Hills right out to Godley Head. There are 6 main tracks in the Port Hills: Godley Head Track, Kennedys Bush, Crocodile Track, Worsleys, Flying Nun and Victoria Park. Many people choose to drive to Evans Pass, while others pack the extra energy bar and ride there from Sumner via the Captain Thomas Track. For more cycle rides in Christchurch go to: **www.ccc.govt.nz/cityleisure/gettingaround**

■ Queen Charlotte Track — Grade 3+, Length 63 to 86km

This is a track that is well documented in the hiking section, but to be fair it's also the longest single-track bike ride in New Zealand. The track itself is tough in places and consists of hard uphill climbs with the reward of wind-in-your-face downhill sections, some of the best scenery in New Zealand and the ability to be picked up or dropped off in different bays by water taxi. The downside is that it is closed to bikers during the peak hiking season — the hot months of December, January and February.

The middle section is a killer to ride and many people bypass it. If you do attempt this section, beware of exposed drop-offs and dangerous precipices — the views, though, are to die for. And for the hardy — save up your reserves for the last section of the trail. It is mainly single track through native forest with enough technical sections to keep the most ardent rider in bike heaven. Track conditions: 3 per cent gravel, 96 per cent shingle, 1 per cent unrideable. You can shorten the drive by catching the Beachcomber Mail Boat or the Arrow Water Taxi. Go to: **www.mailboat.co.nz/mailrun.asp** or **www.arrowwatertaxis.co.nz**

■ The Contact Epic, Lake Hawea, Wanaka — 125km

This bike race is about the challenge of circumnavigating the shores of Lake Hawea, one of the most stunningly beautiful lakes in the South Island, located on the edge of Wanaka. The ride is a 125km journey to explore the land, your biking ability and your self-confidence.

Even though it is held only once a year, it gives you the opportunity to be part of a race and a great day out riding through the Hunter Valley and Dingle Burn high-country farming stations of Lake Hawea courtesy of special permission from the landowners. The course is undulating and varied with waist-deep river and stream crossings, lots of short, hard climbs and long descents.

This is the country's longest circumnavigation of a lake and is the mountain biker's equivalent of the Lake Taupo road-biking challenge. However, this is more of an adventure than a race. Those that are super-fit and want to race hard will be tested over this terrain, while others who see it as a major personal challenge will be able to pace themselves and enjoy the history, scenery and wilderness of this remote region.

This is not the type of course obstructed by big signs and posted with direction arrows — it is left as untouched as possible to allow you to enjoy its natural state. One of the main factors in taking on this event is the knowledge that you will need motivation, common sense and tenacity to get to the finish line. To that end, there will be no official bike checks, no compulsory gear list, and no excuses — just you taking on this challenge on your own terms. The course is held every April and contains over 2000m of vertical ascent and descent. It is varied and rocky and one you have to finish if you want to obtain complete satisfaction.
Go to: **www.contactepic.co.nz**

Mountain biking the Queen Charlotte Track.

Riding beside Lake Hawea
during a mountain-bike race.

SAFETY AND SURVIVAL SKILLS

It's as easy as riding a bike — just don't fall off! At some stage most bike riders have taken a fall off their machines caused by speed wobbles, potholes, brake failure, tyre blowout, gear breakdown, miscalculation and often poor conditions — the list is endless. Remember to keep momentum going, be aware of your route and surroundings, slow down on hills and ride in daylight hours, and in all cases ride more cautiously in wet/icy conditions. Even riders cycling in groups are not immune to being hit by moving vehicles, or for that matter, cycling into stationary ones. But when you are riding alone, especially at night, there are a few obvious things you can do to avoid an accident.

Every year on average 10 cyclists are killed on New Zealand roads and about 750 cyclists are injured in road accidents — so don't become a statistic. Wear a helmet and always stay alert to your surroundings. Have your bike serviced at least once a year by a professional bike maintenance shop. Check your tyre pressure before each ride, carry a first-aid kit if you are mountain biking, a tyre pump, spare inner tube and a small tool kit to carry out minor repairs. Mountain biking has dangers, but if you proceed at your own risk and ride within your ability you will usually be fine and enjoy some of the best scenery in the world. Remember:

■ Wear an approved cycle helmet and protective clothing.
■ Stay on the designated mountain-bike track or roads — do not take short cuts.
■ Take out what you bring in — don't litter!
■ Beware of vehicles when using the roads. Standard New Zealand road rules apply — keep to the left and give way when appropriate.
■ Do not build new tracks or modify existing ones.

Like all sports, cycling has been turned into a multi-million-dollar business. Normal attire nowadays for riders is lightweight garments that include strips of highly reflective fluorescent material. This is the best way for motorists to spot you first, especially if they are distracted reading maps, looking for directions, or just blind to anything as small as a bike. Cyclists need to ride in the direction of traffic and always stop for traffic lights and stop signs. Keep an eye out for pedestrians, as they are usually making sure they don't get run over by a car, bus or big truck. The other obvious problem is people in parked cars opening doors unexpectedly just as you approach.

CYCLE EVENTS HAPPENING AROUND NEW ZEALAND

JANUARY — Tour de Vineyards, Nelson — Go to: www.starandgarterwheelers.co.nz
JANUARY — SRAM Tour de Ranges, Auckland — Go to: www.tourderanges.co.nz
JANUARY — Yarrows Taranaki Cycle Challenge, Taranaki — Go to: www.cyclechallenge.co.nz
FEBRUARY — The REV, Hamilton — Go to: www.therev.co.nz
MARCH — Le Race, Christchurch — Go to: www.lerace.co.nz
MARCH — Twin Coast Cycle Challenge, Northland — Go to: www.twincoast-cycle.co.nz
APRIL — The Forest Estate Graperide, Marlborough — Go to: www.graperide.co.nz
APRIL — Rotorua to Taupo 100 K Flyer — Go to: www.100kflyer.co.nz
APRIL — Around Brunner, Greymouth — Go to: www.aroundbrunner.co.nz
APRIL — Pig and Whistle New Zealand Singlespeed Champs, Rotorua — Go to: www.nzsinglespeeds.com
JULY — Okoroire Mid Winter Fun ride, Okoroire — Go to: www.funcycling.net
OCTOBER — The Wild Coaster, West Coast — Go to: www.nelsonevents.co.nz/WildCoaster.htm
OCTOBER — Tour of the Bay, Hawke's Bay — Go to: http://www.ramblers.co.nz/tob
NOVEMBER — Lake Taupo Cycle Challenge — Go to: www.cyclechallenge.com
NOVEMBER — Roadcraft K2, Coromandel — Go to: www.arcevents.co.nz
DECEMBER — Festival of Cycling — Go to: www.festivalofcycling.co.nz

Mountain biking in Southland.

On two wheels and sailing away in a blokart.

Wheel Weird — Blokarts, Shweeb

The modern 'blokart' (also known as a kite buggy) is another wacky New Zealand invention developed in a back-street garage. Blokarts are land yachts that are capable of speeds up to 100kph. They were invented in 1999 by Papamoa local Paul Beckett, and since then the sport has really 'taken off'. Powered by the wind, these fast, lightweight vehicles look like a cross between a go-kart and a yacht. They can be used on any flat surface — land, grass, or sand. Blokarts are easily steered by a tiller, using your hands rather than your feet.

Beach sailing is the essence of blokarts, yet blokarts also ride well on either small courses or larger beaches, sand flats, and other venues such as grassy parks. Blokarting had its inaugural world championship in Papamoa, Tauranga in October 2008 and is sailed as 2 classes — production and performance (where additional performance parts from the manufacturer are allowed such as carbon-fibre mast sections and an aerodynamic shell). Blokarts have 4 standard sail sizes — 2m, 3m, 4m and 5.5m — with sail choice being dependent on wind strength and sailor weight, as heavier sailors require larger sails, and smaller sails are more efficient in stronger winds. Currently, there are around 12,000 blokarts worldwide. For additional information go to: **www.kitebuggy.co.nz**

There are 12 clubs in New Zealand: Auckland, Thames, Bay of Plenty, Hamilton, Manawatu, Central Hawke's Bay, Wellington, Canterbury and Southland, and some clubs have demo karts available for donations or minimal cost to cover wear and tear. Go to: The New Zealand Blokart Association **www.bai.co.nz**

■ Aqua Air Adventures — Auckland

Blokart sailing is rapidly becoming the world's number one land-based adventure sailing sport. They are so easy to use that anyone from kids to grandparents can have great fun on them. Being light, stable, small and nimble, any open space with wind becomes a funfest. These lads can take you out for an introductory session where you can learn to race other karts. You'll find them having fun at Muriwai Beach or Karioitahi Beach. Go to: **www.gethigh.co.nz**

The fun of racing in blokarts.

■ Blown Away — Takanini, Auckland

For those of us with no sailing experience this is the way to learn about the power of the wind without getting wet or into trouble. With the breeze in your face and your body barely 10cm off the ground, you'll be swept along by the thrill of speeding out of your first jibe or balancing your kart on 2 wheels! Almost anyone can do it regardless of age or physical ability — this is truly an adrenalin sport that will hoist your sails. Hire a blokart and have a good play around their extensive track at Bruce Pulman Park in Papakura, the main centre of blokart sailing in the Auckland region.

Go to: **www.blownaway.co.nz**

■ Game On Activities — Papamoa, Tauranga, Bay of Plenty

This is an all-purpose tarseal speedway concept where you'll receive excellent tuition and enjoy the sensation of pure speed as you handily whip around the track. With 360 degrees of available wind, blokarters can race with any wind direction and have clocked speeds of up to 65–75kph. You can even hire a tandem blokart which is suitable for either Mum or Dad to steer with room for a 5 to 9-year-old by your side. Instructors will match your body weight and wind conditions on the day to the right-sized sail. If this is your first time and you're a little unsure, the instructors may scale the sail size down until you get the hang of it after a few laps.

Go to: **www.gameonactivities.co.nz**

■ Invercargill Land Sailing — Invercargill's Oreti Beach

This adventure is located on Oreti Beach and takes place every weekend 2 hours either side of low tide and when weather conditions permit. Some of the beach shots in the movie *The World's Fastest Indian* were filmed at this location. These guys also offer a Blokart Beach Tour that runs 24km from Riverton back to Invercargill with transport provided from Invercargill. There is a limit of 4 persons per tour.

Go to: **www.jasperstours.com/blokarts.html**

■ Muriwai Surf School — Auckland's West Coast

This is another west coast of Auckland beach location that rents out surfboards, body boards, wetsuits, bikes, kites, and of course blokarts. If you have never tried this type of outdoor sport before, they can also supply professional instruction in a safe and friendly environment. Open 7 days a week.

Go to: **www.muriwaisurfschool.co.nz/Blokarts.html**

Spinning your pedals around the
Shweeb course in Rotorua.

SHWEEB

The Shweeb, it has to be said, is a real one-off
adventure option. It is one of the weirdest-looking
contraptions in the world — in fact, it's the world's
first human-powered monorail racetrack. It consists
of two 200m-long interlocking, overhead monorail
race circuits from which hang highly efficient pedal-
powered pods.

You lie back in a recumbent position for maximum
comfort and minimum aerodynamic drag. The
hard wheels on the smooth track reduce rolling
resistance, so you can click through the 7 gears
and get up to top speed with very little effort. The
track varies in height between 2 and 4m above the
ground. The pods swing freely from left to right, so
as your speed picks up you swing wildly around the
corners and soar high and low over the undulating
terrain. Between 1 and 5 vehicles can be loaded
onto each track, enabling teams to race each other
or compete against the clock.

Due to the minimal resistance riders can reach
speeds of up to 60kph and get up to a 60-degree
angle on the curves, making it a dynamic and
thrilling ride that's truly beyond compare.
Go to: **www.agroventures.co.nz**

CHAPTER 5

FOOTLOOSE

ADVENTURES ON FOOT

These boots were made for walking . . . or climbing or caving or abseiling or skiing! Stepping into the great outdoors is something most of us do every day, whether it's walking to the corner store or heading off to work, but putting your right foot forward requires commitment when you take on some of the down-to-earth adventures and outright challenges presented in this chapter. The best examples of adventurous ground-based activities covering the whole country are clustered together right here. Many of these sports require a certain level of fitness and should not be taken lightly. Some training is definitely worth the effort, so start building up your fitness, strength and muscles — if for no other reason than to find out what our great little country has to offer in this area.

This earth provides us with a huge variety of obstacles to overcome — from climbing mountains, crawling underground, speeding over snow and ice, to hiking in the great outdoors and across man-made structures — and that is what you'll find in this section of the guide. So get out there and put your best foot forward!

Abseiling down to a caving adventure.

BOOT CAMP – HIKING TRAILS

CANYONS & CAVES – CANYONING, ABSEILING, CAVING

ROCK OF AGES – CLIMBING, MOUNTAINEERING

WANDERLUST – BRIDGE CLIMB, OBSTACLE COURSES SKYWALK, ZORB

Boot Camp — Hiking Trails

Many walking tracks in New Zealand have evolved from the oldest Maori trails and early pioneer exploration routes. As a recreational activity, walking was taken up in the early days of European settlement and tramping (hiking) eventually became popular again once the motor car and additional roads heralded a means of getting to more remote places.

Hiking across Masons Bay in Stewart Island.

From the 1950s onwards, tracks, huts and bridges were built in the forested areas of New Zealand to allow easy access for hunters to cull introduced deer, which had slowly become a threat to the biodiversity of the country. As tramping (often referred to as trekking, hiking or walking) grew in popularity, these facilities were increasingly used by travellers. Today New Zealand's long-distance walking tracks are considered world-class and win plaudits for the spectacular scenery, wildlife and native fauna and flora that is encountered en route.

New Zealand's network of public tramping tracks has been developed over many decades throughout the country but most spectacularly in the South Island. All of the major tramping tracks that are on public land are administered by the Department of Conservation (DoC). However, in some cases a small number of tramping tracks also traverse private land either in part or in full.

GREAT WALKS: The 'Great Walks' are 8 of DoC's designated premier walking tracks, through some of the best scenery in the country. The huts and tracks on the 'Great Walks' are of a higher standard than those on other tramping tracks, and consequently have booking systems to manage visitor pressure. The seasons are: High season, 28 October to 29 April; Winter season, May to end October.

HUTS: There is a network of over 950 back-country huts throughout New Zealand operated by DoC on public land. Some areas also have privately owned huts on public land used for commercial tourism operations. The majority of the huts were built by the now defunct New Zealand Forest Service. Others were constructed by alpine clubs, schools and ski clubs. Trampers are expected to leave all huts and campsites clean and tidy and to pack out whatever is packed in as there are no rubbish disposal facilities on most trails. Please be considerate of other visitors. Smoking is not permitted in the huts or shelters on most tracks. You'll also sometimes find DoC staff stationed at huts in the summer or walking the tracks in winter. They are equipped with radios for use in emergencies and for weather forecasts. For your own safety, please sign the hut books on arrival.

The primary distinction between hiking and backpacking is that the backpacker carries everything needed to stay out overnight or for days in the wilderness: clothing, rain gear, gas stove, tent, cooking equipment, ground mats, flashlights, freeze-dried foods, water, sleeping bag etc. The hiker usually carries a day pack with rudimentary needs and as such has to find food and shelter by nightfall. If you are heading out with an outfitter, make sure you know what you need to take and what you need to leave behind, as your shoulders will do most of the carrying.

TE ARAROA — THE LONG PATHWAY — LENGTH 3000km

At the end of 2010 there will be a national walking trail 3000km long extending from Cape Reinga in Northland to Bluff in Southland making it one of the world's longest walking trails. The original concept was the brainchild of Geoff Chapple who proposed the idea of a national walkway as far back as the mid-1990s. Te Araroa now traverses coastline, forest, farmland, volcanoes and mountain passes, river valleys, and green pathways across 7 cities. Most of the work has been completed by volunteers in the last 10 years. It will offer people the opportunity to connect with the history of our country and for visitors to better understand our landscape and culture. An 18km section known as the Pirongia Track also features one of the country's longest and highest boardwalks. Mt Pirongia is not only the tallest mountain in the Waikato but one of the Tainui tribe's most sacred sites, and the track includes an 800m-long boardwalk at almost 1km altitudes. For further information go to: **www.teararoa.org.nz**

CLASSIC LONG DISTANCE HIKING TRACKS

■ Abel Tasman Coastal Track — Length 52km

This is one of DoC's designated 'Great Walks'. The Abel Tasman Coastal Track is located in Abel Tasman National Park on the South Island's northern coastline. All streams are bridged but there are tidal crossings which can only be traversed within a few hours either side of low tide. The track takes an average of 3 to 5 days to complete and can be walked in either direction.

While the Abel Tasman Coastal Track is a one-way track, it can be combined with the Abel Tasman Inland Track to form a 5 to 6-day circuit. By road it takes 2.5 hours to drive between Totaranui or Wainui and Marahau (approximately 100km). This road is narrow, winding and unsealed in places. By water taxi it takes 90 minutes to travel between Totaranui and Marahau.

Places to stay

DoC provides a range of accommodation along the Coastal Track, including 4 huts: Anchorage Hut (24 bunk), Bark Bay Hut (34 bunk), Awaroa Hut (26 bunk) and Whariwharangi Hut (20 bunk), as well as 18 campsites.

All huts have toilets, cooking benches, tables and heating. Communal bunkrooms contain platform bunks and mattresses. Ablution blocks have flush toilets and washbasins with cold water only. There are no cooking facilities or lighting (candles or torches are needed). Potable water is usually provided at huts. However, be prepared to boil, treat or filter drinking water if the DoC water filters are not working correctly. 'Backcountry Hut' tickets and passes are not valid for use on the Coastal Track; however, hut spaces still need to be booked all year round and overnight stays are limited to 2 consecutive nights. There is no charge for day walks.

All campsites have a water supply and toilets and some campsites have cooking shelters and fireplaces. Open fires are only permitted where fireplaces are provided and when there is no fire ban in force.

NOTE: Campers are not permitted to use hut facilities. Campsites need to be booked all year round. Camping at Totaranui is limited to 1 night all year round, and at other campsites 2 nights in any 1 campsite between 1 October to 30 April and 5 nights from 1 May to 30 September.

Walking Season

The Coastal Track is open all year. Transport, activity, equipment and accommodation operators are available year-round. The number of walkers on the track between Torrent Bay and Bark Bay peaks each January with over 250 people per day and drops in August to fewer than 25 people a day.

In peak season (October to April) DoC hut wardens and staff are based at the huts and Totaranui Camp Office. Bookings can't be made at the DoC Totaranui Camp Office due to unreliable internet access and restricted office hours. In winter, wardens rotate among the huts.

The advantages of visiting the Abel Tasman coast in the winter include fewer travellers, calmer water, less water traffic, hardly any insects and off-peak hut and campsite fees. The main disadvantages are the shorter daylight hours and cooler temperatures.

Getting there

Either take public transport to the track or walk into the park from the car parks at each road end. Alternatively, catch a water taxi to one of the beaches along the track.

Bus services operate in summer from Nelson and Motueka to major road ends at Marahau and Kaiteriteri and connect with Takaka transport to Totaranui and Wainui. Bookings are recommended. In winter, bus services operate daily to Marahau and Kaiteriteri but not so regularly to Wainui and Totaranui.

Water taxis operate year-round from Marahau and Kaiteriteri. The scheduled water-taxi pick-up locations are: Anchorage, Torrent Bay, Bark Bay, Onetahuti, Awaroa and Totaranui.

VEHICLE PARKING: DoC provides a car park at Marahau, Totaranui, Wainui and Awaroa road ends. Cars are parked at the owner's/driver's risk, but secure parking can be arranged at various Marahau businesses. The Coastal Track is accessible by road at 4 points, each with a car park:

- Marahau, the southern gateway, is 67km from Nelson on a sealed road.
- Wainui is 21km from Takaka. For the last 2km, the road is unsealed.
- Totaranui is 32km from Takaka. For the last 13km, the road is unsealed.
- Awaroa estuary is 31km from Takaka. The last 12km of road is rough and unsealed. There are 2 fords, which flood after heavy rain. From the Awaroa car park on the northern side of the estuary, it's 25 minutes of tidal walk to the DoC Awaroa hut and campsite, which are on the southern side of the estuary.

◼ Dusky Track — Length 84km

Dusky Track offers trampers a challenging 84km tramping track which requires at least 8 days to complete. It links Lake Hauroko with Lake Manapouri, as well as offering a 2-day detour to Supper Cove in Dusky Sound that traverses 3 major valley systems and crosses 2 mountain ranges.

The track crosses exceptionally mountainous country rising to 1600m. The U-shaped valleys were carved by deep glaciers during the Ice Ages, the last of which ended some 14,000 years ago. The glaciers and sheet ice have left behind hanging side valleys, horned peaks and high basins now filled by lakes. There are 21 three-wire bridges on this track. You can expect to encounter fallen trees, deep mud, tree roots and river crossings. The track is suitable only for well-equipped and experienced individuals and groups.

NOTE: This is not one of DoC's 'Great Walks'.

Places to stay

There are 7 huts on Dusky Track: Hauroko Hut (10 bunk), Halfway Hut (12 bunk), West Arm Hut (6 bunk), Upper Spey Hut (12 bunk), Kintail Hut (12 bunk), Loch Maree Hut (12 bunk) and Supper Cove Hut (12 bunk). Each hut is supplied with mattresses and a pit toilet. Hut users must pay hut fees. All the huts are standard huts, requiring 1 Backcountry Hut ticket per night or a Backcountry Hut pass. Tickets should be purchased in advance from any DoC office or approved retailer. Dusky Track is not suitable for camping.

Getting there

Dusky Track can be reached from the south by a scheduled boat service on Lake Hauroko, 64km west of Tuatapere. From the north a launch operates daily across Lake Manapouri. It is also possible to fly in to or out from Supper Cove or Lake Hauroko by float plane or helicopter.

◼ Greenstone-Caples Track — Length 50km

The Caples and Greenstone valleys are linked by McKellar Saddle, a subalpine pass that makes a moderate 4 to 5-day round trip. The Greenstone Valley is a wide, open valley with tussock flats and beech forest. In comparison, Caples is a narrower valley filled with forest interspersed with grassy clearings. Either of these tracks can be linked with the Routeburn Track or they can be walked as a one-way track starting or finishing at the Divide.

The grassy river flats of the Caples and Greenstone valleys are private farmland. Please respect this fact and stay on the tracks which follow the forest edge. Fiordland National Park begins at the southern end of Lake McKellar. The superb diversity of natural features in this area was recognised internationally with the establishment in 1991 of the Te Wahipounamu–South West New Zealand World Heritage Area. World Heritage status means this part of the country has been recognised as being among the world's foremost natural landscapes.

NOTE: This is not one of DoC's 'Great Walks'.

Places to stay

There are 4 huts on the Greenstone Track: Mid Caples Hut (12 bunk), Upper Caples Hut (12 bunk), McKellar Hut (12 bunk) and Greenstone Hut (20 bunk). The DoC huts on the track are serviced with coal fires for heating only. All huts have mattresses. There is running water in summer months at all huts. Hikers should carry their own cookers as gas stoves are not provided. Hut wardens are present on the tracks from late October to mid-April. A Backcountry Hut pass or tickets must be purchased in advance from a DoC office or approved outlet. Camping is permitted along the bush edge, 50m from the track.

NOTE: You cannot camp on McKellar Saddle or on the open valley floors of the Caples or Greenstone valleys — this is private land. There is no fee for camping unless you use the hut facilities. Fires are only to be lit in recognised fireplaces and must be kept small and be properly put out before leaving the area.

Walking season

Although the tracks are not closed in winter, snow may make travel very difficult, even on the valley floors. Check and register your intentions with a DoC visitor centre before you start your trip and enquire about snow conditions. Side streams on these track systems may also flood due to heavy rains, so always check the weather forecast before entering the area. Remember to sign out at the end of your trip.

Getting there

The Caples and Greenstone tracks start from the car park at the end of Greenstone Road, 86km from Queenstown via Glenorchy. Alternatively, they can be started from Howden Hut on the Routeburn Track, which is 1 hour's walk from the Divide, 80km from Te Anau on the road to Milford Sound. In summer, both ends of the tracks are serviced daily by various transport companies and a boat service operates from Glenorchy to the Greenstone Wharf. Go to: **www.glenorchyinfocentre.co.nz/tracktransport.pdf**

▓ Heaphy Track — Length 78.4km

The Heaphy Track, located in Kahurangi National Park at the northwest corner of the South Island, is the longest of DoC's 'Great Walks'. For 78km the track traverses the park's lush landscapes from the junction of the Brown and Aorere rivers, over expansive tussock downs, through lush forests, to the nikau palms of the wild West Coast.

The track is well formed and suitable for fit, well-equipped people. All rivers and major streams are bridged. This popular hiking track takes 4 to 6 days to complete.

Places to stay

There are 7 DoC huts on the Heaphy Track: Brown Hut (16 bunk), Perry Saddle Hut (24 bunk), Gouland Downs Hut (8 bunk), Saxon Hut (16 bunk), James Mackay Hut (26 bunk), Lewis Hut (20 bunk) and Heaphy Hut (28 bunk), as well as 9 campsites en route. Hikers must have a 'Great Walk' ticket to stay in huts or campsites. On longer hikes walkers usually stay at Perry Saddle, Saxon, James Mackay and Heaphy huts. A popular 2-day trip on the western side is from Kohaihai to Heaphy Hut and return to Kohaihai.

All huts have heating, toilets, bunks, mattresses and water. Gas cooking facilities are available at Perry Saddle, Saxon, James Mackay, Lewis and Heaphy huts but not at Brown and Gouland Downs huts. None of the huts have lighting or pots and pans so take your own. Backcountry Hut tickets and passes are not valid for use on the Heaphy Track, yet hut spaces still need to be booked all year round. Overnight stays in huts along the Heaphy Track are limited to 2 consecutive nights.

All campsites need to be booked. Overnight stays in campsites along the Heaphy Track are limited to 2 consecutive nights at any 1 campsite and campers are not permitted to use hut facilities. All campsites have a water supply and toilets and some campsites have fireplaces. Open fires are only permitted where fireplaces are provided.

Ahead of the pack on the Heaphy Track in the Nelson region.

ANCIENT SETTLEMENT: Trampers staying at Heaphy Hut are resting right next to one of New Zealand's oldest and most interesting archaeological sites. The nearby bank of the Heaphy River was once a 13th- or 14th-century village, settled by people whose parents or grandparents could well have been born in Polynesia.

Walking season

The Heaphy Track is open year-round — however, transport, activity, equipment and accommodation businesses operate mainly in the summer. All huts and campsites must be booked. In summer (November to April), DoC rangers rotate among the huts, while in winter they are on the track or at the huts less frequently.

Getting there

As the ends of the track are 463km apart by road access, the Heaphy is a one-way track. Bus and taxi services are available to reach either end from nearby towns, with regular bus services linking Nelson and Westport. Air services make it possible to walk the track one-way and return by air close to your starting point. You can start the Heaphy Track either from Brown Hut, Golden Bay or from Kohaihai. Both ends of the track are accessible by road and have telephones.

To reach the eastern end of the track, take the road up the Aorere Valley from Collingwood. From Collingwood to Brown Hut is 28km. Three small creeks must be forded on the way but do not attempt to cross these when the river is in flood. The fords may remain impassable for several days, blocking access to and from the track. To reach the western end, head north from Karamea for 15km to the car park and campsite at the Kohaihai River.

◼ Hollyford Track — Length 56km

The Hollyford Track is the only major track in Fiordland at low altitude which can be walked in any season and also connects to the Fiordland coastline. It starts from the Lower Hollyford Road end to the old abandoned port of Martins Bay.

Stepping into the dramatic Hollyford Valley is like entering a world that's remained largely untouched for thousands of years. Geologically spectacular and ever changing, the sheer diversity of vegetation and wildlife in this one valley is truly unparalleled.

Beginning among the sheer rock walls of the Darran Mountains, the track follows the Hollyford River (Whakatipu Ka Tuka) on its journey to the sea. Features of the track are the 2 lakes, Alabaster (Waiwahuika) and McKerrow (Whakatipu Waitai). The latter is the site of the now abandoned Jamestown which was established in 1870. The forest is a mix of native lowland species yet there are also spectacular views of the Darran Mountains. The remote and often wild coastline is inhabited by seals, penguins and herons.

Picking a route forward on the Hollyford Track, Fiordland.

You can walk the track independently or as part of a guided group tour lasting 3 days. This is an all-inclusive experience where you'll enjoy fine cuisine prepared and served by friendly lodge hosts while relaxing in their well-appointed and comfortable bunk-style accommodation. A maximum number of 16 people in each group provides for a personal experience, with an experienced guide sharing their intimate knowledge of the area with the group.

NOTE: This is not one of DoC's 'Great Walks'. Go to: www.hollyfordtrack.com

Places to stay

DoC provides and maintains 6 huts on the Hollyford Track: Hidden Falls Hut (12 bunk), Lake Alabaster Hut (26 bunk), Demon Trail Hut (12 bunk), Martins Bay Hut (12 bunk), Hokuri Hut (12 bunk) and McKerrow Island Hut (12 bunk). Each is supplied with mattresses, running water, wood-burning stoves and toilet facilities. The platform bunks are designed to accommodate the number of people shown for each hut. Everyone who uses the huts must pay hut fees. Tickets should be purchased in advance from the Fiordland National Park Visitor Centre in Te Anau or any DoC office or approved outlet.

Walking season

The Hollyford Track is unusual among Fiordland's major tracks in that it is largely flat and accessible year-round. However, sections of the track can become impassable after heavy rain, especially the Demon Trail area. Travellers should also take care with three-wire river crossings. If in doubt, sit it out. Take adequate food and clothing and allow for weather changes and possible delays. Personally guided trips only operate between October to April each year.

Getting there

The track starts at the end of the Lower Hollyford Road. Turn off State Highway 94, the Milford Road, at Marian Corner. Allow 2 hours to drive from Te Anau to the road end. A number of companies offer an on-demand service from Te Anau to Hollyford Road end or Gunns Camp. Cabin accommodation and campsites are available at Gunns Camp on the Lower Hollyford Road.

▦ Kepler Track — Length 60km

The Kepler Track, designated one of DoC's 'Great Walks', traverses a circular route through spectacular scenery in Fiordland National Park. It is also part of the Te Wahipounamu–South West New Zealand World Heritage Area.

The Kepler Track is an easy tramping track that takes 3 to 4 days to complete. Today over 8000 people walk the track each year.

Places to stay

There are 3 DoC huts on the track: Luxmore Hut (55 bunk), Iris Burn Hut (50 bunk) and Moturau Hut (40 bunk). During the peak season (28 October to 29 April), huts are supplied with gas cookers, tables, benches, cold running water, lighting and heating in the main kitchen/ dining hut. Bunkrooms have communal sleeping arrangements with mattresses provided. Ablution blocks have flush toilets and washbasins (cold water only) but there are no showers.

There are 2 camping possibilities on the Kepler Track at Brod Bay and near Iris Burn Hut. Campers share an open cooking shelter with an adjacent water supply and a pit toilet and are not permitted to use hut facilities. Camping or staying overnight in the day shelters at Forest Burn and Hanging Valley is not permitted.

Walking season

The peak period is 28 October to 29 April. The Kepler Track can be walked in either direction as a 3-night/4-day walk, staying in all 3 huts, or as a 2-night/3-day walk, staying at Luxmore and Iris Burn huts and finishing the track at Rainbow Reach. Bookings are essential for all overnight stays on the track and can be made online or by post, fax, email or phone. The winter season is May to mid-October and during these months hut tickets are necessary but bookings are not required. High snow loadings and avalanches can affect the track, especially between Luxmore Hut and Hanging Valley Shelter, and may make it impassable.

NOTE: Some facilities are removed from the huts during winter.

Getting there

The Kepler Track is accessed from the Lake Te Anau control gates, either by road or a 50-minute walk from the Fiordland National Park Visitor Centre in Te Anau, or over the swing bridge across the Waiau River at Rainbow Reach, a 12km drive from Te Anau. Shuttle buses also operate during the summer months to entry and exit points on the track and a scheduled boat service provides access to Brod Bay.

▦ Lake Waikaremoana — Length 46km

Designated one of DoC's 'Great Walks', Lake Waikaremoana is a 3 to 4-day tramping track which follows the shore of the lake for most of its length and can be walked in either direction. The lake was formed 2200 years ago by a huge landslide, which blocked a narrow gorge along the Waikaretaheke River. Water backed up behind this landslide to form a lake up to 248m deep. The lake edge has since been modified by a hydroelectric development which lowered the level by 5m in 1946.

Places to stay

There are 5 huts along the track: Panekiri Hut (36 bunk), Waiopaoa Hut (30 bunk), Marauiti Hut (26 bunk), Waiharuru Hut (40 bunk) and Whanganui Hut (18 bunk). All huts provide bunks, mattresses, a wood-burning stove or gas heater, water supply (if rainfall is sufficient), cooking benches and vault toilets. Users of both huts and campsites need to carry their own portable cooking stoves. It is recommended that you boil or treat all drinking water.

To stay overnight at a hut or campsite on the Lake Waikaremoana Track you must have a booking prior to starting the track for everyone who is intending to do the walk. This includes those children and young people under 17 years who do not have to pay fees. The 5 designated campsites have cooking shelters, grassed tent sites, water supply (if rainfall is sufficient) and vault toilets. Camping on the track is only permitted at these campsites.

For those wanting a guided tour, try the 4-day hike on the lake with 'Walking Legends' through the North Island's largest untouched native forest. This is a wilderness hiking experience for small groups, with spectacular scenery, great food and wine and small backpacks! Go to: **www.walkinglegends.com**

Walking season

Magnificent scenery and plenty of opportunity for swimming and fishing ensures the walk is well used throughout the year. To enjoy your trip in all weathers, you will need to be reasonably fit and have good equipment. The walk is a moderate tramp with a climb and descent of about 600m over the Panekiri Ridge. If you are hiking independently you can expect to walk 4 to 6 hours a day carrying a pack of up to 15kg. If you are camping you will also need to carry a tent and a sleeping mat. Please note that it can snow in summer — so go well prepared.

Getting there

Located in the southwest corner of the 212,673ha Te Urewera National Park, Lake Waikaremoana can be approached from 2 directions. State Highway 38 links Wairoa and the East Coast with the central North Island, and passes the lake and the Aniwaniwa Visitor Centre. The highway has a 2-wheel-drive gravel surface for about 90km between Murupara and Aniwaniwa. There are well-marked side roads to the main boat ramps, campsites and walk entrances. Privately owned shuttle buses and water taxis provide transport to either end of the walk throughout the year. This allows walkers to leave their vehicles at the Waikaremoana Motor Camp, where they are more secure than at the walk ends.

■ Milford Track — Length 53.5km

One of DoC's designated 'Great Walks', the Milford Track is in the heart of spectacular Fiordland National Park, part of the Te Wahipounamu–South West New Zealand World Heritage Area. The track starts at the head of Lake Te Anau and finishes at Milford Sound.

The epithet 'The finest walk in the world' first accompanied an article by poet Blanche Baughan which was published in the *London Spectator* in 1908. Today the Milford Track is New Zealand's best-known walking track, with over 14,000 independent and guided trampers completing the walk each year. 'Ultimate Hikes' hold the only DoC-approved concession for overnight guided walks on the Milford Track during the peak walking season. Go to: **www.ultimatehikes.co.nz**

Places to stay

There are 3 DoC huts on the track: Clinton Hut (40 bunk), Mintaro Hut (40 bunk) and Dumpling Hut (40 bunk). Facilities for guided walkers are not available to independent walkers. During the peak season huts are supplied with gas cookers, tables, benches, cold running water, lighting and heating in the main kitchen/dining hut. Bunkrooms have communal sleeping arrangements with mattresses provided. Ablution blocks have flush toilets and washbasins (cold water only) but there are no showers. For your own safety, please sign the hut books on arrival. Camping and staying overnight in the day shelters is not permitted on the track.

Walking season

During the peak season (October to late April) the Milford Track can only be walked as a 3-night/4-day package, starting at the head of Lake Te Anau and finishing at Sandfly Point, Milford Sound. Bookings

The views of Lake Waikaremoana are worth the hike.

Packs waiting to be transported on the Queen Charlotte Track.

MINERS WHARF

ENDE

are essential and can be made online or by post, fax, email or phone. A maximum of 40 people may start the track each day. During the winter season (May to late October) hut tickets are necessary but bookings are not required. The track can be walked in either direction during this time. High snow loadings and avalanches can occur and may well make the track impassable.

Getting there

The Milford Track requires boat transport at both ends. Bus or private transport is required to Te Anau Downs and also from Milford Sound. During the summer there are regular transport services to and from the track.

▩ Queen Charlotte Track — Length 71km

DoC-administered Queen Charlotte Track lies deep in the heart of the Marlborough Sounds at the top of the South Island. Stretching from Ship Cove to Anakiwa, home of the renowned Outward Bound School, the track passes through lush coastal forest, around historic bays and along skyline ridges, affording travellers unsurpassed views of both Queen Charlotte and Kenepuru sounds.

Much of the track's charm is due to its relative ease of access, which allows visitors to walk or bike it in sections. It is also possible for visitors to arrange for a boat operator to transport their packs between accommodation places. Historic Ship Cove is the favoured point for beginning the track.

As you journey the track, you will pass through a variety of vegetation types, ranging from undisturbed native forest to gorse-covered hills with regenerating forest and grassy farmland, all of which are typical of the New Zealand landscape. Both ends of the track begin in forested reserves. At sea level the forest is particularly lush: ferns, tree ferns, nikau palms, climbing kiekie and perching plants flourish, making up a spectacular coastal domain that has been lost in so many other places.

Queen Charlotte Track is classified as being wide and benched. All the major streams are bridged; however, stout walking boots and a good level of fitness are required.

NOTE: This is not one of DoC's designated 'Great Walks'.

Places to stay

There are many places to stay along the way, either in private accommodation or in DoC campsites. A number of accommodation houses are marked on the map, providing hostel, cabin, motel and hotel lodgings and tent sites. The private tracks that leave the main track to private accommodation are not constructed to the same standard as the Queen Charlotte Track and may be narrow, steep and slippery when wet. Some private accommodation sites may not be signposted, so make sure you get clear directions when you book.

There are 6 DoC-managed, 'self-registration' campsites on the track, each with toilets and water supply. The campsites at Bay of Many Coves and Black Rock are not at sea level. There are no cooking facilities at the campsites so you need to carry your own cooker. Camping fees for DoC campsites are to be deposited in the self-registration box at each site or prepaid at the Picton i-Site or at the DoC office in Picton.

Walking season

The Queen Charlotte Track is open all year round and is an easy walking track suitable for both walkers and mountain-bike riders, taking 3 to 5 days to complete walking, or 2 to 3 days for mountain bikers.

Getting there

Private transport: Anakiwa, Mistletoe Saddle, Torea Saddle and Kenepuru Saddle are all accessible by road. Anakiwa, Mistletoe Bay, Torea Bay, Camp Bay, Endeavour Inlet, Resolution Bay and Ship Cove can be accessed by sea. Many of the short walks can be enjoyed from these places.

A number of companies offer boat transport to and from points along the track, including Ship Cove. Regular and on-demand bus services link Anakiwa with Picton.
Go to: **www.destinationmarlborough.com**

■ Rakiura — Length 36km

Rakiura Track, a designated DoC 'Great Walk', is located on Stewart Island, just a 20-minute flight from Invercargill or an hour by ferry from Bluff. Stewart Island (Rakiura) is home to New Zealand's most southerly national park, Rakiura National Park, and the Rakiura Track. Although the trail is a 29km tramping track, suitable for anyone with moderate fitness, the entire circuit is actually 36km

in total, including road walking. It takes 3 days and provides a good introduction to the diverse scenery of the island.

Stewart Island is remarkable for its almost complete overall coverage of natural vegetation extending from the sea to cloudy, windswept summits. The highest mountain of the island, Mt Anglem (Hananui), reaches 980m and is visible from a section of the track along the open coast. The Rakiura Track, however, does not involve travel above the bush line. It traverses mainly rimu and kamahi forest with a rich diversity of tree ferns, ground ferns and perching orchids. Rata only becomes more common at higher altitudes.

Places to stay

There are 2 huts on the track: Port William Hut (24 bunk) and North Arm Hut (24 bunk). Bunks are claimed on a first come, first served basis, with a limit of 2 consecutive nights in any hut. They are supplied with mattresses, a wood-burning stove for heating, running water and toilets. Cookers and cooking utensils are not supplied so it's essential to carry your own portable stove, fuel and utensils.

Camping is permitted only at the designated campsites at Maori Beach, Port William and Sawdust Bay. A cooking shelter, water supply and toilet have been provided at each site. Once on the island, sea kayaks and water taxis are available for hire and can be used for access to the Rakiura Track huts.

Walking season

Rakiura Track is suitable for tramping all year round, but Stewart Island's weather is very changeable and difficult to predict. Strong winds, hail and heavy rain can occur at any time of the year so you should go equipped for the very worst weather conditions. Remember, exposure and hypothermia can affect anyone. Stewart Island waters are extremely changeable and should be treated with the utmost respect.

Getting there

The track begins at Lee Bay, the official entrance to Rakiura National Park. To commence the track, turn right from the island's DoC visitor centre, heading towards the waterfront. Follow the road over a series of hills to Horseshoe Bay, then on to Lee Bay.

◼ Routeburn Track — Length 32km

Designated one of DoC's 'Great Walks', the Routeburn Track traverses 32km of Mount Aspiring and Fiordland National Parks, part of the Te Wahipounamu–South West New Zealand World Heritage Area.

The Routeburn Track is today considered one of New Zealand's most popular tracks, with over 13,000 walkers completing the track each year. You can travel the track independently or as part of a guided group. Ultimate Hikes hold the only DoC-approved concession for overnight guided walks on the Routeburn Track during the peak walking season. Go to: **www.ultimatehikes.co.nz**

Places to stay

There are 4 DoC huts on the track: Routeburn Flats Hut (20 bunk), Routeburn Falls Hut (48 bunk), Lake Mackenzie Hut (50 bunk) and Lake Howden Hut (28 bunk). During the Great Walks peak season (late October to late April) huts are supplied with gas cookers, tables, benches, cold running water, lighting and heating in the main kitchen/dining hut. Bunkrooms have communal sleeping arrangements with mattresses provided. Ablution blocks have flush toilets and washbasins (cold water only) but there are no showers. For your own safety, please sign the hut books on arrival.

There are only 2 designated campsites on the Routeburn Track — sited near the Routeburn Flats and Lake Mackenzie huts. Campers share an open cooking shelter with an adjacent water supply and a pit toilet. The use of hut facilities by campers is not permitted.

Walking season

Peak season is late October to late April. Most walkers take 3 days to complete the track, usually staying at Lake Mackenzie and Routeburn Falls huts. However, the trip can be extended by also staying at the Lake Howden and Routeburn Flats huts. Those walking the track from one end and finishing at the other will need to make transport arrangements, as it is 350km by road between the track's two ends. Bookings are essential for all overnight stays on the track and can be made online or by post, fax, email or phone. Winter season (May to late October) hut tickets are necessary but bookings are not required. High snow loadings and avalanches can occur, especially between Lake Harris and the Mackenzie Hut, and may well make the track impassable. Some facilities are removed from the huts and track during winter.

Getting there

The Routeburn Track is located in the southwest of the South Island and extends between the head of Lake Wakatipu and State Highway 94, the Te Anau to Milford road. The nearest townships of Queenstown, Te Anau and Glenorchy offer a full range of accommodation. Access the track by road at either the Routeburn Shelter (the starting or finishing point at the Mount Aspiring National Park end of the track), or at the Divide (the starting or finishing point at the Fiordland National Park end of the track).

◼ Tongariro Northern Circuit — Length 41km

Also designated one of DoC's 'Great Walks', the Tongariro Northern Circuit winds its way over the Tongariro massif and around Mt Ngauruhoe. This walk passes through unique and stunning landforms which include volcanic craters and glacial valleys.

The Tongariro Northern Circuit is considered a challenging hike, largely on open exposed terrain, much of it on uneven track surface. It can be subject to sudden rapid weather change. You should be at least moderately fit. If you are considering taking on the Circuit make sure you have good warm clothing, a waterproof and windproof parka, leggings, comfortable well-constructed hiking boots, hat and sunscreen.

The Tongariro Northern Circuit connects with the Round the Mountain Track at 2 points — Whakapapa Village and Waihohonu.

Places to stay

There are 4 huts on the circuit: Ketetahi Hut (26 bunk), Mangatepopo Hut (23 bunk), Oturere Hut (26 bunk) and Waihohonu Hut (29 bunk). There is rainwater for drinking at the huts but you need to bring cooking pots, utensils, sleeping bag, food and toilet paper. Gas cookers and gas heating are installed at the huts.

Campsites have been established near each of the huts on the circuit. Facilities at the huts can be used when camping but camping is prohibited within 500m of the track. Hut and camping fees go towards servicing and maintenance to ensure that these special back-country facilities remain available. DoC visitor centres provide further information and hut or campsite pass sales.

Walking season

The peak season is late October to early June. Dated 'Great Walks' passes for huts and campsites are required during the Great Walks season and should be purchased before commencing this trip. There is a surcharge for passes purchased from hut wardens. Backcountry Hut passes and tickets are not accepted at huts on the Tongariro Northern Circuit during the Great Walks season.

A range of trips can be planned around the Tongariro Northern Circuit: day trips, overnight trips, or a 3 to 4-day walk around the complete circuit. The safest and most popular time of year to walk the Circuit is during the summer months (December to March) when the tracks are normally clear of snow and the weather is less severe. In winter, snow and ice make this a full alpine trip requiring ice axes and crampons. During and after heavy snowfalls, avalanches are possible. With adequate clothing, equipment and experience, people can visit and enjoy the area at any time of year. Please check the weather forecast, track conditions and avalanche hazard before departure.

Getting there

The Tongariro Northern Circuit can be accessed from Whakapapa Village, Mangatepopo Road, Ketetahi Road and the Desert Road (State Highway 1).

SAFETY AND SURVIVAL SKILLS

The Mountain Safety Council who help advise search-and-rescue authorities warn all hikers venturing into the bush or on remote back-country trails to set a 'panic button' so that in the event a hiker has not returned by a particular time and date, a search can be triggered. Remember to write down the route you are taking, how long you intend going for and where you've parked your vehicle, and then leave the information with a responsible person. Always sign and date hut books.

Before departing have a bad-weather alternative to fall back on and check with DoC, local hiking clubs, regional authorities or district councils about the track and hut conditions. Monitor the weather forecast in the days before you leave, watch and respond to weather conditions during the trip, and keep to the tracks. If you become lost, stop, find shelter, stay calm and wait for searchers to arrive. Do not move away from the area unless you're absolutely sure of direction and location. During winter, tracks are often impassable due to snowstorms, slips, ice and avalanches. New Zealand's weather changes rapidly. It can be very cold at any time of the year. Always be physically and mentally prepared for the worst conditions and be ready to change your plans if necessary. Beware of rivers, especially when they are swollen — know when, where and how to cross one. If in doubt, stay out.

Carry at least a reliable means of communication such as a mountain radio, satellite phone or 406MHz emergency beacon and as a back-up a fully charged mobile phone. Always make sure the emergency communication device is securely fixed to your person so that it can't get dislodged when hiking through scrub brush or in the case of a fall. Always pack additional food rations and a full first-aid kit, a space blanket and additional warm clothing. In most outfitting stores you'll be able to buy a waterproof 'dry bag' in the event you need to wade across a river or you are caught in extreme weather. Learn how to make an emergency bivvy tent, and ration food supplies if you are too injured to walk out. Always carry waterproof matches and an all-purpose multi-tool.

When things go wrong, use the STAR Model for making decisions:

■ STOP: Take a breath, sit down and remain calm.
■ THINK: Look around you, listen, brainstorm ideas.
■ ASSESS: Evaluate the options and their potential consequences.
■ RESPOND: Take the best alternative.

Some people with this knowledge have been known to survive for 7 days under adverse circumstances.

Canyons & Caves — Canyoning, Abseiling, Caving

These three topics are related in more ways than one. Inevitably, if you go canyoning in New Zealand you'll need to know some basic methods of abseiling, and luckily most companies that arrange such trips teach it to you in next to no time at all — then all you need to do is overcome your fear of heights! The same thing applies to caving, as many times you will abseil down into a cave to start off your adventure. The only real difference is that canyoning and abseiling can be practised above ground and in a relatively short time and in a relatively safe environment. Caving, as the name implies, is a dark world often hundreds of metres underground — however, it can be a dangerous activity even for the very experienced. Cavers can become trapped by rising floodwaters and in some instances inexperienced cavers venture places they shouldn't go.

Thankfully, there are many clubs, organisations and operators who cater to tourists wanting to experience new adventures, whether it is above or below ground. New Zealand has been blessed, as most Kiwis know, with some of the world's most spectacular scenery to go exploring in as well as some hidden caverns that rival the very best overseas. So jump into streams, slide down chutes, abseil your way beneath waterfalls and wade and float through blackwater rivers. There is a plethora of these amazing opportunities just waiting for you to discover, so dive on in.

ASCENTS AND DESCENTS — NORTH ISLAND

■ Auckland Adventures — Multiple Sites

This operator is a flexible, small group adventure company offering a personalised service and a variety of adventure tourism products. They recommend a number of abseiling sites with heights ranging from 26 to 75m, usually Auckland-based — however, they can arrange adventures to Wharepapa, Waitomo or anywhere else there are suitable cliff sites. An average of 8 people can abseil or rap jump per hour and there is no necessary experience required as full instruction and moral support is supplied. All their instructors are fully (NZOIA) New Zealand Outdoor Instructors Association qualified, and equipment is monitored and replaced regularly.
Go to: **www.aucklandadventures.co.nz**

■ Canyonz — Blue Canyon, Auckland

This is one of Auckland's premier wilderness-outdoor adventures. Discover for yourself a superb

Abseiling down waterfall at Piha, near Auckland

Holding back the water at Piha, near Auckland.

gorge called Blue Canyon only 40 minutes from the city. Canyonz is the only company licensed to operate tours in the Blue Canyon — a hidden subtropical region in the heart of the Waitakere rainforest. The adventure is via an amazing natural playground with 18 waterfalls and more abseils, jumps and waterslides than any other river in Auckland. No experience is necessary for this 3-hour adventure, just an average level of fitness. The company provides a wetsuit, neoprene socks, and shoes for canyoning, harness, helmet, as well as lunch at Karekare Beach — one of the locations for the movie *The Piano*. Departs year-round at 9.30am. Go to: **www.canyonz.co.nz**

■ Canyonz — Sleeping God Tour, Thames

This canyoning expedition is the ultimate adrenalin rush — one of those exciting New Zealand adventures that is just screaming out to be experienced. It is located near Thames in the absolutely amazing and dramatic Kauaeranga Valley. The Sleeping God tour is a vertical descent of over 300m down a steep set of spectacular waterfalls that involves abseiling up to 80m drops. These small group trips allow you to jump into deep pools from up to a height of 13m, as well as a series of exhilarating water slides. The tour is aimed at people with a good level of fitness who are water-confident and want a real taste of adventure. This is an all-day tour leaving Auckland at 7am. Big jumps

are optional, abseils are not. All gear is provided, along with expert guides, transport and lunch. Go to: **www.canyonz.co.nz**

■ Piha Canyoning — Auckland

Just 40 minutes from downtown Auckland you'll find yourself at the foot of the largest commercial waterfall abseil in the Waitakere Ranges. The Piha Canyon in which the waterfalls are located is a majestic subtropical rainforest. During this adventure you'll spend an exhilarating day abseiling or rappelling down showering waterfalls that fall on moss-covered volcanic rocks below. Remember, jumps and abseils are optional and there is no experience required. Day trips depart at 9.30am. Go to: **www.awoladventures.co.nz**

■ Taranaki Outdoor Adventures — Fossil Canyon, Taranaki

This little gem that includes abseiling, water sliding, river floating and a hiking adventure all rolled into one could turn out to be a real classic. The top section of the river is a masterpiece of nature and certainly a place largely undiscovered. This is a region you are going to have to go and see for yourself. Even the guys from Outdoor Adventures admit it's the most amazing piece of river they have seen in Taranaki replete with beautiful waterfalls, gorges, swimming holes and limestone water slides. Go to: **www.toa.co.nz**

Wet, wet, wet on a canyoning adventure at Wanaka.

ASCENTS AND DESCENTS — SOUTH ISLAND

■ 12 Mile Delta Canyoning — Queenstown

Imagine descending into a canyon, plunging into pools, sliding down cascading chutes, abseiling waterfalls and swimming in narrow passageways. You don't actually need any abseiling skills either. It's just a gentle walk through 10 minutes of native bush to the beginning of this canyoning experience. However, you'll need a willingness to try new things and a desire to explore. If you are the daring type, this will certainly challenge your highly tuned ego. Lastly, take a moment to soak in the splendid vista of Lake Wakatipu as you exit the canyon onto the 12 Mile Delta. Go to: **www.canyoning.co.nz**

■ Deep Canyon — Wanaka

Deep Canyon offer all-day canyoning experiences that are mainly geared to adults. Canyons in Wanaka are world class, with steep drops and deep pools. The trip in Niger Stream involves 40 minutes' travelling and then you'll kit up. It's then a 40-minute uphill hike followed by 1 hour's instruction on how to abseil. The trip itself is 4 hours of canyoning, after which you'll get changed and have lunch and return to town. There are 8 abseils, 5 of which are over 15m; while 1 is an optional slide or jump. Big Nige is similar but the walk in is 1 hour plus 5 hours spent canyoning. The main difference is the upper section which contains abseils directly in the waterfalls, meaning it's less suited to beginners and is more intermediate level. Their trips are focused on small groups as they rev up the excitement factor with heaps of fun in a unique and fabulous natural setting.
Go to: **www.deepcanyon.co.nz**

■ Live-Life Experiences — Nelson

This company claim there is only one uniquely suitable place for their activities in the top of the South Island region and Live-Life Experiences has found it. They offer a number of options from caving, rock climbing and hiking to abseiling and canyoning as part of a trip they have developed into the distant Merino Mountains. It truly is an awesome place and one that very few locals know about. You'll discover water-sculpted limestone holes, bowls, spires and cliffs. The fact that you're abseiling through this area is only part of the thrill. The canyon gets so tight that it's virtually only shoulder distance apart. Go to: **www.live-life.co.nz**

■ Routeburn Canyoning — Glenorchy

In the small town of Glenorchy 50km from Queenstown is a relatively new adventure in the area. Utilising the Routeburn Track to gain access into the canyon, adventure junkies don wetsuits and harnesses to navigate a way through the tight and steep bedrock, which has created beautiful sculpted walls and spectacular waterfalls. You'll make your way through this river tributary by walking, scrambling, climbing, abseiling and swimming. Don't forget your camera as there are some wonderful photographic opportunities. Go to: **www.gycanyoning.co.nz**

SAFETY AND SURVIVAL SKILLS

Canyoning and abseiling can present considerable risks, especially to the unsupervised or inexperienced. According to German mountaineer Pit Schubert, about 25 per cent of climbing deaths occur during rappelling — most commonly due to failing anchors.

Another frequent cause of accidents is abseiling beyond the end of the rope. Abseiling is prohibited or discouraged in some areas of New Zealand, due to the potential for environmental damage and/or conflict with climbers heading upwards, or the danger to people on the ground. Always check first — and unless you are experienced with your own equipment, join an organised group.

CAVING IN NEW ZEALAND

Cavers from all corners of the globe recognise just how really spectacular our world-class caving systems are. No matter what your plans, whether it's a wander through a cavernous cathedral-like grotto or squeezing through subterranean cracks in the earth's crust, New Zealand will deliver some memorable moments and heart-racing adventure opportunities. Virtually every part of the country, except for Otago (excluding North Otago) has caves. The most important caving areas are at Waitomo, northwest Nelson and north Westland. So slip below the surface and discover the best regions to explore.

CAVE TYPES: The vast majority of caves in New Zealand are formed in limestone, or in its metamorphic variety, marble. Other than this, there are some lava caves formed in volcanic rocks as they cool, principally in and around Auckland City.

Delving into history

On 1 October 1949 the New Zealand Speleological Society came into existence. It had one member, Henry G. Lambert, who was declared President, Secretary, Treasurer and Editor of the *NZSS Bulletin*. At that time very little was known about caves in New Zealand. Information was gleaned from borough councils, museums, university geologists, geological surveys and private citizens. The Society was set up to collate this information and make it available to earnest enquirers to stimulate further exploration and to add to this knowledge. There are currently about 300 members.

In the Society's early days, the sport was very much based around Auckland and activities were limited to the Auckland and Waikato regions. Before long, though, a strong core of active cavers began developing and exploring the Waikato, particularly at Hamilton and Waitomo.

During the 1960s, caving clubs were formed in Wellington, Nelson and Christchurch, and these became affiliated to the Society, gradually extending its influence across the country. Nowadays, most caving activity is at Waitomo, Mahoenui (North Taranaki), northwest Nelson and north Westland. The Society's structure reflects its broad geographical base, though most of the membership resides in the northern North Island.

Sunbeams enter the Waitomo Caves.

Anga near the coast, contains most of the North Island's best-known caves, including the longest, Gardners Gut, which is 12km long. Other major caves are the stream caves of Mangapu and Mangawhitikau and the Waitomo headwaters system.

To the south towards Awakino, the limestone block narrows. Popular areas in north Taranaki include Puketiti, Matawhero and Mahoenui, containing several caves more than 4km long.

On the East Cape is the Whakapunake area, containing the Te Reinga Cave and the Mangaone Valley with the Mangaone Cave. To the south, between Coonoor and Makuri in the northern Wairarapa, there are numerous small caves.

Other small North Island caving areas include Pohangina (north of Palmerston North), Taihape, Martinborough and Mauriceville.

CAVING LOCATIONS — SOUTH ISLAND

Caves are found in both limestone and marble throughout northwest Nelson. The marble areas — Takaka Hill, Mt Arthur and Mt Owen — are alpine in character, with caves found up to 1700m above sea level. These three marble mountains contain all of New Zealand's deepest caves, as well as the three longest — Bulmer Cavern (39km) at Mt Owen, Ellis Basin System (28km) and Nettlebed Cave (24km), both at Mt Arthur.

There is an important limestone area with numerous caves, mainly easy and well decorated with stalagmites and stalactites, at Paturau, west of Collingwood, as well as significant areas of limestone in the Aorere, Anatoki, Takaka and Cobb valleys. Moonsilver Cave in the Cobb is about 5km long.

The other major South Island area is north Westland. At Karamea is the 13km Honeycomb Hill Cave, with 70 entrances that include New Zealand's largest limestone arches. To the west of the Paparoa Range, a band of limestone stretches from Charleston to Punakaiki, containing caves such as The Metro near Charleston, with 8km of mainly large passages, and Xanadu Cave near Punakaiki, which

The Society's members, officers and affiliated clubs organise both exploratory and recreational trips to caves throughout New Zealand (and occasionally overseas). Caves are explored and surveyed, and the information gathered is disseminated through the Society's publications and stored in its archives. Go to: **www.caves.org.nz**

CAVING LOCATIONS — NORTH ISLAND

In Northland, there is a small limestone block containing some popular caves at Waipu. Beneath Auckland City and environs are lava caves, formed as the lava cooled. The region around Waitomo, extending southward to north Taranaki and to Te

Straddling the cauldron during a caving expedition in Waitomo.

is 5km long. To the east of the Paparoas is a smaller area of limestone, with Profanity Cave at Inangahua nearly 3km in length.

CAVING CLUBS

Auckland Speleo Club: **www.asg.org.nz**
Hamilton Tomo Group: **www.htg.org.nz**
Manawatu Speleological Group: **www.massey. ac.nz/~sglasgow/welcome.htm**
Wellington Caving Club: **www.caving.wellington. net.nz**
Nelson Speleological Group: **www.nsg.org.nz**
Canterbury Caving Group: **www.ccg.50webs.com**

SAFETY AND SURVIVAL SKILLS

The average visitor would be hard pressed to even find most of the caves in New Zealand, and then, once inside, would have difficulty either getting through or back out again. Some caves can flood very quickly, some have unstable rock falls, many have mazes of passages that confuse even those familiar with the system, and many have difficult, exposed climbs. Caving is best carried out with the guidance of local cavers, who know the caves, know the conditions and know the landowners. It is the local cavers who will have to rescue a visitor if anything goes wrong and one of their greatest annoyances is putting themselves at risk rescuing people who are inexperienced and ill prepared. So join a club and go underground with experienced cavers and you'll have the time of your life.

Rock of Ages — Climbing, Mountaineering

Gone are the days when climbing in leather boots with old worn rope was the norm, but harking back to those years is something that many climbers nowadays do with fondness, as more and more routes become crowded and favourite spots are much too accessible. Here, then, is an opportunity to highlight some known and unknown spots worth considering out of the many thousands of cliff faces, big rocks, alpine routes and bouldering hot spots across the country.

It was Sir Ed Hillary who lifted the adventure level to new heights when he scaled Mt Everest with Tensing Norgay in 1953. Yet, years earlier, Hillary had joined the Auckland branch of the New Zealand Alpine Club, taking part in the first ascent of the southern ridge of Mt Cook and undertaking several other high climbs in the Southern Alps. It was this technical rock and ice climbing experience that gave him the confidence to go to the Himalayas on the unsuccessful 1951 Everest expedition and two years later on the successful 1953 expedition — from which he is famously quoted as saying, '*We knocked the bastard off.*'

As a sport, rock climbing is relatively new in New Zealand but it has grown in popularity year on year with the explosion of indoor rock-climbing centres and TV coverage. A contributing factor is the modern version of extreme sports coupled with equipment advances and new grading systems, some of which are different overseas. Grading in New Zealand is based on the Australian EWBANK system. If you are planning a visit to New Zealand to go rock climbing, don't start at the top and work your way south, do some homework and pick the regions that suit your style, technical ability and desire to improve. With over 3000 possible sites throughout the country, you need to be choosy, so pick a region and check out some websites first. For further information go to: The New Zealand Alpine Club: **www.alpineclub.org.nz** or a popular website such as: **www.climb.co.nz**

CLIMBING LOCATIONS — NORTH ISLAND

■ Mangaraho — Northland

This is a big chunk of volcanic plug that boasts the oldest recorded climb in Northland. However, it wasn't until the 1990s that Mangaraho and nearby Tokatoka became popular and generated a growing reputation for what some people consider to be the best climbing region in the North. Nowadays it has a mixture of pitches and new sporting routes that demand respect. The plug is about 120m high and the rock is generally sound, with some flaky patches at lower elevations. There are upwards of 20 different slab routes including the classic 115m north face route known as Green Eggs and Ham which can take over 3 hours for even the most experienced climber. This is also a good area for bouldering. It's about 150km from Auckland.

DIRECTIONS: From Whangarei, drive to Dargaville, and then turn left onto Provincial Highway 12 towards Maungaturoto. Follow this for 15km to the Mititai turnoff. Both Mangaraho and Tokatoka are large volcanic plugs easily spotted from the main road. Go to: **www.alpineclub.org.nz**

■ Mt Eden Quarry

The home of Auckland rock climbing has always been the old Mt Eden Quarry. The basalt rock face varies from 5 to 20m. There is a good range of rock climbs here with about 80 routes (some are bolted routes or top-roped using the bolted anchors provided), on what are known as the Long Side and the Short Side. The Long Side is located on the lower fields of Auckland Grammar School on Mountain Road. The Short Side rock-climbing area is located on the other side of Auckland Grammar School and access can be gained from the upper fields and down the concrete path near the

Half-way to the top at Wharepapa in the North Island.

incinerator. Permission must be obtained from the school: phone David Hunt, property manager, (09) 623 5400 ext. 415.

◼ Titahi Bay, Lower Hutt

For those of you who want to climb cliffs and abseil back down afterwards — or if you're more extreme and that way inclined try 'rap jumping' (abseiling down a cliff facing forwards and running down as fast as you can) — these dudes at Hang Dog will teach you how. Titahi Bay is Wellington's best real rock-climbing area that is suitable for all levels of ability and fitness. Under their instructors' guidance beginners can learn to tackle Grade 9 routes up small cliffs through to hard Grade 23 routes. They offer climbing, canyoning and abseiling adventures in the Upper Hutt as well. If the weather is a tad nasty, they also have their own indoor climbing wall. Go to: **www.hangdog.co.nz**

◼ Wharepapa

For outdoor adventure enthusiasts, Wharepapa is a region you should definitely stick on your itinerary, especially if you fancy some great rock climbing. It's considered one of the best rock-climbing areas in New Zealand. The list of well-known crags includes Bayleys Road, Bosch, Gower, Secret Valley, Sheridan Hills, Smith Rock and Waipapa. This is a rural area and a very popular climbing region offering almost 800 routes with easy access and short hikes to the climbs. Wharepapa South is located between Te Awamutu and Mangakino.

Directions: From Te Awamutu, travel south to Kihikihi, turn into Arapuni Road and travel towards Mangakino/Rotorua. Turn right after about 9km into the road opposite the Parawera (Stone) Store and then drive almost 15km to the Wharepapa Outdoor Centre and Café. Go to: **www.rockclimb.co.nz**

Alpine Guides — Mt Cook

In operation since 1966, this company is New Zealand's longest-established mountain and ski guiding company. Alpine Guides is a small, privately owned New Zealand outfit who are passionate about the mountains. All their trips and courses are realistic — and they need to be when set against the scale of the terrain and range of conditions that this dynamic climate can deliver. They've developed, tested and refined their guiding programme over 40 years to give you the best chance of success. Summer (November to April) is the most popular period for mountaineering in the Southern Alps. This is the time to learn the basics, or bag the big peaks.

Winter (mid June to mid October) is for ski touring, ice climbing, ski mountaineering, avalanche courses and climbing trips. There are also half- and full-day adventure hikes and rock climbing around Mt Cook Village (November to March).
Go to: **www.alpineguides.co.nz**

Alpine Recreation — Lake Tekapo

If you're looking to get some first-time experience or if you already have some mountaineering know-how under your belt, Alpine Recreation can deliver the goods. They offer 4 or 6-day climbing instruction courses for those who have tramping or hiking experience and wish to venture higher or those who seek to improve and extend their mountaineering skills and prepare themselves to climb technical peaks independently. For an initial taste of mountaineering, try the 3-day Ball

Up the rock face near Queenstown.

Pass Trek, where you'll learn how to use crampons and ice axe, and get to spend 2 nights in a private hut straight opposite the mighty Caroline Face of Aoraki/Mt Cook. Their winter snowshoe tours use the same venue. If you already have mountaineering experience, then recruit one of their professional UIAGM/IFMGA mountain guides for a guided ascent of Aoraki/Mt Cook, Mt Tasman, Mt Sefton or Mt Aspiring. All costs include equipment.
Go to: **www.alpinerecreation.com**

■ Aspiring Guides New Zealand — Wanaka

This company have almost 20 years of history in leading and teaching people about mountaineering in the Southern Alps. Aspiring Guides offer guided wilderness walks, mountaineering and ski touring run by professional and fully qualified mountain and ski guides. Whether your desire is to take those first steps into the world of mountaineering, develop your climbing techniques, reach a summit, join an expedition, learn ice climbing, or just take time out in the mountains — they will handle any request to ensure a safe climbing experience. Their climbing instruction courses include: Mountain Skills — an introduction to mountaineering; Winter Waterfall — an ice introductory course; Mt Aspiring Expedition — advanced climbing; Steep Alpine Ice — intermediate/advanced course; Private Instruction on all levels from 2 to 4 climbers; Summit Week on all levels from 1 to 2 climbers; Darran Mountains climbing week advanced 1 to 2 climbers; and a 1-day Sharpen Up programme.
Go to: **www.aspiringguides.com**

■ Climbing Queenstown

This outfit offer beginner to advanced courses through to 1 to 3-day expeditions. Try their introduction to rock climbing, learn to walk on snow with and without crampons, using an ice axe, basic terrain and travel analysis and basic rope work. This company is all about getting people into the mountains to learn some essential skills and have heaps of fun while taking in the amazing views. A high point will be a full day out on Wye Dome — the leading rock-climbing area in the Wakatipu which now has over 150 routes. It can challenge the beginner right through to the advanced climber looking for steep overhangs. No experience is required but you do need a moderate level of fitness. The mountain skills trip is a full day of 8 hours plus. Go to: **www.climbingqueenstown.com**

■ Hukawai Glacier Centre, Franz Josef — Indoor Ice Climbing

This is a spectacular way for beginners to experience ice climbing. The wall is 10m high with over 15 different climbing routes. This temperature-controlled chamber is the only one in the Southern Hemisphere. Routes vary from easy (for absolute beginners) through to the monster overhang only for adventurous and experienced climbers. They provide all the climbing gear and an expert instructor to guide you up the ice wall. If you can fit into a size 5 or above climbing boot (usually ages 10 and above), you can have a go at it. Ice-climbing courses last approximately 1.5 hours.
Go to: **www.hukawai.co.nz**

■ Southern Alps Guiding — Aoraki/Mt Cook

Based in the Aoraki/Mount Cook National Park, this mountaineering school is located among some of the most spectacular alpine terrain in the world. A personalised service, with low client-to-guide ratios on their courses and guided ascents, ensures that your safety, enjoyment and expectations are fulfilled. Climbing and ski mountaineering with a guide is the safest and most informative way to extend your climbing and skiing abilities. Whether you are contemplating a transalpine crossing, ascending the highest peaks, ski touring the glaciers or climbing technically demanding routes, these people will show you the way.
Go to: **www.mtcook.com**

■ The Rung Way — Via Ferrata, Queenstown

Definitely give this a go as it is an all-weather climbing system and has grades suitable for every fitness level, age and gender. The Southern Hemisphere's only Via Ferrata is an inspirational climbing experience located in a truly majestic landscape. This is an Italian climbing system where all the routes are constructed of rungs, ladders and wire ropes, making the rocky cliffs and grassy ledges high above Queenstown accessible to anyone of moderate fitness. Challenging, rewarding and fun, the Via Ferrata is a year-round activity that is perfect for families, groups or individuals.
Go to: **www.climbingqueenstown.com**

■ Wanaka Rock Climbing

If you aspire to the vertical world of rock climbing and abseiling, this is the place to hook up your karabiner. Wanaka Rock Climbing offer 1, 3 and 5-day rock-climbing courses in the Matukituki Valley. This glaciated valley is over 40km long and contains numerous random outcrops of ice-scoured and weatherworn rock, more commonly known as Otago Schist. Their instructors keep the client-to-guide ratio low so you'll learn more and get a better personal service. They also put together guided trips to other top climbing areas around the Southern Lakes region such as The Remarkables Range and Wye Creek near Queenstown, Chinamans Bluff near Glenorchy and Sebastopol Bluffs near Mt Cook. You get to choose from half-day, full-day or 3-day courses as well as multi-day alpine adventures. Go to: **www.wanakarock.co.nz**

Mountaineering and Climbing Clubs

If you are planning on learning 'the ropes' it is always advisable to seek out the best courses, guides and clubs to learn from. The Federated Mountain Clubs of New Zealand is the national association of over 80 tramping and mountain-climbing clubs, representing a total of over 11,000 individual members. Go to: **www.fmc.org.nz**

SAFETY AND SURVIVAL SKILLS

NEW ZEALAND WEATHER AND AVALANCHE SITES
■ For latest avalanche information from the New Zealand Mountain Safety Council — Go to: www.avalanche.net.nz
■ DoC (MetService forecasts broken into mountain and national park regions useful for outdoor types) — Go to: www.doc.govt.nz/templates/page.aspx?id=44798
■ MetVUW weather and climate service — Go to: www.metvuw.com
■ Mean monthly temperatures around New Zealand — Go to: www.niwa.co.nz/edu/resources/climate/meanairtemp
■ Search-and-rescue national body — Go to: New Zealand Land Search and Rescue Inc (LandSAR) www.landsar.org.nz
■ Search-and-rescue coordinators — Go to: New Zealand Police www.police.govt.nz/service/sar/index.html
■ Search-and-rescue Queenstown area — Go to: Wakatipu Search and Rescue www.wakatipusar.co.nz

As with so many adventures, it becomes pretty obvious even to a novice that the sport of climbing is a potentially hazardous activity carrying a risk of personal injury or even death. Climbing should only be undertaken with a full understanding of all inherent risks. It is recommended that novice climbers seek proper training from recognised sources or join clubs to gain the requisite knowledge and expertise to attempt many of the climbs in New Zealand.

Do not underestimate this country's mountains. There are many peaks around 3000m in height, and although they appear small in comparison to the higher peaks of the Himalayan or Swiss Alps, our mountains offer similar valley-to-summit altitude gains. Weather is also another major contributing factor to accidents when climbing, so it is imperative you seek information on the region you are climbing in before undertaking a climb of any sort. If you plan on tackling this type of activity, check out the websites listed above — know before you go!

On an ice climb near Wanaka.

Wanderlust — Bridge Climb, Obstacle Courses, Skywalk, ZORB

Is it any wonder New Zealand has pioneered so many new and inventive ways to push the boundaries for thrill seekers? As the world becomes wackier, we just become wiser and invent a new adventure each time to keep you all coming back for more! Here are just a few of our more unusual activities you can experience.

BRIDGE CLIMB

■ Auckland Harbour Bridge Climb

One of Auckland's leading adventure tourism attractions has to be the Auckland Bridge Climb. This ultimate social climb that takes you onto, into, up, around and over the historic 1959 harbour icon lasts 2.5 hours. Expect to be blown away by the view from the top across the City of Sails, as well as by the wind. Once you're attached to the harness in your special climbing suit you'll feel that once-in-a-lifetime thrill when you reach the 134m high point. From here you'll have stunning views of the Waitakere Ranges, the Hauraki Gulf islands including volcanoes such as Rangitoto, estuaries, beaches and bushy suburbs — oh, and all that busy traffic below.
Go to: **www.aucklandbridgeclimb.co.nz**

OBSTACLE COURSES

The army has them and so do the navy, and while I'm not so sure about the air force the good old obstacle course has sure been around for a long time. Scrunching under barbed wire in mud often comes to mind — that and balancing on moving logs and climbing rope netting, hopping in and out of old tyres, aerial rope bridges, flying foxes, and of course swinging Tarzan-like across ditches or canyons is what we all typically envisage. Well, nowadays it can be done in a few select places in New Zealand and purely as an adventure attraction.

■ Adrenalin Forest — Christchurch

This is your chance to experience a high on Adrenalin Forest's multi-level aerial obstacle course and test your gravity, balance and agility. There are 6 pathways in the treetops, each posing different challenges and differing in height from 1.5 to 20m. In total there are 100 challenges that you have to overcome and it can take an average of 3 hours to cover the 2km course. Expect hire wires, commando netting, Tarzan swings,

Bridging the gap across the Auckland Harbour Bridge.

hanging loops, a 15m-high stirrup bridge, a monkey bridge, and finally the 90m-long flying fox.
Go to: **www.adrenalin-forest.co.nz**

■ Rock'n Ropes, Taupo

Part obstacle course, part rope course, part high wire — it's hard to categorise this adventure playground on the outskirts of Taupo! Rock'n Ropes has a wide range of adventure options for you to choose from and, as their website points out, 'what is quite acceptable is an average degree of unfitness and a genuine fear of heights!' To start off with, try some of these beauties on a half-day visit: the Wire Bridge, Rickety Bridge, High Log, Giant Trapeze, Multi Vine and the Chicken Walk.
Go to: **www.rocknropes.co.nz**

■ Ultimate Challenge — Canterbury

So you want to push yourself in true SAS commando style? Well, you've arrived at the right place! At Ultimate Challenge you'll have the opportunity to take on the 'Beast'. Their purpose-built 1400m obstacle course includes a unique figure-of-eight design that features 45 obstacles which test your physical strength, balance, agility, stamina and mental problem-solving skills in a safe and fun

Waving away a fear of heights on the walk around Auckland Sky Tower.

environment. This activity is suitable for families or teams and anyone over 10 years old (which is strictly enforced). All participants are accompanied by one of their qualified Instructors.
Go to: **www.ultimatechallengecentre.co.nz**

Skywalk — Auckland Sky Tower

Look Mum, no hands! Yes, this little escapade might put the wind up you as there are no guardrails, just the air that you breathe 192m up on the 1.2m-wide Sky Walk outer ledge. If you want to experience life on the edge, then give this a try. It's a 360-degree walk around the tallest tower in the Southern Hemisphere. Besides taking in the amazing views and looking down to the teeny-tiny cars below, you'll also learn about some of the history of Auckland and what landmark is what, as well as how the Sky Tower was constructed. If you have the nerve, you'll certainly have the chance to hang your bum off the edge with just the harness holding you aloft. Go to: **www.skywalk.co.nz**

ZORB

ZORB Rotorua

Zorbing in New Zealand is on a roll — like a giant football out of control! People of all ages are now adding this unique activity of rolling downhill in a transparent globe to their must-do list. ZORB is performed on a grassy slope with pre-designed zigzag tracks or on a straight track. For adventure seekers there are 2 types of globe — the harnessed and non-harnessed. The non-harness globes can have up to 3 riders, whereas the harness variety is constructed for only one rider. The globe is double-sectioned, with one ball inside the other and a layer of air in between. This acts as a shock absorber for the rider. A typical sphere is about 3m in diameter, with an inner sphere size of about 2m, leaving a 50 to 60cm air cushion around the riders.

THE RIDES: **1. Zydro** — Expect to get wet! You have different track options and up to 3 people can ride in a single globe — and, oh yes, this is an extreme ride. **2. Zorbit** — You stay dry as you're strapped into a specially designed safety harness within the globe. You ride alone, and while you have only 1 track option you can wear what you want. ZORB Rotorua is the only globe riding site in New Zealand.
Go to: **www.zorb.co.nz**

CHAPTER 6

There is always a flurry of excitement from the skiing fraternity when heavy dumps of snow start building up a good base on our skifields before the start of any New Zealand winter season. Unlike the Northern Hemisphere, our season is from mid-June to mid-September. We are blessed with some very high mountains and volcanoes that make skiing in this part of the world a real adventure. You can also be as extreme as your heart desires — from groomed runs on intermediate skifields to cat-skiing, glacier skiing and heli-skiing.

The geographical diversity of New Zealand lends itself to snow experiences in a variety of environments. It's safe to say that there are very few places in the world where you can ski on an active volcano, yet in the North Island at Mt Ruapehu the two skifields of Turoa and Whakapapa are literally positioned on either side of one. Mt Ruapehu is New Zealand's largest and most developed ski region. It also allows for cross-country ski traversing as well as snowboarding and alpine skiing. The highest point in the North Island at 2797m, it is also one of only three mountains in the world boasting a crater lake encircled by snow and ice.

Most skifields in the South Island are situated high on the slopes of the Southern Alps. It is further afield in remote environments that heli-skiers relish the deep powder and astonishing locations. Elsewhere, skiers and riders can choose to ski a glacier, ride the tubes, or schuss their way down varied groomed slopes. New Zealand's only Nordic ski area (Snow Farm) and an area reserved for freestyle skiing and riding (Snow Park) are found near Wanaka. Coronet Peak and Snow Park also offer the only night skiing in the country.

WHITE OUT
ADVENTURES ON SNOW

CARVING IT UP – SKIING, SNOWBOARDING

FIRST TRACKS – HELI-SKIING, SNOWCAT-SKIING, SNOWMOBILING

PUT ON ICE – GLACIER HIKING, GLACIER SKIING, ICE LUGE

SMOOTH GLIDE – SKI TOURING, DOG SLEDDING, SNOWKITING

Skiing at Mt Hutt.

Carving It Up — Skiing, Snowboarding

SKIING IN NEW ZEALAND

Due to its high latitude, mountainous terrain and a well-developed and established tourism infrastructure, New Zealand is a major Southern Hemisphere skiing destination. While there are several skifields in the North Island, most are found in the South. Alongside major commercial skifields and smaller club skifields which provide access to affordable skiing for club members, there are also specialist back-country skiing areas such as Mt Potts and Invincible Snowfields which provide heli-skiing and snowcat-skiing for adventure seekers. There are now 15 commercially operated downhill and cross-country skifields in New Zealand. However, commercial skifields were slow to be developed and it took over 30 years until some of them could be considered world class.

New Zealand has competed at most Winter Olympics since first sending a team to the 1952 Oslo games in Norway. In 1992, New Zealander Annelise Coberger became the first person from the Southern Hemisphere to win a medal at the Winter Olympics when she won silver in the slalom at Albertville in France — a feat that is of particular significance in our part of the world and one that is hard to emulate.

The first basic ski tow was trialled briefly at Mt Ruapehu in 1938. Until then most keen skiers hiked their way up the slopes to get a few good runs in each day. After WWII other commercial skifields were slowly developed as more people took up this emerging sport and outdoor pastime. By 1947, a rope ski tow was designed by inventor Bill Hamilton and installed at Coronet Peak. At Mt Ruapehu, in the North Island, the first chairlift was opened in 1954 and the first drag lift was installed in 1961. Additional T-bar lifts were also gradually introduced on other commercial skifields around the country. The first ever modified plane with ski sleds flew from Mt Cook Village in 1955. This innovation eventually turned New Zealand's most famous glacier, Tasman Glacier, into one gigantic ski run.

The South Island has the biggest concentration of commercial skifields including Rainbow Skifield in the Nelson region. Canterbury has Hanmer Springs, Mt Lyford, Porters, Mt Hutt and Mt Potts. The Mackenzie region has Mt Dobson, Roundhill and Ohau. The best-known commercial skifields are located in the Southern Lakes region and include Coronet Peak, The Remarkables, Snow Farm, Snow Park, Cardrona and Treble Cone.

Unlike other parts of the world, New Zealand doesn't have designated 'ski resorts' — here they are mainly known as skifields. The country's first ski club was formed in 1913 by two ski mountaineers at Mt Ruapehu, and even though many skifields today are commercial, there are still a good number of private club skifields which require membership including Tukino on Mt Ruapehu and Manganui on Mt Taranaki/Egmont in the North Island. In the South Island there's Broken River, Craigieburn, Temple Basin, Mt Cheeseman and Mt Olympus in the Canterbury region, while the Mackenzie region is home to Fox Peak and Awakino.

Typically, our ski season runs from mid-June to the end of September. However, in 2008 Turoa didn't close until 16 November! As the mountains are higher they generally attract snow-laden weather systems. Not only does this mean they're well positioned to receive the best snowfalls, the quality of snow is also generally very high. To boost nature's efforts, most skifields now have extensive snow-making equipment on hand. In 2009, our skifields recorded their best season ever with 1.5 million visits to the slopes.

As New Zealand's skifields are high in the mountains and many are on environmentally protected land, there is very little on-mountain (ski-in/ski-out) lodging except some apartment accommodation at Snow Park near Wanaka. Après-ski activities are catered for around the nearby full-service resort towns located at the bottom of the skifields. Finding what fits your ski itinerary has just been made a whole lot easier — so buckle up your boots and check out the slopes!

Youngsters learn the basics
on Mt Ruapehu.

COMMERCIAL SKIFIELDS — NORTH ISLAND

Mt Ruapehu — Whakapapa and Turoa

Mt Ruapehu, located in the central North Island, is home to New Zealand's two largest skifields, Whakapapa and Turoa, one of which has the highest lift access in New Zealand and the other the longest vertical descent in Australasia. It is situated in Tongariro National Park, classified as a dual World Heritage Site for its natural beauty and cultural significance. From here you can enjoy spectacular views over the entire central North Island including adjacent Mt Ngauruhoe which featured as Mt Doom in the *Lord of the Rings* movie trilogy. Mt Ruapehu offers something for everyone along with some of the best natural terrain in the country. One Mt Ruapehu lift pass gives you access to both skifields.

■ Whakapapa Skifield

On the northwest-facing slopes of Mt Ruapehu is the largest skifield in New Zealand. Whakapapa has 14 lifts and more than 30 groomed trails and New Zealand's largest learners' facility, Happy Valley. It has its own rental facility, café and snow school and a dedicated slow-moving learners' chairlift.

LIFTS: 1 Fixed Grip Quad, 1 Express Quad, 5 Doubles, 4 T-bars, 2 Platters, 1 Rope Tow. Skiable area: 900ha, Elevation: 2300m, Vertical: 675m drop, Terrain: 25% Beginner, 50% Intermediate, 25% Advanced.
Go to: **www.mtruapehu.com**

■ Turoa Skifield

On the southwest face of the mountain is the second-largest skifield in New Zealand with the longest vertical descent in Australasia at 722m. In 2009, Turoa had a record season, drawing 237,000 visitors. Turoa is home to the High Noon Express, a 6-seater chairlift with the biggest uphill capacity in Australasia, providing access to New Zealand's highest lift at 2322m.

LIFTS: I x 6-person Express, 2 Triples, 2 Quads, 1 T-bar, 2 Platters, 1 Carpet Lift. Skiable area: 900ha, Elevation: 2322m, Vertical: 722m drop, Terrain: 25% Beginner, 50% Intermediate, 25% Advanced.
Go to: **www.mtruapehu.com**

Cardrona Alpine Resort

With a base elevation of 1670m above sea level, Cardrona is high, cold and renowned for its natural snow plus wide open spaces. Known as the friendly mountain, it has superb runs and modern resort facilities, a certain amount of mountain accommodation, an extensive terrain park and also boasts some brilliant children's facilities.

On the mountain you'll find great terrain and good natural snow enhanced by man-made snow in the main basin. Cardrona is suitable for all levels and abilities. Three Magic Learner lifts, a beginner quad chair and the widest and most scenic learner runs make Cardrona a great place for beginners. More than 50 per cent of the terrain is suitable for intermediates with trails groomed daily.

LIFTS: 1 Quad Fixed Chairlift, 2 Quad Express Chairlifts, 3 Magic Learner Lifts, 1 Platter Beginner Lift, Lift capacity: 7800 per hour. Skiable area: 320ha, Elevation: 1894m, Vertical: 390m vertical drop, Terrain: 25% Beginner, 55% Intermediate, 20% Advanced.

You'll find the skifield located on the Cardrona Valley Road, 35km from Wanaka and 55km from Queenstown. Drive time from Wanaka — allow 45 minutes. Drive time from Queenstown — allow 1 hour. Shuttles operate daily from both Queenstown and Wanaka. Go to: **www.cardrona.com**

Coronet Peak Skifield

Queenstown's Coronet Peak is the South Island's most popular skifield and with good reason. Diverse terrain, fantastic views, proximity to Queenstown and a cosmopolitan ambience create a superb winter experience for every level of snow sport enthusiast. Coronet Peak's base building offers superb facilities — its larger and improved food and beverage service areas, ticketing, storage, rentals, a huge sundeck and expanded childcare facilities and crèche have elevated this mountain to true world-class status.

The skifield provides access to some of the best and most varied terrain of any mountain in the region. Its series of multiple interconnected bowls presents all sorts of surprising challenges and hidden delights to ski or ride. The mountain's longest run, the M1-Big Easy, is still very popular with beginner and intermediate skiers and riders. There's also a dedicated terrain park.

Coronet Peak hosts many sporting and social events including the FIS-rated Southern Cup and the Southern Hemisphere's ultimate winter celebration, the American Express Queenstown Winter Festival. It's also the training ground of New Zealand's national ski team. There's skiing on Friday and Saturday nights from July to mid-September (weather and conditions permitting) offering illuminated trails that include the M1 and Big Easy.

LIFTS: 1 High Speed 6-seater Chair, 1 Express Quad Chair, 1 Double Chair, 1 T-bar, 3 Surface Conveyor Lifts and 1 Beginner Tow. Skiable area: 280ha, Longest run: 2.4km, Elevation: 1649m, Vertical: 462m vertical drop, Terrain: 20% Beginner, 45% Intermediate, 35% Advanced (excludes back bowls). A snow sports school and dedicated children's programme are among the world-class facilities. Children aged 6 and under enjoy free day passes.

The skifield is an easy 25-minute drive from Queenstown on a sealed road, its ease of access, proximity and extensive facilities making it a logical and convenient choice for all ages and families. Go to: **www.nzski.com**

Mt Dobson Skifield

This is one of New Zealand's best-kept secrets. Mt Dobson has been owned and operated by the Foote family of Fairlie since 1985 and they've made it their mission to turn this skifield into one of the most accessible and friendly around. Peter Foote oversees the mountain operation that includes the cafeteria, ski and board rental, ski patrol, and the ski and board school. The top of the skifield is renowned for its spectacular panoramic views as you can gaze out across Lakes Pukaki and Tekapo to the magnificent peaks of New Zealand's highest mountains, Aoraki/ Mt Cook and Mt Tasman.

LIFTS: 1 Triple Chair, 1 T-bar, 1 Platter, 1 Tow Rope. Skiable area: 400ha (excludes Rakaia Saddle Chutes of 107ha), Elevation: 2110m, Vertical: 415m, Terrain: 25% Beginner, 50% Intermediate, 25% Advanced.

You'll find the skifield just off the Christchurch to Queenstown highway, 26km from Fairlie and

43km east from Lake Tekapo. Mt Dobson is a short 40-minute drive on a smooth mountain road — one of the best alpine roads in the country. There's plenty of parking available and shuttle transport available on weekends and holidays.
Go to: **www.dobson.com**

Mt Hutt Skifield

The slopes of Mt Hutt are renowned for some of the best snow combined with spectacular views across the Canterbury Plains to the Pacific Ocean. The mountain has an amazing sense of space and regularly posts one of the longest and most consistent seasons in the Southern Hemisphere. Opening early June to late October, it boasts some of the best spring skiing in the country.

Mt Hutt claims to offer New Zealand's most complete mountain experience. The big bowl-shaped mountain caters well for advanced skiers with adrenalin-pumping Black Diamond runs and pretty awesome off-piste skiing. It has wide open trails for novices, an extensive terrain park including a beginner park and halfpipe, and the immense runs off the Triple Chair are a favourite with freestyle and big mountain riders whether on one plank or two!

LIFTS: 1 High Speed 6-seater Chair, 1 Quad Chair, 1 Triple Chair, 1 Magic Carpet. Skiable area: 365ha (excludes Rakaia Saddle Chutes of 107ha), Snowmaking: 42ha, Terrain park: 10,000sqm, Longest run: 2km, Elevation: 2086m, Vertical: 683m, Terrain: 25% Beginner, 50% Intermediate, 25% Advanced.

You'll find the skifield an hour and a half from Christchurch, and 35 minutes from the local ski resort village of Methven, commonly known as Mt Hutt Village. From Christchurch airport look for the 'Inland Scenic Route 72' to Mt Hutt and Methven. Mt Hutt Village offers a lively après-ski atmosphere and is known for its warm and friendly hospitality.
Go to: **www.nzski.com/mthutt**

Mt Lyford Skifield

This is New Zealand's first true alpine development — and it has a very leisurely feel to it with a variety of intermediate terrain plus advanced skiing and riding in the Terako Basin. This is an ideal

Deep powder skiing at Mt Hutt.

Snowboarders at Cardrona.

family skifield which is great for learners yet with challenging runs for intermediate and advanced skiers. Wild Ride Terrain Park has a natural chute lead-in, jumps, rails, half- and quarterpipes as well as a great little tubing area. There's an enclosed kindergarten, cafeteria restaurant 'Chamois Café', day shelter lodge, ski and snowboard rentals, heli-skiing on demand, and skidoo hire.

LIFTS: 1 T-bar, 1 Poma, 2 Platters, 1 Fixed Grip Learners Tow, 1 Rope Tow. Skiable area: 180ha, Elevation: 1750m, Vertical: 350m, Terrain: 30% Beginners, 40% Intermediate, 30% Advanced.

You'll find the skifield located 26km from Waiau and 60km from Kaikoura. Go to: **www.mtlyford.co.nz**

■ Ohau Skifield
Mike and Louise Neilson took sole charge of the Ohau skifield in 1990, but their love affair with the property started in 1985 when Mike bought the field with some friends. The slopes originally opened in 1956 when pioneer tourism operator Harry Wigley of the Mount Cook Company installed a rope tow. Ohau is considered a 'club field', which is a private patch of mountain managed by individual ski clubs but open to the public.

The field has a reputation for advanced back-country skiing with access to around 600ha of powder bowls.

Ohau is also a popular year-round destination with extensive hiking opportunities and dramatic views from Lake Ohau across to Aoraki/Mt Cook.

In 2009, NZ$2 million was spent on snow-making, which included 23 snow guns. The next two steps of a three-stage development will see an extra 55 snow guns and a second chairlift installed, as well as a new three-storey base building and snow school.

LIFTS: 1 Chairlift, 1 Platter and 1 Snow Mat, and 2 progressive terrain parks. Skiable area: 125ha, Elevation: 1825m, Vertical: 400m, Longest run: 2.5km, Terrain: 20% Beginner, 50% Intermediate, 30% Advanced.

You'll find the skifield situated below the Ohau Range on the Southern Alps main divide, and not far from Aoraki/Mt Cook. Go to: **www.ohau.co.nz**

■ Porters Skifield
As far as great skiing goes, Porters offers 2 of New Zealand's most famous runs — Bluff Face and Big Mama. They have a wide range of slopes to suit a variety of skier or rider abilities, and the good news for you is that skiing here is very affordable. Many people don't know it, but Big Mama is the longest, steepest single slope in the Southern Hemisphere. Whatever your ability level, you'll feel right at home at Porters. There are gentle runs and easy lifts for beginners

and kids, with long cruising runs for the intermediates and super-challenging runs for the advanced. Skiing and snowboarding facilities are comprehensive with a very friendly staff and community atmosphere. The Porters Community Park also offers a challenge for the more adventurous boarder for boosting, popping and cruising to show off your best freestyle skills.

LIFTS: 3 T-bar, 1 Platter, 1 Learners Ski Mat, 1 Rope Tow. Skiable area: 230ha, Elevation: 1980m, Vertical: 350m, Terrain: 30% Beginners, 30% Intermediate, 40% Advanced.

You'll find this skifield the closest one to Christchurch, which is only 96km away — in fact, at that distance, it's a wonder it hasn't lost any of its local charm! Go to: **www.skiporters.co.nz**

■ Rainbow Skifield

This is a great little skifield which was voted best small skifield in 2004 and 2005. It overlooks Lake Rotoiti and Nelson Lakes National Park so the views from the summit are all the more spectacular. The main attraction here is the uncrowded slopes. They provide well-groomed trails that are ideal for beginners and intermediates, but that's not to say

advanced skiers are overlooked as they can access powder runs and more difficult chutes.

LIFTS: 1 Main T-bar, 1 Platter Lift, 1 Tubing Park Lift, 1 Learners Rope Tow, 1 Handle Terrain Park Tow, 1 West Bowl Access Tow. Skiable area: 300ha, Mountain car-park elevation: 1540m, Vertical: 322m, Terrain: 25% Beginners, 55% Intermediate, 20% Advanced.

You'll find the skifield less than 2 hours' drive from Nelson or Blenheim or just 17km from the State Highway 63 turnoff. Chains must be fitted or carried by all vehicles at all times from the base car park where shuttle buses operate multiple trips daily. Go to: **www.skirainbow.co.nz**

■ Roundhill Skifield

This small skifield is situated in the heart of the Mackenzie Country and provides the perfect setting for a relaxing day's skiing or snowboarding on their gentle, rolling hills. Nestled in the Southern Alps, Roundhill has everything a skier needs for a spectacular winter alpine getaway including New Zealand's longest T-bar as well as undulating slopes that are perfect for beginners and intermediates. Central Park on Roundhill also offers boxes, rails and jumps for skiers and snowboarders.

Junior skiing lessons at Roundhill.

Dramatic aerial views from
Ohau skifield.

LIFTS: Main T-bar, Beginners Platter, Kiddies Lift.
Elevation: 1620m, Vertical: 255m, Terrain: 20%
Beginner, 80% Intermediate, 0% Advanced.

You'll find the skifield located just 30 minutes' drive
from the lakeside alpine village of Tekapo, 230km
from Christchurch. Go to: **www.roundhill.co.nz**

■ Snow Park

Snow Park NZ opened to the public in 2002 as the
first dedicated freestyle terrain park in the world,
a Mecca for snowboarders and skiers. It features
2 superpipes, a quarterpipe, big kickers, 40+ rails,
hits, jumps and more — in fact, Snow Park has
something for everyone. They've added a Half Pint
beginner park and a playground of boxes, jumps
and rails designed specifically for the novice skier or
snowboarder. The world-class design and shaping
crew are dedicated to providing innovative and
progressive terrain for all levels throughout the
winter season. Snow Park NZ boasts a world cup
standard superpipe — 160m long at a 17-degree
pitch — designed and cut to perfection by resident
pipe guru Frank Wells (the beginner superpipe is
90m long at 15 degrees pitch). The quarterpipe is
suitable for all levels. The resort offers an ever-
changing landscape of jumps and hits throughout

the season. However, the mainstays are the jumps
in the infamous triple line. Also scattered around
the park is a selection of intermediate jumps up to
10.5m as well as those in the Half Pint Park.

LIFTS: 1 Quad Fixed Chairlift (Doppelmeyer),
Lift capacity: 2100 per hour. Skiable area: 60ha,
Elevation: 1530m, Vertical: 110m, Snow guns: 35,
Average snowfall: 50cm, Terrain: 20% Novice, 50%
Intermediate, 30% Advanced.

One of the few resorts in New Zealand capable of
relying 100 per cent on snow-making, Snow Park NZ
has an impressive fleet of 33 snow guns covering 60
acres of land. This system ensures that Snow Park
is one of the first resorts to open each season with
consistent coverage throughout the winter.

You'll find the skifield located in the Pisa Range on
the Cardrona Valley Road, 35km from Wanaka and
55km from Queenstown. The last 11km (the Snow
Park access road) is unsealed, but kept in good
condition. Chains may be required at times. Drive
time from Wanaka — allow 45 minutes. Drive time
from Queenstown — allow 1 hour. Shuttles operate
daily from both Queenstown and Wanaka.
Go to: **www.snowparknz.com**

Showing how it should be done;
Telemark Ski Instructor, Taz Dawson.

■ The Remarkables Skifield

At The Remarkables it's all about the 3Fs — fun, families and the freestyle love of a big mountain environment. The Remarkables is a splendid skifield where you can expect to find a true alpine atmosphere. They cater superbly for the beginner and intermediate market with 3 quad chairs and 3 surface conveyor lifts to ferry you to the trails. There is also a wealth of big mountain possibilities for off-piste enthusiasts. Here you'll enjoy a relaxed alpine ambience with DJs, live music, festivals and heaps of entertainment throughout the season. In addition, it has possibly the best southern views around, the country's longest back-country run 'Homeward Bound', and some of the most challenging, advanced skiing in the country.

In 2008, 'The Stash', a 1km-long Burton signature terrain park, opened — the first of its type in the Southern Hemisphere and only the third in the world. The Stash creates an avenue of features unique to the local environment for all jibbers. The parks and free-ride facilities include a 150m Parklife Superpipe, Beginner Park and advanced Terrain Park, catering to freestylers of all ages and abilities.

The Remarks' kids' programmes and learning facilities are located within full view of the café sundeck, and the licensed Skiwiland crèche provides full care for kids 3 months and upwards, including an introduction to snow for 3 to 6-year-olds. This, coupled with its wide groomed trails, provides an awesome facility for families or the first-timer on snow and a great place for parents to watch the little ones learn. For a not-so-serious snow experience, glide down cut trails in an inner tube in the Ozone Tubing Park.

Snow-making increased substantially in 2009 ensuring consistent snow cover on main trails. There's an award-winning ski and snowboard school, café, retail shop and equipment hire.

LIFTS: 3 Quad Chairs, 3 Surface Conveyor Lifts, 1 Handle Tow, 1 Snow-tubing Fixed Grip. Skiable area: 220ha, Longest run: 1.5km, Elevation: 1943m, Vertical: 357m, Terrain: 30% Beginner, 40% Intermediate, 30% Advanced.

You'll find the skifield a 15-minute drive from Queenstown and usually open late June to October. Brand-new 4-wheel-drive shuttle buses mean you can leave the car at home and ride to the skifield daily from Queenstown. Go to: **www.nzski.com**

Dropping off a cornice, up high on Treble Cone Skifield.

■ Treble Cone Skifield

The largest skifield in the South Island has some of the most exhilarating runs in the country. Treble Cone offers the longest vertical rise in the Southern Lakes, uncrowded slopes, wide intermediate groomed trails and legendary powder skiing unrivalled in Australasia.

From the slopes expect spectacular views of Lake Wanaka, Mt Aspiring, and the Southern Alps. The proximity to the last allows for reliable snow and weather conditions coating the mountain with fluffy powder snow. Treble Cone is spread over 3 large basins, covering 550 hectares, offering more advanced terrain than many other skifields. It boasts a purpose-built learners' area, providing long groomed runs for beginners and intermediates through to plenty of off-piste powder conditions to challenge the most advanced skiers.

LIFTS: Volkswagen 6-seater High-speed Detachable Chairlift, Saddle Quad Chairlift, Nice and Easy Platter and Magic Carpet. Skiable area: 550ha, Elevation: 1960m, Vertical rise: 705m, Terrain: 10% Beginner, 45% Intermediate, 45% Advanced.

Treble Cone also has a state-of-the-art snow-making system with 20 snow guns covering an area of 50 hectares ensuring early-season snow reliability.

You'll find the skifield located in the Matukituki Valley 26km west of Wanaka (approximately 35 minutes' drive), near the gateway to Mount Aspiring National Park. Go to: **www.treblecone.com**

First Tracks — Heli-skiing, Snowcat-skiing, Snowmobiling

The South Island is still one of the most accessible places on the planet to heli-ski and heli-snowboard. In this part of the world you'll experience some incredible powder runs against a backdrop of awe-inspiring mountain ranges.

Heli-skiing is off-trail, downhill skiing that is accessed by a helicopter, not a ski lift — essentially, it's about skiing in a natural, albeit highly selective, environment without the effort or gear compromise required for hiking into these areas associated with ski touring or ski mountaineering. Most heli-skiers are seeking specific, pleasurable skiing conditions that are hard to replicate on skifields. In particular, adventuresome skiers are looking for light, fluffy powder snow. You'll experience long descents in natural terrain, some steep and extreme slopes at altitude in a pristine environment, and will probably get between 5 to 9 runs in any 1 day with lunch included. This is free-form skiing and snowboarding at its best.

HELI-SKIING — SOUTH ISLAND

■ Harris Mountains Heli-Ski

You may be a first-time heli-skier or heli-snowboarder, or a regular — it doesn't matter. With exclusive access to terrain stretching from Queenstown to Aoraki/Mt Cook, Harris Mountains Heli-Ski will find the perfect terrain to suit your ability. They offer 3, 4, or 7-run options. If you fancy starting your day with an awe-inspiring scenic flight from either Queenstown or Wanaka to Mt Cook, this trip is for you. Aoraki/Mt Cook is New Zealand's highest mountain and the area offers high-altitude

Untracked powder awaits the heli-skiers.

Heli-skiing the Tasman Glacier.

heli-skiing and boarding. After an alpine lunch you'll get the chance to upgrade and add a few more runs before your flight back to Wanaka.
Go to: **www.heliski.co.nz**

■ Heli-Ski With Heli-Guides — Southern Alps, South Island

Heli-Ski Queenstown in association with helicopter company Over The Top have designed skiing tours and itineraries 'far from the madding crowd'. This company works with small groups to ensure some exceptional skiing and snowboarding on untracked virgin snow in a breathtaking natural environment.

They offer 3 and 5-run packages with guaranteed vertical as well as a personalised heli-skiing package. Your personal helicopter and guides will ensure unlimited runs on virgin snow at your pace — yes, you get your own helicopter in their terrain. The price includes a gourmet lunch in alpine splendour.
Go to: **www.flynz.co.nz**

■ Methven Heliski — Mt Hutt

This offering is from the same company who operate Wilderness Heliski, Alpine Guides (Aoraki) Ltd. Your choices range from multi-day trips for the experienced skier and snowboarder through to single runs for those new to heli-skiing. Here's your chance to heli-ski 3 mountain ranges with over

250 named runs that includes ideal terrain from intermediate to advanced with amazing 'in your face' views along the Southern Alps to Aoraki/Mt Cook. From the top of at least two runs it's possible to see both the Pacific Ocean and Tasman Sea.

The 'Perfect Day' is a 5-run standard package and includes transfers from Methven to their helipad at Glenfalloch Station. Go to: **www.methvenheli.co.nz**

■ Southern Alps Guiding — Aoraki/ Mt Cook

The Southern Alps are a range of extraordinary mountains which together form the backbone of the South Island. The centrepiece, surrounded by spectacular glaciers, is Aoraki/Mt Cook — New Zealand's highest peak.

On this experience, skiers and boarders first report to the Old Mountaineers Café at Aoraki/Mt Cook. While there, you'll receive a full safety briefing on all aspects of the day's operation. The heli-ski director then divides you into small, compatible groups, each led by a professional guide, before flying out for the day's first run.

In general, expect great powder from July to early September and spring snow from September to early November. Go to: **www.mtcook.com/heli.html**

Heading for perfect ski terrain.

■ Southern Lakes Heliski & Heliworks

This heli-ski company have been operating premium heli-skiing in the Southern Lakes region of New Zealand for over 20 years. Each guide rides and skis with a group size of just 5 people, thereby maximising your experience. It also allows for a more flexible and personable service to meet everyone's ability from skiing gentle slopes for beginners to steeper runs for experts. Besides operating on several mountain ranges, Southern Lakes also have exclusive rights to the Central Harris Mountains on Branches Station and the famed Towers Ridge beyond the Treble Cone skifield, which is arguably the best free skiing and snowboarding terrain around. Most of their ski terrain is between 1400m and 2200m, and gourmet lunches are also provided. Go to: **www.heliworks.co.nz**

■ Wilderness Heliski — Aoraki/Mt Cook Region

Wilderness Heliski is operated by New Zealand's helicopter skiing pioneers — Alpine Guides (Aoraki) Ltd. They are the only company offering heli-skiing and heli-boarding in Aoraki/Mount Cook National Park, the big mountains of the Southern Alps. With small groups of 5 guests per guide, heli-skier numbers are seldom more than 20 on a busy day. Every run they'll seek out fresh vertical, the best snow and the most suitable terrain for your ability. Run length will vary through the season due to changing snow cover, with some terrain boasting runs over 1000m vertical. The regular Big Vertical package includes 5 runs. This 'standard day' — where the average drop is around 800m vertical — is one you'll never forget. Lunch and transfers are included. Go to: **www.wildernessheli.co.nz**

SAFETY AND SURVIVAL SKILLS

All heli-ski operators consider safety to be the number one priority above customer satisfaction, and the safety infrastructure in place provides you with an unsurpassed level of assurance. All guides are well trained in avalanche hazard evaluation and control, route selection, weather analysis, emergency first aid, mountain survival, rescue, and ski instruction techniques. Radio repeaters give them voice communication throughout the heli-ski area. Snow pack and weather are analysed daily and forecasts made accordingly, with slope assessment conducted prior to skiing. Remember, you'll be skiing or boarding in a very high alpine region, so warm clothing is of prime importance.

SNOWCAT-SKIING — SOUTHERN ALPS, SOUTH ISLAND

In essence, 'cat-skiing' offers access to terrain similar to that offered with heli-skiing, differentiated mainly by its price tag and transportation — making this half the cost of heli-skiing and double the fun!

■ Alpure Peaks Snowcat — Sherwood Range

Snowcat-skiing with this crowd starts with an exhilarating 30-minute ride on a Hagglund all-terrain vehicle such as those used in Antarctica which can handle the most demanding of conditions. Passengers then transfer to a powerful snowcat for the final grunt up the mountain. The cat can take on virtually any terrain and can also build ski jumps with ease. It has been fitted with a custom-built, fully enclosed rear canopy and forward-facing seats for maximum passenger comfort.

Powderhounds have exclusive access to more than 2600ha of private land near Fox Peak skifield, just 30 minutes from State Highway 8 between Christchurch and Queenstown. The terrain features spectacular views of the Southern Alps, huge bowls between Fox and Butlers Saddle, a 2220m peak with a vertical 650m run and a 1500m base area in which to ski, board, snowshoe and telemark.

Alpure Peaks, the company who run these trips, ensure each group enjoys fresh tracks, and fun and challenging runs. You'll be given full safety instructions and also supplied with an avalanche transceiver. Go to: **www.alpurepeaks.co.nz**

SNOWMOBLING — SOUTHERN ALPS, SOUTH ISLAND

■ Nevis Snowmobile Adventure

No special skills or fitness level is required to operate snowmobiles. Simply squeeze the accelerator and you're mobile; squeeze the brake and you stop. When you join a Nevis Snowmobile Adventure, you get to drive your own snowmobile into a unique, rarely visited part of New Zealand — and when you reach the 1700m plateau with 360-degree vistas of the southern South Island you'll think you're on top of the world! Expert guides will lead you on the journey into this intriguing

Snowmobiling in the mountains.

alpine region flanked by mountain ranges and distant valleys, and the flat to gently rolling terrain is also ideally suited to novices.

Trips depart from Queenstown Airport on a 12-minute exclusive helicopter flight over The Remarkables to land at their base camp on the Old Woman Range. Here professional guides help familiarise you with the snowmobile operation. Special thermal snowmobile suits, gloves, boots and helmets are provided to keep out the cold and then it's off on your great adventure partaking in an unparalleled experience from the comfort and safety of a modern fleet of snowmobiles.
Go to: **www.snowmobilenz.com**

Put on Ice — Glacier Hiking, Glacier Skiing, Ice Luge

GLACIER HIKING — WEST COAST, SOUTH ISLAND

■ Franz Josef Glacier Guides

From its origins high in the Southern Alps, the Franz Josef Glacier descends deep into the lush rainforest of Westland National Park, from a height of 2700m above sea level to only 240m in as little as 11km, making it the world's steepest and fastest-flowing commercially guided glacier.

Franz Josef Glacier Guides was founded in 1990 — so with that much experience under their belts, they know how to traverse glaciers. Plus, they operate on what is widely considered the gem of New Zealand's West Coast glaciers. Your great trip options include a full-day adventure, half-day hiking experience, ice climbing, heli-hiking and glacier valley walks. To be honest, you'd be hard pressed to find a better all-round adventure in New Zealand.
Go to: **www.franzjosefglacier.com**

■ Fox Glacier Guiding

This is your chance to take an ice-cold guided glacier walk onto one of the world's most famous ice flows, Fox Glacier. The company offer 9 variations from half- and full-day walks, a heli-hiking combo, a terminal face walk, ice climbing adventures, an overnight heli-trek, Chancellor Dome heli-trek and mountaineer adventures. You'll encounter ice crevasses — chasms and clefts in the glacier made when the ice flows over rough rocks and ledges — along with something to suit all fitness levels on these trips.

Fox Glacier is New Zealand's largest commercially guided glacier, situated on the West Coast only 21km south of Franz Josef.
Go to: **www.foxguides.co.nz**

Traversing a snow cave on Fox Glacier.

GLACIER SKIING — SOUTHERN ALPS, SOUTH ISLAND

Dating from the Pleistocene ice age, the 27km-long Tasman Glacier is two million years old and in places 650m thick. It's also the longest glacier in New Zealand, making it the perfect place to powder ski or snowboard, and quite possibly this country's most definitive skiing experience ever.

■ Ski The Tasman — Aoraki/Mt Cook

By the time the ski plane has landed, your small party will be looking down the longest and widest ski run you've ever seen — all 10km of it (yes, 10km, really). The glacier is not too steep, meaning anyone with intermediate ability can ski the Tasman. Nowadays, fat skis also make the transition to off-piste easy, relaxing and very cruisey. You'll also stop often to take in the scenery, so this makes it a great introduction and learning curve for the transition to heli-skiing.

Alpine Guides has introduced generations of skiers to this incredible experience at the heart of Aoraki/ Mount Cook National Park.
Go to: **www.skithetasman.co.nz**

ICE LUGE — CENRAL OTAGO, SOUTH ISLAND

If you need a break from skiing or you just have a hankering to try something new, head to Naseby, the ice sport capital of New Zealand, to try out the only ice luge in the Southern Hemisphere.

■ Maniototo Ice Rink & Luge — Naseby

Opened in 2008, Maniototo Ice Rink's 360m-long luge track has 10 bends and drops 25m from top to bottom. Lugers travel feet-first on single sleds and take an exhilarating trip on a specially built track through Douglas fir, pine and larch trees. The 1-hour session allows time for 3 short runs learning how to stop and direct the sled, followed by 2 full runs. Helmets are supplied but bring gloves and reasonably sturdy footwear. The adrenalin action doesn't stop here when the sun goes down, so enquire about luging under lights in the evening.

Up to a dozen people can use the luge track at a time, but Maniototo Ice Rink also offer curling indoors or skating outdoors if there's a wait. The luge is open every winter from June to August.
Go to: **www.nasebyicesports.co.nz**

The need for speed on the Naseby Ice Luge.

Dog sledding at Snow Farm.

Smooth Glide — Ski Touring, Dog Sledding, Snowkiting

As anyone who's ever clipped into cross-country skis will tell you, the rhythmic flow pushes up the heart rate as your body heats up in the cold mountain air. The terms cross-country skiing and ski touring are synonymous, and while this snow activity is probably never going to surpass skiing or boarding, if you feel like getting away from the downhill speedsters, this is a great way to go about it. And let's face it — ski touring is also easier to learn and a much safer sport.

■ Waiorau Snow Farm — Cardrona

Cross-country skiers at Waiorau are blessed with some of the best-prepared trails in the world, groomed and snow fenced to give the best possible conditions. Trails have been designed for all levels of cross-country skier — young, old, beginner or expert — in fact, pretty much anybody can push/glide/push/glide their way around this wonderful environment. There are magnificent views of the Southern Alps, river valleys and rolling slopes. Offering 55km covering 18 different well-groomed trails, Snow Farm has become New Zealand's cross-country skiing showpiece. Their base lodge houses a café, restaurant, ski hire and tuition as well as accommodation for over 70 guests in en suite and shared facility rooms. The main season is July to September.

The River Run & Loop

Out of the 18 trails this is a must-do if you're looking for a great workout and to put some distance under your belt. Its 12km length runs through the picturesque Meg River valley. The Meadow Warming Hut, nearly 4km from the lodge, is situated to catch the sun and is a great resting place, overnight hut, or stop-off point to make yourself a quick brew or sip a hot toddy. In good weather return via the Loop and enjoy the contrasting views of the Alps.

Located in the heart of the Cardrona Valley, Snow Farm can be easily accessed from both Queenstown, 1 hour's drive away, and Wanaka, which is 34km or 45 minutes in the opposite direction.
Go to: **www.snowfarmnz.com**

DOG SLEDDING

For something that the whole family can do that is different yet quite an adventure, how about experiencing a slice of the Arctic down under and head out dog sledding?

■ Quiet Running Adventures — Dog Sledding

Based at Snow Farm in the Cardrona Valley (see p.113), Quiet Running gives you a taste of what it's like to ride with their sled dogs — a mixture of Siberian and Alaskan huskies. After meeting the dogs and learning a little about them — along with the customary dog cuddle for the photo album — they will harness up a team and take you for a ride with these amazing four-legged athletes.

There are 3 tours to choose from: a 1-hour Basic Beginners trip; a 1-hour Basic Beginners Family trip — 2 adults, 2 sleds, 2 guides; and an overnight trip to the upper reaches of the Roaring Meg Stream. Quiet Running operates in limited time slots so a prior booking is essential.
Go to: **www.quietrunning.co.nz**

SNOWKITING

Catching on very fast in New Zealand, and especially in the Pisa Range at Snow Farm in the Cardrona Valley (see p.113), snowkiting already has a decade-long history in this country.

■ Wanakite Snowkite Freeride

Wanaka is a world-class snowkite destination and it's there that the annual Wanakite Snowkite Freeride is held, with 2010 marking the 10th anniversary of the event.
Go to: **www.kitesports.co.nz**

SAFETY AND SURVIVAL SKILLS

Whether it's skiing, snowboarding, heli-skiing, heli-boarding, snowcat-skiing or ski touring, it isn't uncommon in any one day for medical staff to treat a range of neck injuries, broken ankles, legs and wrists, plus an assortment of sprains associated with all forms of skiing but especially with heading downhill at speed on a hard-pack groomed trail. At least you can't ski headfirst into a tree on New Zealand skifields as they're all treeless — but do use some common sense and ski to your ability all the same.

It's well known that heli-skiing is an inherently dangerous sport — just think avalanches — which is what makes it such an exciting thing to do. Nevertheless, the New Zealand heli-skiing industry had recorded just two fatalities in two decades until in 2009 alone two people were lost to avalanches, including one who was an experienced guide. Thus, it should go without saying that keeping your wits about you off-piste is the way to stay alive. Obey the rules and don't go out of bounds when the signs clearly indicate them. Follow your guides' instructions in the event of avalanche or emergency.

For back-country skiing of any type you'll be carrying an avalanche transceiver (locator beacon), a simple homing device to enable rescue teams to locate you faster. A small backpack should also contain energy drinks or bottled water, energy bars, a whistle, and sometimes even a folding snow shovel and probe. Always travel in a group or in pairs and never alone.

Dressing appropriately affords your best chance of survival should you become lost or disoriented. Layer your clothing as it allows you to take things off as you start perspiring when it grows hot. Go out and buy the best thermal socks, leggings, body top and hat, add a good fleece jacket and then finish off with a technical high-neck ski suit and pants. Also carry goggles and sunglasses to prevent eye damage and protect you further in a snowstorm.

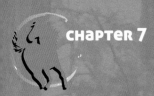

CHAPTER 7

A horse is a horse, of course, of course . . . So when saddles and equine endeavours are mentioned, it goes without saying that people are more than passionate about the mighty steed. When tourism took off in New Zealand in the 1990s, horse riding schools and remote farms saw the potential to offer visitors a way of seeing parts of the country literally hidden from view. If there is one thing that is pure about horse riding it's that it leaves no carbon footprint — just a hoofmark in the ground. This must surely be one of the most pleasurable and exciting modes of travel on the planet. Whether galloping along beaches, crossing mountain ridges, or wading through rivers, all you need is open space — and in Kiwi-land that's in plentiful supply, plus a whole heap of options to boot.

There are literally thousands of horse trails in every corner of New Zealand. Perhaps the fairest way to present some of the wildest trails and best spots in the country is to concentrate on some of the little-known multi-day riding areas. Multi-day horse treks can be of any duration with at least a 1-night stop en route on 2-day adventure rides through to 12-day riding and camping expeditions. The longest and highest rides are in the South Island including regions with beach access like the West Coast, or on farms and high-country sheep stations in places like Southland, the Mackenzie Country and Queenstown — but they usually only offer trips during the summer months because the winter weather is too severe. Conversely, in the North Island there are numerous options for wilderness trekking year-round in places like Northland and the Bay of Islands, Pakiri Beach and South Kaipara near Auckland, as well as parts of the East Cape and in the Taupo region. So put your feet in the stirrups and discover what this glorious country has to showcase in the way of equine escapades.

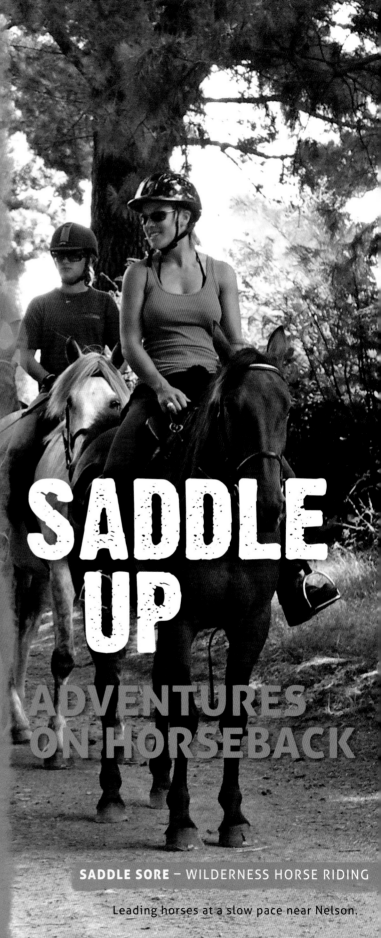

SADDLE UP
ADVENTURES ON HORSEBACK

SADDLE SORE – WILDERNESS HORSE RIDING

Leading horses at a slow pace near Nelson.

Roaming the upper reaches of the Mackenzie Basin, near Lake Tekapo.

Saddle Sore — Wilderness Horse Riding

Every year, hundreds of riders retrace the footsteps of New Zealand's early settlers across some of the country's most remote and dramatic landscapes in what has become an annual pilgrimage for many New Zealanders. The Goldfields Cavalcade journey is a popular event based on the first Cobb & Co stagecoach trip which left the Provincial Hotel in Dunedin to cross the Dunstan Trail to Central Otago's Dunstan Goldfields on 22 November 1862.

A decision to re-enact that journey in 1991 saw 220 people, 240 horses, coaches, wagons, carts, gigs, buggies and packhorses take part in the first Goldfields Cavalcade, which has now developed into a golden opportunity to mix history with intrepid travel. Organisers liken the experience to that of the old pioneers who were thrown together in migrant ships — Irish, Scots, Welsh and English wayfarers who normally had nothing much to do with each other.

Central Otago was the scene of New Zealand's biggest gold strike and the discovery of the yellow metal in the 1860s led to a rapid influx of foreign miners. Remnants of the mining heyday are still very much in evidence, and each year the Goldfields Cavalcade selects a different destination or host town so participants have the opportunity to learn more about the region's association with that golden era.

Nine different trails make up the Goldfields Cavalcade. Four of those are riding trails that take 6 to 7 days crossing Otago's dramatic hills and rivers with another 2 trails that are suitable for wagons

that take 5 days each — a good option for anyone wanting to enjoy the scenery with an element of comfort. The trails cover the rugged hills, rock-faced gullies and tussock-covered plains of Central Otago, a region famed for its vast open spaces, dramatic scenery and sparsely populated settlements.

The Cavalcade starts in late February to early March. Logistics means catering for large numbers is difficult, and organisers limit each trail to between 50 and 80 people. Most of those taking part ride their own horses but there are also a few mounts available for hire.

A moderate to high level of fitness is required for all horse riding, but especially for multi-day trails — for both horse and participant. If you are taking part in an organised trail ride it will be led by a 'trail boss', several wranglers and leaders who have planned the route and guide the cavalcade. The journey is considered more apt for the 'intrepid traveller' as no civilian luxuries (including showers) are available en route. Go to: **www.cavalcade.co.nz**

HORSE TREKS — NORTH ISLAND

■ Dromgool Horsemanship — Paihia, Bay of Islands

If you're looking for something slightly different — like learning horsemanship — this could be the place to saddle up. Horsemanship is essential to all riding disciplines from dressage to western, Clydesdales to miniatures. So no matter what your tastes, at Dromgool Horsemanship you can learn from the master, Ken Dromgool. Besides their 2 to 5-day clinics they also offer the Dromgool Horsemanship Experience, a spectacular week of riding and fun. It includes 3 full days of clinic instruction in a great facility with a covered 20m arena, 70m x 35m outdoor arena and round pen, plus trail riding over the farm and through native bush. Day 4 is a day of travel as you enjoy a relaxed journey to Henderson Bay in the Far North. The next 3 days are spent riding on spectacular Henderson Bay and Ninety Mile Beach followed by a relaxation day on the return to Paihia to spend as you wish. There are a number of options including bringing your own horse. Go to: **www.horseman.co.nz**

■ Eastender Horse Treks — Rangitukia, East Coast

This unique Maori-based outfit endeavours to enable you to experience the tribal Ngati Porou culture and hospitality on a day's trek. For a more rustic overnight riding and camping excursion they offer a 1-night, 2-day trip. The riding time is approximately 4 hours on Day 1 and 2 hours on Day 2. Once you've enjoyed a hearty campfire meal, this is your chance to rough it, sleeping under the stars by the flames of the fire. The trail eventually leads you to the highest lookout in the area with 360-degree views all the way to the East Cape Lighthouse, Mt Hikurangi and the Waiapu River, to a long stretch of the coastline towards Tokomaru Bay You'll need to be a confident and experienced rider to undertake this ride as the hills and trails are very steep. It's only offered in the summer, when weather permits, and for groups of 5 people or more. Eastender Horse Treks are located off the beaten track on the North Island's beautiful and isolated east coast. Go to: **www.eastenderhorsetreks.co.nz**

■ Ngahere Adventures — Taneatua, Whakatane

Based in the Bay of Plenty, Ngahere Adventures offer a unique horse trekking experience through the remote and mystical Te Urewera National Park as you journey along and through the Whakatane River, flanked on both sides by native bush, on either a day or overnight trek. On the Overnight Trek you'll ride 4 hours to their campsite, and the rest of the day is spent at your leisure. You complete the return leg the following morning. You'll need to bring along your own lunch, dinner, water bottle, sunscreen and additional warm clothing, solid footwear, swimming togs/towel, torch and sleeping bag. Sheets, pillows, mattresses, breakfast and light refreshments of tea/coffee and biscuits are provided.
Go to: **www.ngahereadventures.co.nz**

Riding in the waves on an East Coast beach.

Pakiri Beach Horse Rides — North of Auckland

For adventurous souls wanting a full week in the saddle, this epic 'coast to coast' journey might be for you. Their 7-day horse ride follows the mighty Hoteo River from the white sands and blue Pacific waters in the east, across rugged high-country hills to the black sands of the wild west coast. You'll negotiate lush forests and valleys as your guide follows trails made by the ancient Maori and by early European settlers. The landscape includes fertile farmland, tranquil native bush and exotic pine forests. Each day you'll spend between 4 to 6 hours in the saddle. This ride is not for novice riders. You must be able to mount and dismount unaided and be comfortable at all gaits. A maximum weight limit is 90kg and a minimum number of 4 riders is required. Included are all country-style and BBQ meals, some wine, plus accommodation in the beach house, country lodges and a motel as well as transport to and from Auckland City. Half- and full-day tours are also available. Go to: **www.horseride-nz.co.nz**

Ruahine Adventure Horsetreks — South of Taupo

This is a multi-day horse trek that started in the summer of 2010. It offers a 7-day, 7-night chance to really explore the beautiful Rangitikei high country the way it should be enjoyed — on horseback. Their horse trails lie nestled below the magnificent Ruahine Range and forest park, at the head of the Upper Kawhatau Valley. The 240ha property is a mix of river flats, hill country and native beech forest. Ruahine Adventure Horsetreks are part of a genuine working high-country farm. As well as the horses, sheep, dairy goats and cattle are run — including the renowned Meersbrooke Highland cattle. Go to: **www.ruahineadventurehorsetreks.co.nz**

South Kaipara Horse Treks — Helensville, Northwest of Auckland

This family-run crowd offer a 2-day horse trek that begins with an easy Woodhill Forest ride to the picturesque local lakes. Lunch is usually beside a lake or in the forest. In the afternoon the forest tracks open onto a historic farm of 1012 ha. The night is spent in shearers' quarters that sleep up to 12 people in 6 rooms with showers, toilets and a large kitchen/dining area. Next day the return journey takes you to the tip of the South Head peninsula where the Kaipara Harbour meets the Tasman Sea. Crossing the wilderness flats you will pass (and ride on if you want) sand dunes up to 20m high. Finally, it's out onto the open beach with nothing but sand and surf. The last leg is 16km of Muriwai Beach before re-entering Woodhill Forest on your homeward trail. Half- and full-day treks or weeklong 'riding holidays' are also on the itinerary. Go to: **www.horserides.co.nz**

HORSE TREKS — SOUTH ISLAND

Cape Farewell Horse Treks — Wharariki, West Coast

The Explorers Route is a 4-day trip that affords riders the chance to follow the same route Thomas Brunner, one of New Zealand's first adventurers, traced along the rugged West Coast, where the beaches seem to stretch out forever. The trip takes in remote Kahurangi Point, within the Kahurangi National Park, where you'll overnight in what was once the lighthouse keeper's house, now renovated into a bunkhouse and administered by DoC. With a little luck, freshly netted fish will be on the menu that evening. Wander up the Kahurangi River and feast your eyes on what they call the 'beer pool', where the water drops some 3m into a round pool where the native bush is astonishingly beautiful. You'll also not want to get out of the saddle until you're galloping full tilt down Wharariki Beach — something not to be missed!
Go to: **www.horsetreksnz.com**

High Country Horse Adventures — Rakaia Gorge, Canterbury

High Country Horse Adventures offer longer treks on quiet, friendly horses. Treks start at Ryton Station and range from 1 hour to 3 days. Ryton Station is beautiful horse riding country amid truly stunning mountains and majestic scenery. There are also translucent lakes and tarns to be visited — or to swim in if you like. Riders on the multi-day trek can overnight at Harper Village or camp at the Monck Hut. Both locations are very private and set in lovely environs. The Harper Village is a modern accommodation complex, and Monck Hut a historical musterers' cabin.
Go to: **www.horsetrek.co.nz**

Hurunui Trails and Adventures — Hawarden, North Canterbury

This outfitter has pioneered horse treks through some of this country's most spectacular wilderness

High country adventures on horseback.

for over 25 years. They offer a variety of multi-day horse riding adventures from overnighters to 9-night trips traversing the mountains, rivers and lakes in the spectacular high country of North Canterbury. The attraction of one of their rides, The Adventurer, is that you get to stay at 4 separate stations, giving riders the opportunity to see how the station owners survive in this rugged wilderness while experiencing their wonderful hospitality. The Adventurer is 5 days long and includes accommodation, dinner, bed, breakfast and packed lunch along the Hurunui River, lakes and mountains. Or try The Weekender, a romantic break that includes 2 nights' accommodation, dinner, bed, breakfast, packed lunch, a bottle of sparkling wine, chocolates and 2 days trekking in the high country and rivers. Note: This can be booked on weekdays as well.
Go to: **www.nztreks.co.nz**

■ Mackenzie Alpine Horse Trekking — Lake Tekapo

From the teal blue waters of Lake Tekapo to the high-country station in the Mackenzie Country is some of the most picturesque and natural scenery in the Southern Alps. This is your chance to ride across private high-country stations beneath the majestic 'Main Divide'. Day 1: The morning is spent riding across the tussock plains of Balmoral Station and over the Old Man Range. Day 2: You'll now ride across Braemar Station up to Maryburn Hut where you can look across Lake Pukaki to the mighty Ben Omar Range. Day 3: From Maryburn Hut you'll drop into the Forks River Valley on Glenmore Station. Day 4: Head down the Forks River and cross through Mt Joseph onto the edge of the Cass River, a tributary of Lake Tekapo. Day 5: A shorter half-day ride as you amble from the Cass River down through Godley Peaks Country to the edge of Lake Tekapo. Day 6: The final day — you'll cross the Cass River and follow the shores of Lake Tekapo on the homeward leg. Go to: **www.maht.co.nz**

■ Mt Lyford Horse Riding — Mt Lyford

On this outfit's Rustic Adventure ride you'll stay in huts, cook your own food (which is provided) and sleep occasionally in sleeping bags — in other words, it has adventure written all over it! The route is long, high and very impressive, passing through 7 working farming properties as you journey from Mt Lyford to Hanmer Springs. From Mt Lyford to the Sherwood Huts you'll ride along the foothills of the Amuri Range. On the second day the ride is from the Sherwood Huts to Moriarty's Farm Cottage that takes 7 to 8 hours while passing the highest point on the whole route. Finally, the stretch from Moriarty's Cottage to Chatterton Farm just outside Hanmer Springs township lasts between 4 and 5 hours.

All accommodation, food, riding gear, transfer of gear and return to Mt Lyford is arranged. A 6-day ride includes the return trip following different trails.
Go to: **www.lyfordtreks.co.nz**

Horse trekking in the South Island's high country.

■ Time Out Tussock Tours — Ranfurly, Central Otago

Mustering is still carried out on horseback today, rounding up merino sheep and cattle with working dogs at the blow of a whistle. As the local folk and the guides' families have been in this area for four generations and know the region's history well, these southern men and women have always got a few tales and yarns to share. This is one of those rare chances to go on a muster as you visit historic dwellings and pubs en route, following in the footsteps of 19th-century gold miners as you sleep in their original stone huts and out-of-the-way musterers' camps.

The Time Out Tussock Tour is held only twice a year and takes up to 40 riders on a 4-day trek. A minimum of 15 riders is required.
Go to: **www.highcountrytours.co.nz**

SAFETY AND SURVIVAL SKILLS

As many people are all too aware, falling off a horse can result in broken bones, serious injuries, or at times end in a fatality. It is always best to learn to ride with some reputable operators. Remember to stick to your route and always travel in a group in case of an emergency. Ride to your ability and in particular request a horse with a good disposition.

Some suggestions on avoiding aches and pains:
- Wear pantyhose, tights or Lycra bike pants under your riding pants to help reduce chafing.
- Avoid wearing new or freshly starched jeans — those seams can be a killer!
- Lengthen stirrup leathers a notch or two to reduce stress on knee joints.
- Take the opportunity to walk when possible and do some simple stretching exercises before mounting.
- Bring some Vaseline, talcum powder or similar for chafed bits.
- A small cotton neckerchief can help keep sunburn at bay when you have an open-neck shirt. Protect all other exposed skin from the sun.

CHAPTER 8

Splashing about in water is something that most Kiwi adults continue to do long after their childhood paddling days in the backyard pool over summer or walking home from school sloshing through muddy puddles. The progression is usually from diving into favourite swimming holes in the local river, to swimming or snorkelling in the sea that sometimes leads to scuba diving. Kids often mess about in a dinghy before they are 10 years old and that soon becomes addictive (look across any harbour in summer). Before long a dinghy leads to Hobie Cats that progress to trailer-sailers that morph into bigger and better yachts. Yachting truly is a rite of passage for many New Zealand kids and for our world-class professional yachtsmen it means ocean sailing.

With waves and coastline waters on just about everybody's doorstep in these islands, it's not surprising that as a nation we have embraced adventurous water sports such as surfing, windsurfing and kitesurfing. Sea kayaking, on the other hand, is today an incredibly popular outdoor activity and one in which the whole family can get involved, as double kayaks offer the chance for parent-child bonding unlike some other adventures. Then there are boat-related sports such as water skiing and wakeboarding that seems to have a solid following year on year. However, it's the chance to swim with dolphins and whale watch that particularly captivates the visitor to our shores, especially as they can get closer to them in the wild than in Sea World-like aquariums. So if you're the kind of person looking to ride the crest of a wave or dive on underwater wrecks, then get your feet wet and dip into this chapter.

BLUE WATER

ADVENTURES OUT AT SEA

FULL SAIL AHEAD – SAILING

INTO THE BLUE – SCUBA DIVING, SNORKELLING

MARINE ENCOUNTERS – SWIMMING WITH DOLPHINS, WHALE WATCHING

OFF THE BOW – JET SKIING, KAYAK FISHING, OCEAN ADVENTURE BOATING

PADDLE POWER – SEA KAYAKING

SURF'S UP – KITESURFING, SURFING, WINDSURFING

WAKES & WAVES – WATER SKIING, WAKEBOARDING

Kitesurfing at New Brighton Beach.

Full Sail Ahead — Sailing

Younger people have always been the backbone of the sailing community in our little country, and they start to learn to sail at a very early age, usually between 7 and 13 years old. They are often first taught in the snub-nosed New Zealand-designed P Class sailing dinghy, first introduced in 1923, and eventually progress to bigger keelboats. If you want to learn to sail a keelboat, then a proper course will teach you more than just the basic skills. You'll learn how to manoeuvre the yacht out of the marina on engine power alone, plus how to reef the sails as the wind increases as well as anchor the boat correctly and safely.

With so many Kiwi sailors having taken to the world stage it would be hard not to mention a few of them, for they are an inspiration to thousands of ordinary New Zealanders. Sir Peter Blake who was both a Whitbread Round the World Race winner and achieved two successive America's Cup wins for Team New Zealand is without question our best-known sailor. Sadly, he was murdered in Brazil in 2001.

Russell Coutts, Olympic gold medallist in the Finn Class, has won the America's Cup four times, 1995, 2000, 2003 and 2010, and is still considered by many to be the best sailor in the world. Grant Dalton, currently Managing Director of Emirates Team New Zealand's America's Cup syndicate, is another name synonymous with round-the-world sailing. Bruce Farr is another individual who first learned to sail in the P Class dinghy and then went on to become one of the world's most successful racing yacht designers. His yachts have won the Whitbread Round the World Race in 1986, 1990, 1994 and 1998. In 2001 the event was renamed the Volvo Ocean Race and a yacht designed by Farr Yacht Design was victorious in 2002. His yachts have also won the Sydney to Hobart Yacht Race 15 times and many America's Cup races over the years.

One of Auckland's best-known personalities and sailors is Penny Whiting who owns the Penny Whiting Sailing School and in more than 40 years has not missed one of her classes. With the assistance of her yacht *Endless Summer*, Penny has provided sailing tuition and instruction to over 20,000 students. A complete learn-to-sail course comprises five 3-hour practical lessons. You can do it on afternoons or at weekends and the total fee includes a book, DVD and navigation lesson. Go to: **www.pennywhiting.com**

There are so many wonderful sailing spots in New Zealand as virtually every region of our fine country boast locations that are equally as good as the next one — the list is pretty much endless. With nearly 16,000km of coastline, it's almost impossible to escape the sea down here — and with such stunning bays and islands, sheltered harbours, mountain fiords and lakes, who would want to avoid it?

SAILING SWEET SPOTS — NORTH ISLAND

■ Bay of Islands — Northland

An idyllic group of 144 islands in 'winterless' Northland in the Bay of Islands is rated one of the world's best cruising destinations. It's usually the first port of call for hundreds of yachts dropping down from the tropics in the cyclone season. Secluded white-sand beaches are everywhere. It's also famed for its big game fishing — in 1926, American novelist Zane Grey dubbed its waters the 'Angler's Eldorado'. Every year, competitive yachties sail from Auckland to Russell, the 'capital' of the Bay of Islands, in the country's most popular inshore race, the 119-nautical-mile Coastal Classic. From Auckland to Northland up the east coast there's a plethora of perfect sailing spots — such as the Cavalli Islands, Poor Knights Islands and Hen and Chicken Islands.

■ Hauraki Gulf — Auckland

First-time visitors are usually awestruck to find a maritime paradise so close to a major city. There are 47 islands dotted around the Hauraki Gulf Maritime Park — some, like Waiheke and the volcanic peak of Rangitoto, less than an hour away under sail. Other islands like Tiritiri Matangi, Little Barrier and Great Barrier Island are refuges for rare and endangered wildlife. Dolphins, blue penguins and, occasionally, orca can be seen in the Gulf's sparkling waters. Auckland is known as the 'City of Sails', and rightly so as on any given day the Waitemata Harbour sparkles with triangles of white sailcloth. There are also a number of skippers in Auckland who charter

Racing America's Cup yachts on Auckland's Waitemata Harbour.

out yachts or offer sailing experiences from a few hours to a few days in duration.

▦ Mercury Islands — Coromandel Coast

This beautiful region of New Zealand is often overlooked as a sailing destination, but besides the Mercury Islands there's the small group known as the Aldermen Islands and further south Slipper Island, while further south still is the marine reserve known as Mayor Island. However, it's the coastline of the Coromandel itself that makes for some wonderful sailing adventures extending from Cathedral Cove, down past Hot Water Beach and on to Pauanui and Whangamata.

▦ Wellington Harbour — Capital City

Wellington holds the dubious distinction of being one of the windiest cities in the world — making it both a haven and a hazard for sailors. New Zealand's capital perches on a 'river of wind', with the Cook Strait between the North and South Islands creating a wind corridor that sweeps into its harbour. However, the city's wide and deep harbour bays are perfect for dinghy and board sailing. Wellington was a short stopover in the 2005/2006 Volvo Ocean Race as the fleet sailed through Cook Strait on the way to the Southern Ocean.

SAILING SWEET SPOTS — SOUTH ISLAND

▦ Marlborough Sounds — Upper South Island

Encompassing one-sixth of New Zealand's coastline, it's been called one of the world's best-kept maritime secrets. The Marlborough Sounds at the top of the South Island comprises 3 main waterways: Queen Charlotte Sound, Pelorus Sound and Kenepuru Sound — a veritable labyrinth of islands, bays, coves and waterways fringed by native forest. A collection of submerged river valleys, the Sounds are a sanctuary for some of New Zealand's endangered wildlife — South Island robins, fur seals and the Hector's, dusky and bottlenose dolphins. With an area of approximately 150sq km, D'Urville Island is the eighth largest island in New Zealand and is well worth exploring under sail. Just beware of the dangerous French Pass through which water flows at up to 8 knots.

Lion New Zealand sailing into a good wind.

■ The Southern Fiords — Westland

Fiordland, in the southwest corner of the South Island, is like nowhere else in New Zealand. It is a World Heritage Park with inlets from the Tasman Sea running into wild, dramatic, unspoilt 'sounds'. Waterfalls cascade hundreds of metres into the primeval forest which were once gouged out by enormous glaciers. Of the 12 'sounds', Milford Sound is the best known, described by Rudyard Kipling as the 'eighth wonder of the world'. Here mountains rise out of the water and boats can sail past huge rock overhangs and tumbling cascades. Doubtful Sound is the deepest of the fiords (421m) and a haven for bottlenose dolphins, fur seals and crested penguins.

SAFETY AND SURVIVAL SKILLS

Sailing and boating rank among New Zealand's greatest pastimes and sports, but staying safe no matter what form of vessel you're skippering or crewing means keeping track of the weather. The national weather service, MetService (www.metservice.co.nz) and local area authorities offer important marine weather updates that all boaties should be aware of before and during any expedition on our beautiful gulfs, oceans, rivers, back bays and inland lakes. Check on the internet before you depart, or check the satellite weather forecast if you have SKY TV available. Most radio stations in New Zealand also update the weather forecast hourly and nationwide talkback radio often updates the marine forecast too.

Boaties should always have access to a VHF marine radio and if possible a hand-held one in a plastic bag. Also take along a fully charged mobile phone (again in a plastic bag) as a backup in an emergency — this has saved lives in the past — plus some red hand-held flares (check the expiry date). No matter what body of water you are on in New Zealand, take a hand-held GPS on the trip and you'll never get lost. Lastly, know and study the region's tide charts before leaving shore and you'll be shipshape.

If you are going out to sea and are not part of an organised charter boat, file a trip report with the coastguard and tell family and friends to raise the alarm if you are not back by a certain time. Wear a lifejacket and be well prepared. Know the rules. Check out the safety bylaws for the region in which you plan to boat, including the harbours, coastguard and marine radio information, marine reserve details, tides, emergency channels, marinas, weather, or boat ramp locations. One great way to obtain marine forecasts while out at sea is to ring MetService: 0900 999 + your area code.

- ■ Maritime New Zealand — Go to: www.maritimenz.govt.nz
- ■ New Zealand's Boating Website — Go to: www.boaties. co.nz
- ■ New Zealand Coastguard — Go to: www.nzcoastguard.co.nz
- ■ Water Safety Council — Go to: www.watersafety.org.nz/ goodadvice/boating.asp
- ■ Yachting New Zealand — Go to: www.yachtingnz.org.nz

Sailing *Arcturus* on the
Hauraki Gulf, Auckland.

CHARTER SAIL BOATS — HERITAGE CRUISING

■ *Arcturus* — Auckland

This ship was built in Maine in 1930 and is one of only nine boats from the John Alden 390 series. General George Patton and his wife sailed the yacht to Hawaii where he was stationed. At a later date he sailed her back to the west coast of the USA when war seemed imminent. Her accommodation includes 2 cabins, the aft serving as a guest suite. With its fine woodwork the galley is also faithful to the original design but incorporates all the benefits of modern appliances. Her expansive teak decks are the perfect spot on which to relax and enjoy the stable cruising for which she is renowned.

With timeless, elegant looks and a history that links her with one of America's greatest war heroes, the classic schooner *Arcturus* is still making her living in style, offering landlubbers a first-class sailing vacation. Go to: **www.classicboatcharter.com**

■ *Breum* — Auckland

A traditional 1925 gaff ketch of wooden construction, built of oak in Denmark, originally as a North Sea fishing vessel, *Breum* is 22.2m long and weighs 50 tons. She is a strong, stable and comfortable craft with large deck areas and wheelhouse seating options. For overnight coastal voyaging and longer passages, 13 passengers can experience sailing further afield — possibly Great Barrier Island, Coromandel Peninsula, or the Bay of Islands. You'll get to enjoy the unique experience of a large traditional yacht or assist with the boat handling and sail control.

The boat can be chartered for 2 and 4 hours or full-day sails for up to 30 passengers, allowing you to experience the beauty of the Waitemata Harbour or the full splendour of the islands of the Hauraki Gulf. Go to: **www.breum.co.nz**

■ *Fox II* — Akaroa, South Island

Fox II is a 15.2m gaff-rigged ketch that was built in Auckland in 1922 by WA Elley. She was originally built as a sailing cargo carrier with a single mast, a 2.7m bowsprit and a steel centreboard. Named *Iris Eileen* after the builder's daughter, only the best kauri was used in her construction, with much of it also made from pohutukawa with copper fastenings. The *Iris Eileen* was later sold to the Fox Fishing Company and became the second boat for the company fleet and renamed *Fox II*. She is New Zealand's oldest gaff-rigged ketch and is certified to carry 30 passengers. This is your chance to sail with dolphins in the crater of an extinct volcano in Akaroa Harbour. See Hector's dolphins, yellow-eyed and blue penguins, New Zealand fur seals, albatross and other sea birds. Go to: **www.akaroafoxsail.co.nz**

■ *Soren Larsen* — Auckland

The ship is the 19th-century brigantine star of the BBC's *Onedin Line* series and *Shackleton* docudrama. Built in Denmark in 1948/49, the vessel is 44m long, 7.8m wide with 29.8m-high masts, uses both diesel and auxiliary sail every summer and accommodates 13 crew and 22 guests. She is one of the most magnificently restored tall ships still sailing. She has sailed Cape Horn, explored the Pacific in the wake of Captain Cook and has sailed in New Zealand for the last 20 years. The *Soren Larsen* operates from Princes Wharf from Christmas onwards offering 4 to 5-day sailing adventures between Auckland and the Bay of Islands until the end of February and shorter 3 to 5-night voyages through March and April. Go to: **www.sorenlarsen.co.nz**

■ *Spirit of Adventure* — Auckland

Technically, she is a reproduction of a tall ship, having been built in 1986. Each year between 1000 and 1200 young people aged 15 to 19 and hailing from a wide range of ethnic and social backgrounds throughout the country participate in the Youth Development programme on the Spirit of Adventure Tall Ship sailing programme. In the past 30 years, 50,000 young people have taken part. The Spirit of Adventure Trust was established to provide the youth of New Zealand access to a character development programme through sail training. During the course of each voyage, the Trust aims to give young New Zealanders an equal opportunity to learn and develop from each other qualities of independence, understanding and community spirit through the medium of the sea. Although the Trust describes itself as a 'sail training organisation', the focus of learning for 'trainees' on its trips is on personal skills such as teamwork and communication. Go to: **www.spiritofadventure.org.nz**

■ *Ranui* — Auckland and Bay of Islands

Here is a 70-ton traditional Norwegian pilot ketch with a wonderful history. She was designed and built in 1936 by whaling Captain Korinius Larsen in Stewart Island. Crafted mostly of native kauri and totara, the *Ranui* is enormously strong and has long been renowned for her seaworthiness. An expedition aboard this vessel combines unparalleled service and comfort with a unique opportunity to sail the seas aboard one of New Zealand's maritime treasures.

The *Ranui*'s spacious hand-rubbed teak and kauri interior is superbly appointed and fully air-conditioned. The Milford Saloon provides ample room for internal relaxation and is equipped to cater for sizeable groups. There is accommodation for 12 people. She is only available in the Hauraki Gulf and Bay of Islands during the summer months. Go to: **www.ranui.co.nz**

SAFETY AND SURVIVAL SKILLS

There are strict guidelines and safety precautions for all trainees and passengers on board tall ships and older charter sailing boats. For further information on staying afloat and staying alive at sea go to: www.watersafety.org.nz

BARE BOAT YACHT CHARTERS

As in other parts of the world, chartering your own yacht or launch in this country is growing in popularity. There are 3 main cruising grounds in which bare boat yacht charters operate — Auckland's Hauraki Gulf, the Bay of Islands in Northland, and Marlborough at the top of the South Island — making coastal cruising one of the best ways to see our unique and diverse landscape. Most good yacht charter companies will give you a thorough briefing before departure and depending on your destination supply you with appropriate charts and advice. Most also offer a range of itineraries with a variety of go-ashore options and other activities. Go to: **www.charterlink.co.nz** or **www.charterguide.co.nz** or **www.chieftaincruises. co.nz** or **www.compass-charters.co.nz**

Into the Blue — Scuba Diving, Snorkelling

Scuba diving isn't everybody's cup of tea, but for all those that do dive with tanks there are probably ten times as many people who go snorkelling instead. Once a pastime for a privileged few, this water sport can be expensive, especially with all the gear you need: wetsuit, regulator, vest, dive mask and tanks and so forth. Then you need a boat to head out to reefs or sunken wrecks on. Snorkelling, however, is a pastime you can start at any age as long as you can swim. All you need is snorkel, mask and fins and the ability to launch yourself off any beach in New Zealand — now that's what makes this pastime a no-brainer! It's no wonder it's such a popular pursuit for beach-goers each summer.

For those of you who fancy diving to deeper depths, there's only one way to go about it if you haven't already done so. Take a certified course and learn to dive from the experts so that you don't make the mistakes that can lead to life-threatening situations. As you can snorkel and dive just about anywhere, highlighted in this section are a number of the best marine regions in our sparkling waters together with some of the wrecks offering premier scuba diving sites. So slip below the surface and discover what lies beneath . . .

BEST DIVE SPOTS — NORTH ISLAND

■ Gisborne — East Coast

This part of the country is often overlooked when it comes to diving but there are a few hidden spots that are worth discovering. About 10 minutes south of Gisborne on State Highway 35 you'll find Tatapouri Beach where Dive Tatapouri is based. The truly adventurous can drop into their purpose-built shark cage for a close look at some of the world's most feared marine creatures — mako and blue sharks. No experience is required but allow a whole day for the activity. Bookings are essential and it is weather dependent. All dive trips leave from the base as the ramp is situated just to its right.
Go to: **www.divetatapouri.com**

■ Goat Island — North of Auckland

It would be remiss not to mention this very popular marine reserve where generations of Aucklanders have learned to dive and snorkel. Not only is its close proximity to Auckland an attraction but the fact that it has been protected since 1975 means the marine life has had ample opportunity to flourish. Goat Island is an easy swim and a superb dive spot with very clear visibility in depths ranging from 10 to 20m. The seabed exhibits a variety of habitats: deep reefs, underwater cliffs, canyons and sand flats. Marine life can vary from seaweed forests to deeper waters where sea squirts, anemones, sponges and shellfish are found. Even the wily crayfish know they are protected where schools of snapper play in your bubbles.
Go to: **www.goatislanddive.co.nz**

■ Great Barrier Island

Here's one out of the 'catch bag' for you. Remote Great Barrier Island or Motu Aotea, the fourth largest island in Aotearoa, is a glittering gem at the far eastern edge of the Hauraki Gulf making it a truly brilliant dive spot. If you are just diving for crayfish and shellfish, then you won't be disappointed as they exist here in abundance. For wreck diving there is the TSS *Wiltshire*, a twin-screw steamer of 7801 tons, which struck a rock off Windy Hill, north of Rosalie Bay, in 1922. The rear half of the wreck constitutes the main section and is still fairly intact. As it lies in 15 to 28m, divers can tailor their dives to a variety of depths. The wreck of the SS *Wairarapa* is to be found at the top of the west coast, lying in about 15m of water. It is pretty broken up and well picked over by visiting divers but lots of small items can still be found. Other dive sites include Rabbit Island, The Pigeons, Rosalie Bay and Arid Island.

The *Sundancer* is a large 11.6m commercial charter dive/fishing boat based at Whangaparapara Harbour; however, there are a number of medium- to smaller-sized boats that can also be chartered at Claris, Tryphena and Port FitzRoy. A *Sundancer* charter offers a half-day or full-day excursion including tank hire.
Go to: **www.greatbarrierlodge.co.nz**

GEAR: You can bring all your own equipment on the ferry or hire wetsuits, regulators, BCD, weight belts, mask, fins, boots and catch bags at Hooked on Barrier Adventure Centre located in Claris township. Tanks can also be refilled in Port FitzRoy, Claris and Tryphena. Go to: **www.sealink.co.nz**

Diving at Poor Knights Islands, off Tutukaka.

▨ Poor Knights Islands Marine Reserve — Tutukaka, Whangarei, East Coast

When the legendary diver Jacques Cousteau declared the Poor Knights Islands one of the world's 10 best dive spots he wasn't kidding. As you'd expect, the water temperatures up here are warmer than normal, visibility is crystal clear and a complex underwater landscape provides an environment perfect for scuba diving. Just 2km north of Tutukaka Heads is the wreck of NZ Navy ship the *Tui*, which was designed for hydrological survey and submarine-hunting spy work and at one point protected New Zealand's anti-nuclear protest fleet at Mururoa Atoll. At 62m long she now lies in 30m of water and is ideal for investigating some of the best undersea marine life you'll find. This dive outfit will meet you at their white catamaran called *Shadowfax* moored at berth M4 next to the small boat ramp. Go to: **www.pkdive.co.nz**

▨ *Rainbow Warrior* — Cavalli Islands

The *Rainbow Warrior* was the Greenpeace ship that was bombed in Auckland Harbour by French secret service agents on 10 July 1985, at the height of the Pacific nuclear tests being conducted by France. The wreck was sunk off the Cavalli Islands some years later. This artificial reef has matured and is now host to an ever more populous and diverse assortment of marine life including a magnificent array of jewel-coloured anemones in hues of deep purple, iridescent blues and golden yellows. It is also a favourite haunt of golden snapper, giant kingfish and john dory. Don't miss the opportunity to dive on one of the Southern Hemisphere's most famous wrecks. Go to: **www.divenz.com**

▨ The Aldermen Islands — Tairua, Coromandel Coast

This awesome dive location is often referred to as the vanishing volcanoes. It is a group of precipitous, rocky islands which Captain Cook named The Court of Aldermen as he sailed past in 1769, and from the sea they are certainly a very impressive sight. There are numerous dive spots around with weird and wonderful names: the Sugarloaf, the Rambles at Ugly Point, the Jungle and the Dromedary, the Sieve (Elephant Bay) and the Flat Island Caves (but both of these last two need the sun to be in the right place for maximum enjoyment). Probably the best known is the Honeycomb Caves which are ideal for intermediate entry divers.
Go to: **www.divethecoromandel.co.nz**

Up-close diving off
Whale Rock, Coromandel.

■ White Island — Whakatane, East Coast

This is one of the ultimate dive spots due to the proximity to New Zealand's only active marine volcano which has been steaming away for centuries. Located 48km from Whakatane, this unique environment is world class with clear waters, prolific marine life and the underwater volcanic terrain. Expect to see huge kingfish, plenty of stingrays and massive schools of blue maomao along with some of the biggest crayfish you'll ever meet. Visibility is generally 20m or better in this fascinating locale where underwater hot-tub action from the open fissures just adds to the 150m drop-offs and easy reef dives.
Go to: **www.divewhite.co.nz**

BEST DIVE SPOTS — SOUTH ISLAND

■ Fiordland — Milford Sound

Of the thousands of visitors a week to Fiordland each summer, most are not aware that below the tide line there is an altogether different underwater world rich in fauna and flora. Much of its uniqueness is caused by the light-absorbing freshwater layer (unique to fiords) that restricts algal growth and allows deepwater or light-avoiding species to become established at much shallower depths. Approximately 160 species of fish have so far been recorded by divers within 45m of the surface of the fiords. Cold-water species include copper moki, trumpeter, banded wrasse and pigfish. Species usually confined to 100m-deep water include sandpaper fish and spiny sea dragons. Warm-water species include splendid perch and blue-dot triplefin. Go to: **www.tawakidive.co.nz**

■ Kaikoura — East Coast

Well known for its award-winning whale watching and swimming with dolphins charters, it's no wonder Kaikoura on the east coast of the South

Island has also made a reputation for snorkelling and diving. For a diver, Kaikoura's undersea community is an opportunity to observe a plethora of astonishing and unique marine creatures — this is sea life at its best. The rich underwater diversity of the rocky coastline means that every day there is a chance to see and experience the fascinating world of marine mammals from dolphins and the cheeky and inquisitive fur seals through to giant sperm whales. Go to: **www.divekaikoura.co.nz**

■ Marlborough Sounds — Upper South Island

The Russian cruise ship *Mikhail Lermontov* ran aground on 16 February 1986 as it tried to sail through a narrow/shallow channel off the tip of Cape Jackson and is now an artificial reef perfect for divers. The *Lermontov* just managed to make it as far as Port Gore after sustaining damage hitting an underwater rock, causing two gashes, both about 12m long and around 30m back from the port beam. The ship eventually sank in 30m of water and now lies fully intact resting on her starboard side. Diving on the *Lermontov* is a fantastic experience, with the propellers, funnel, bridge and pool area all easily accessible. There are 3 other wreck sites in the Marlborough Sounds: the *Lastingham* lying in 10 to 12m of water, the *Koi* down about 12m, and the *Rangitoto* at a 12 to 16m depth. They are all rated good dive sites with plenty of crayfish and fish life such as blue moki and red moki, sea perch, butterfly perch, marble fish, blue cod, leatherjacket, triplefin, banded wrasse, scarlet wrasse, and tarakihi. Go to: **www.godive.co.nz**

■ Stewart Island

This is a must-do for serious divers. As the third largest island in Aotearoa and a largely untouched wilderness, Stewart Island offers some great scuba diving and snorkelling off its coastline although many of the sites are very weather affected. Dive sites are located around Port Pegasus, Halfmoon Bay and Port Adventure, all on the east coast of the island. One good place to pull on a mask and tank is the *Marine Maid*, a 20m cargo ship that sank in 2000, which sits in 30 to 35m of water near Barclay Rocks at the entrance to Halfmoon Bay. Leask Bay, near Oban township, also offers a good shore-based dive site. Sandhill Bay is another easy dive among kelp forests with plenty of blue cod, southern pigfish, spotties, small sharks, barracuda, blue moki and other marine life.

Water temperatures vary from 14°C in summer to 7°C in winter so wear a thick wetsuit. You can book Stewart Island dives online or from Bluff or Invercargill as well as Oban itself. Regular ferry services operate to the island.
Go to: **www.tawakidive.co.nz**

SAFETY AND SURVIVAL SKILLS

Scuba diving is inherently risky due to many factors which are fairly obvious even to a layperson. Staying safe will help you make the most of your time diving around our pristine coastline. As well as observing the safety aspects of diving and snorkelling, bear in mind your obligation to protect and preserve the marine environment:

- ■ If you haven't dived for a while, do a local dive or refresher course with a reputable dive company. Dive within your limits and don't push your depth or bottom time limits.
- ■ Never dive alone. If you're inexperienced, always dive with an experienced 'buddy', and if you're snorkelling be aware of your surroundings and don't get pulled out of your depth or stray off alone.
- ■ Practise and maintain proper buoyancy control and avoid overweighting.
- ■ Stay warm both in and out of the water and drink plenty of fluids to avoid dehydration.
- ■ Avoid flying for at least 24 hours after your last dive (to avoid decompression sickness) and also avoid driving from sea level to altitude (above 150m) immediately after a dive.
- ■ Take care in underwater caves, archways and ledges, which can be especially dangerous during heavy surges.
- ■ Secure gauges and the regulator so they're not dangling — they can damage reefs and become entangled in kelp.

Although you don't necessarily need to be experienced to dive in New Zealand, some sites are only available to divers with the skills and experience to descend safely. Remember to always have your diver's certification card on hand and your dive log as evidence of your skills and experience. If you are not certified, many areas provide a fantastic range of diving schools. Some of the pitfalls to be mindful of while diving include: injuries due to changes in air pressure, decompression sickness, nitrogen narcosis, oxygen toxicity, refraction and underwater vision, controlling buoyancy underwater and losing body heat.

Marine Encounters — Swimming with Dolphins, Whale Watching

The numerous species of dolphin likely to be seen off New Zealand's coastline include the common dolphin, bottlenose dolphin, Risso's dolphin, dusky dolphin, Hector's dolphin and the not too common striped dolphin. Due to their sociable nature and ability to interact with humans, these marine mammals are regarded with special affection in our waters.

To this day, people refer to two individuals in particular — a Risso's dolphin known as Pelorus Jack who made a name for himself as he accompanied ships and ferries sailing through Pelorus Sound between the 1890s and 1912; and the equally famous and very friendly female bottlenose called Opo who gained her reputation in the summer of 1955 by first accompanying fishing boats in Hokianga Harbour before progressing to frolic and play with bathers on a daily basis. Up till recently, a resident dolphin in Whakatane called Moko caused a stir among surfers and lifesavers with her playful antics.

You'll find dolphin excursions on offer in many places around the country including the Bay of Islands, Auckland's Hauraki Gulf, the Bay of Plenty, Marlborough Sounds, Kaikoura, and in Southland and Fiordland. Most (but not all) of the operators in this section offer swimming with dolphin options. This activity is very much dependent on two main factors — the weather and the demeanour of the dolphins themselves. All the boats are regulated by DoC to allow you to swim with dolphins, but if it is deemed at all risky and possibly harmful to the mammals the crew will not allow you into the water.

WHALE & DOLPHIN ENCOUNTERS — NORTH ISLAND

■ Auckland Whale & Dolphin Safari — Auckland

Established in 2000, this crowd's record says it all: dolphins are viewed on over 90 per cent of trips and whales are viewed on 75 per cent. Once on board their comfortable 20m catamaran they'll scour the Hauraki Gulf to locate whale and dolphin activity. This operator specialises in making the most of a day out on the water and claims to have sighted 22 species of marine mammal. However, this is not a swimming experience, just a chance to view the hugely diverse range of mammals that call the Gulf and its harbours their home.
Go to: **www.explorenz.co.nz**

■ Butler's Swim With Dolphins — Tauranga, Bay Of Plenty

Offering a totally natural experience with wild dolphins, this company head out in *Gemini Galaxsea*, at 18m long and very comfortable an extremely dolphin-friendly sailing boat — making this voyage ecotourism at its very best. You also have a chance to see orca, the odd baleen whale, pilot whales and the occasional false killer whale. Although refunds are not offered, in the rare event of not seeing dolphins or whales you can take a return trip at no charge.
Go to: **www.swimwithdolphins.co.nz**

Dolphins in the Hauraki Gulf, Auckland.

Dolphins play in the wake

■ Dolphin Blue — Tauranga, Bay of Plenty

The Bay of Plenty is not only home to dolphins but also hosts an abundance of marine and bird life such as whales, seals, sunfish, sea birds and New Zealand's very own blue penguins. This is a 6-hour dolphin watch and swimming encounter, and to ensure the interaction is enhanced passenger numbers are limited to just 15. Lunch, morning tea and refreshments are provided along with wetsuits and snorkelling equipment.
Go to: **www.dolphinblue.co.nz**

■ Dolphin Discoveries — Paihia, Bay of Islands

These folks are said to have pioneered dolphin swimming and viewing in the Bay of Islands and are the only operator to provide you with a lifetime dolphin viewing guarantee on all trips. You'll cruise among some of the 144 islands in the region on their modern high-speed catamaran, purpose-built for dolphin watching and swimming and offering easy access to the water, which is the warmest in New Zealand. Their crew will assess the behaviour of the dolphins on the day and decide whether swimming with them will be possible under DoC regulations. A portion of your fare contributes to local marine mammal research and conservation.
Go to: **www.explorenz.co.nz**

■ Dolphins Down Under — Whakatane, Eastern Bay of Plenty

This company take great pride in the fact that their Dolphin Swim Tours are personal and exclusive. They operate only in summer in an all-weather 10m Kevlar catamaran that is extremely comfortable and seaworthy. Experienced skippers and guides provide an insight into this magnificent marine environment, with the goal of finding dolphins paramount in their minds — and they can proudly claim a success rate of around 95 per cent during the summer months with the opportunity to swim with the dolphins rated very probable.
Go to: **www.whalesanddolphinwatch.co.nz**

■ Dolphin Explorer — Auckland

Clearly, these guys aren't often wrong, as they reckon dolphins are encountered on 90 per cent of all trips out on the Gulf — if not, they offer another free trip. So go and enjoy the ultimate marine mammal experience, and as a bonus sail in the Hauraki Gulf for between 4 to 5 hours. The

opportunity to swim with dolphins is also rated good and you get to do it in one of the world's most biologically and geographically diverse maritime parks. Snorkel, mask, fins and wetsuit for swimmers are provided, so don't forget your towel.
Go to: **www.dolphinexplorer.com**

■ Dolphin Seafaris — Mt Maunganui, Bay of Plenty

This company has been going for many years and is a leading professional ecotour operator in the Bay of Plenty for watching and swimming with dolphins. Their vessel *Guardian* is a purpose-built, fully licensed, super-fast 15m luxury Cougar catamaran, crewed by expert marine biologists/naturalists and dive masters. Each day your swim encounters are governed totally by the behaviour of the wild dolphins. In good sea conditions it is possible to free swim with the dolphins in small groups of 3 to 8 people only. They will ensure that your experience will be one of the highlights of your visit to the North Island. Go to: **www.nzdolphin.com**

■ Fullers Great Sights — Paihia, Bay of Islands

This half-day cruise is a 'must do' for dolphin lovers. Take the opportunity to swim with common and bottlenose dolphins in their natural habitat. The warm waters of the Bay of Islands are rich in marine life all year round. This tour gives you the opportunity to swim with these incredible creatures in their natural environment (conditions permitting) and cruise the many secluded islands. Should conditions prevent you from swimming with dolphins, a swim refund will be offered to those passengers who have paid to swim, or alternatively a 'go again for free' voucher for another Dolphin Eco Encounter cruise. Snorkel, mask, fins and wetsuit are provided. Go to: **www.dolphincruises.co.nz**

■ *South Sea Vagabond* — Tauranga, Bay of Plenty

Over the summer months (November to May) *South Sea Vagabond* is a fast, comfortable 18m sailing catamaran that runs regular trips out to swim and kayak with the hundreds of common dolphins that inhabit the waters and islands of the aptly named Bay of Plenty. Wetsuit, mask and snorkel and kayaks are all provided on this total marine encounter experience. Go to: **www.southseasailing.com**

WHALE & DOLPHIN ENCOUNTERS — SOUTH ISLAND

■ Dolphin Encounter — Kaikoura

Visitors have been introduced to the delights of a wonderful marine environment, just offshore from the stunning Kaikoura coastline, since the summer of 1989/90. This operator's tours take place in the open ocean and are subject to the elements, so expect cancellations sometimes. A permit system also restricts the number of dolphin swimmers allowed in the water at any one time. During the summer months (November to April) it is essential to plan well ahead if you want to book a dolphin swim. Swimming with or watching the dusky dolphins is something very special and makes you realise that our oceans and their inhabitants are a treasure worth preserving.
Go to: **www.dolphin.co.nz**

■ Dolphin Watch Ecotours — Marlborough

The calm sheltered waters of the scenic Marlborough Sounds are perfect for swimming with dolphins. Help search for the dusky dolphins, bottlenose dolphins, common dolphins and even rare Hector's dolphins that frequent this region. This operator is Picton's only 'swimming with dolphins' charter boat. That means you will be the only boatload of swimmers out with a group of dolphins at any one time. They're also fortunate enough to operate in an area of little to no sea swell and their dolphin swimming success rate is said to be 83 per cent. As with all operators, your equipment is provided. Go to: **www.naturetours.co.nz**

■ Swimming With Dolphins — Akaroa

Black Cat Cruises operate 'Swimming with Dolphins' and have conducted dolphin encounters since 1990, making them one of the first companies to begin taking tourists out to sea for that prime purpose. Here you can swim with the world's smallest and rarest dolphin — the Hector's dolphin — in the beautiful sheltered setting of Akaroa Harbour. All necessary gear is supplied including wetsuits, masks and snorkels. Just take a towel, swimming costume, sunscreen and your digital camera! The water temperature in Akaroa Harbour ranges from 11°C in winter to 17°C in summer. Expect 2 hours on the water.
Go to: **www.swimmingwithdolphins.co.nz**

Up-close with whales at Kaikoura.

■ Whale Watch Kaikoura — Kaikoura

A multiple award-winning nature tourism company owned and operated by the indigenous Kati Kuri people of Kaikoura, Whale Watch was formed in 1987 and has become the best-known marine encounter in New Zealand. On 12 November 2009, Whale Watch Kaikoura was also awarded the year's Supreme Award at the Virgin Holidays Responsible Tourism Awards in London. It is this country's only marine-based whale watching company offering visitors an exciting up-close encounter with the giant sperm whale at all times of the year. Kaikoura's resident sperm whales are the largest living carnivore — equivalent in size to four elephants — and seeing these giants of the deepest ocean up close will leave you in awe. The company's 95 per cent success rate means they guarantee an 80 per cent refund if your tour does NOT see a whale. Go to: **www.whalewatch.co.nz**

Off The Bow — Jet Skiing, Kayak Fishing, Ocean Adventure Boating

JET SKIING

Jet skiing is one of the fastest-growing water sport activities around the New Zealand coastline, purely because it is inexpensive to get started and it doesn't take long to get the hang of the technique required to ride the machine. It's fast and furious and guaranteed to cool you down. Summer's the time when you can hire jet skis at some of the most popular beaches and recreation areas in the country. Some tour companies offer guided jet ski trips of 1 hour, 2 hours or half a day. A few even conduct 3-day tours, specifically in the Marlborough Sounds and the Buller River on the West Coast. On most overnight trips your tour guides will carry two-way radios and have GPS fitted, so you'll be in safe hands. The best way to find out more information is to contact the tourism bureau nearest to the destination you plan on visiting: Go to page 174 for a list of all their websites.

Lake jet skiing in Rotorua.

SAFETY AND SURVIVAL SKILLS

The speeds at which they can travel as well as the sharp turning radius make these wave-hoppers as dangerous as an out-of-control motorbike. Accidents happen every year and swimmers and divers are the usual recipients. Obey the wake speed limits set in harbours and on beaches and keep your eyes peeled for people in the water. Wake and wave jumping is obviously something that comes with experience and you should become proficient first before attempting such manoeuvres. Alcohol and jet skis also do not mix and should be avoided altogether. Remember to always wear a lifejacket.

Fishing from a kayak in Auckland.

KAYAK FISHING

Once you put together a popular sport like kayaking with great scenery and the world's biggest outdoor recreation — fishing — you get a unique new adventure that is catching on quickly in this country. At present many visitors are hiring specially designed kayaks from professional operators that are kayaking and fishing in the Hauraki Gulf in Auckland, with other operators located on the Coromandel Peninsula and in the Bay of Plenty.

The newest kayaks are nowadays made especially for fishing with a range of innovations including rod holders, bait tanks, sealed fishing gear hatches, extra storage space and raised seating to keep you drier. One of the most successful operators is New Zealand Tours and Travel based in Auckland. Their full-day tours offer a door-to-kayak-seat service as they transfer you to their entry point on a North Shore beach. You'll then receive kayak instruction before embarking on a kayaking trip and a fishing adventure all in one. Lunch, snacks, and hot and cold drinks are all included. Expect to catch snapper, gurnard, kahawai, trevally, john dory and kingfish. Go to: **www.newzealandtours.travel**

OCEAN ADVENTURE BOATING

Experience the adrenalin rush as elongated ocean-going speed machines take you on a 90-minute trip through the Bay of Islands. It is one of the fastest — and most spectacular — ways to see the famous Hole in the Rock. This is all about travelling at speeds of up to 100kph. Adrenalin junkies will love the 'extreme seats' at the front — a place to feel the wind in your hair and sea-spray on your face. Both operators stop for photo and video opportunities and to observe the abundant wildlife of this stunning region. Not only will you get to cruise through the Hole in the Rock and explore Cathedral Cave, the trip will take you through the inner and outer islands to the spectacular scenery of Cape Brett. Go to: **www.awesomenz.com** or **www.macattack.co.nz**

Paddle Power — Sea Kayaking

New Zealand Maori were paddling rivers, estuaries and harbours long before Europeans introduced Eskimo-type canoes to this country in the 1880s. As recently as December 2009, a member of the public spotted the remains of an ancient craft sticking out of the sands at the southern end of Muriwai Beach west of Auckland. It turned out to be an old Maori canoe, a 7m-long waka tiwai — a craft made from a single piece of kauri once common on rivers and used for fishing. First indications are that it is likely to be pre-European.

Sea kayaking is a very safe and popular outdoor sport and one that is now embraced globally. You only have to look at all the 4-wheel-drive vehicles heading out of the city towards the beach on weekends or during holiday breaks with kayaks fastened to the roof rack to appreciate how far this outdoor pastime has come. Today's adventurous paddlers have wonderful opportunities to experience our maritime ports and harbours, island and mainland coastlines, backwater estuaries and open sea — and all from a very different perspective.

This is one of the few adventure sports with no rules and no restrictions, other than the sea itself. It's easy to escape clogged roads, city fumes and noisy neighbours, to replace them with lapping waves, deserted islands, quiet inlets, hidden beaches and tidal mangroves where other craft can't venture. It's still a challenging environment, especially as you venture into open seas, but it's only as hard as you want to make it. Some kayaks are basic one-mould open-cockpit plastic shells. Top-end models are technically more advanced with a huge range of

Exploring Cathedral Cove at Hahei by kayak.

options and additions — ocean-going kayaks have spray sheets to enclose the cockpit and sometimes small split sails to harness the wind. With a multitude of sealed compartments, they can more than carry enough gear to spend a week in coastline wilderness.

Thankfully, we are blessed with some of the finest shoreline in the world, and it is all ideally suited to kayaking: the Bay of Islands, the Cavalli Islands, Waiheke Island, Kawau Island, Great Barrier Island, the Coromandel Coast, the Marlborough Sounds and Abel Tasman National Park, Banks Peninsula, Fiordland and Stewart Island are but a few of the wonderful regions you can explore from the seat of a kayak. The kayaker also has the advantage of paddling for a few hours at a time and then pitching camp early or going much further.

Whether you go out on a day trip in an open kayak across the harbour or take to the open waters in an ocean-going touring kayak, you will be carrying on an adventure boom that only really took off in this country about 20 years ago. To find out where to linger longer and explore farther afield, delve into this section to discover some of our great kayaking regions for yourself.

SEA KAYAKING REGIONS

Top End of the North Island

Head up to Northland and you won't be disappointed. There are so many bays, beaches, boat ramps, harbours and private estuaries that you could spend a year exploring this region and barely skim the surface. Even in winter months you'll still find some adventure seekers ocean kayaking here. The Bay of Islands is an obvious place to slide a kayak into the water as the area offers a variety of options from half-day excursions to multi-day open sea journeys. Islands are dotted with picnic spots and campgrounds near secluded beaches. The region stretches from Kerikeri Falls to the outer islands and beyond. Further north are what we call the Three Capes: Reinga, Maria van Diemen, and North Cape. This is an area of exposed open sea beaches with many surf breaks and big swells rolling in from the Tasman Sea. Hokianga Harbour is another dream region in which to kayak, but don't venture out beyond the bar as it's a whole different ball game. Go to: **www.coastalkayakers.co.nz** or **www.baybeachhire.co.nz** or **www.nzkayaktours.com**

The City of Sails, Gulf Harbour and West Coast Beaches

Not surprisingly, our largest city supplies a wealth of hidden gems for kayakers with a myriad of paddling locations from which to choose. Such diversity gives all kayakers a rare chance to embark on a few hours or a few days at sea depending on what part of the city's coastline you decide to explore. There are of course the two distinctly different harbours: Waitemata and Manukau — with the Manukau being more estuarine. The Waitemata Harbour allows you to explore the city's suburban coastlines.
Go to: **www.fergskayaks.co.nz**

Kayaks on the Sealink Ferry to Great Barrier Island.

Further north of Auckland on the west coast is Kaipara Harbour, a maze of inlets, bays, backwater coves and estuaries just waiting to be discovered; or head up the Hoteo River to the base of Mt Auckland. An hour north of Auckland is Mahurangi Regional Park, just perfect for the paddler, with abundant rivers, sheltered bays, sea caves, sinewy estuaries and even a shipwreck to check out. If you fancy an overnight adventure, join a guided tour with the option of staying in a genuine Kiwi bach or at a superb campsite. This kayak company work the northern beaches and offer sheltered-water sea kayak tours or can tailor a trip to suit your specific needs. Go to: **www.seakayakauckland.co.nz**

Other regular and popular destinations to paddle are the Hauraki Gulf islands including Rangitoto, Motutapu, Motuihe, Rakino and further north The Noises. For those craving some solitude, point your bow out to the eastern end of Waiheke Island, where the additional islands of Rotoroa and Ponui offer some really special kayaking adventures. Waiheke is a much bigger island than it looks but offers some unsurpassed secluded beaches ideal for overnight camping. Kayaks can be rented from the foreshore at Matiatia on Waiheke.
Go to: **www.kayakwaiheke.co.nz**

Further out and at the more adventurous end of the scale is the western side of Great Barrier Island, a place of rugged beauty and wild coastlines with a couple of isolated DoC campgrounds. Kayaks can be rented in Tryphena and Whangaparapara Harbour on the island. Go to: **www.islands.co.nz/sea-kayaking**

For the stay-close-to-home big-city kayaker who's in need of an afternoon fix, head into the upper Waitemata Harbour, or paddle your way along the coastal headland around Devonport or Takapuna, or follow the serpentine bays from Auckland to Mission Bay and stop off for lattes or a few cold bevvies along the route. Last but not least are the west coast beaches — if you're into surf canoeing and like the challenge, this will be fulfilling if not hair-raising. Go to: **www.windsurfauckland.com**

Middle of the North Island
For the serious kayaker this region affords some of the best exploration of any coastline in the country. Starting on the east coast with the Coromandel Peninsula, the area features huge rocky outcrops with high bluffs and wonderful sandy beaches

below. These are very exposed shores and should probably only be tackled by experienced paddlers. However, the region also offers some of the most picturesque scenery in the North Island.
Go to: **www.seakayaktours.co.nz**

Further south is the Eastern Bay of Plenty coastline, especially the harbour of Tauranga. One operator offers fully inclusive 1 to 5-day sea kayak holidays along the Coromandel Coast with accommodation each night in a typical Kiwi bach.
Go to: **www.adriftnz.co.nz**

Lower End of the North Island
As windy a reputation as Wellington has, it still offers some enticing challenges for the serious kayaker. This part of New Zealand is especially rugged due in most part to the wild nature of Cook Strait that fuels the winds onto the lower North Island. Don't be fooled by the inner harbour which can swiftly turn from flat calm into a whitecap-whipped gale. North of Wellington is New Plymouth, a region not that well known or defined for paddlers, yet worth exploring to search out the Nga Moru/ Sugar Loaf Coastal Reserve.
Go to: **www.fergskayaks.co.nz**

Top End of the South Island
This is the region where kayakers realise their dreams as there are hundreds of inlets and islands to explore around places like Golden Bay, Tasman Bay, Abel Tasman National Park, and the Marlborough Sounds. Abel Tasman is New Zealand's smallest national park with a coastline that stretches 91km from Wainui Inlet in the north to Marahau Estuary in the south. The granite coastline is characterised by near-shore islands, sheltered waters, estuaries and golden-sand beaches. The marine reserve is home to a fur seal colony; and marine and terrestrial birds are abundant along the coastal margin. There are at least 5 kayak operators in the region who offer either guided or freedom go-as-you-please rentals. Go to: **www.ngaitahutourism. co.nz** or **www.abeltasmankayaks.co.nz**

The Marlborough Sounds, on the other hand, has a 1500km coastline. This ancient system of drowned river valleys is sheer sea kayaking heaven. The vast expanses of water extend from the open seas of Cook Strait, inland through the maze of bays and hidden coves of the Queen Charlotte and Pelorus sounds, to the port towns of Picton and Havelock.

Kayaking in Abel Tasman National Park.

While the intimacy of the coves and bays provides the ideal day trip, the vast expanses of the Outer Sounds are perfect for either day trips or guided trips of unlimited duration where it is common to see dolphins and seals.
Go to: **www.soundswild.com**

East Coast of the South Island

Kaikoura is located on a rocky peninsula, protruding from lush farmland beneath snow-capped mountains. In the waters below, a complex marine system provides an abundantly rich habitat for marine mammals and sea birds making it an ideal place for getting close to nature — and for kayakers there is no better way to experience it. Chances are also high that you'll see dolphins and whales on your outing. Go to: **www.seakayakkaikoura.co.nz**

With its myriad assortment of bays and coves offering infinite possibilities for exploration in a diverse and fascinating coastal environment, Akaroa Harbour is another superb location. Whether you're a seasoned paddler or just getting started, you can explore nature, view sea birds, dolphins and penguins, or go for a swim at remote sandy beaches. There is now a guided safari tour of this wonderful coastline.
Go to: **www.akaroakayaks.co.nz**

Further down this coastline, the Banks Peninsula also offers some stunning waters in which to paddle. Flea Bay and the Pohatu Marine Reserve is a small coastal region and the site of New Zealand's largest mainland penguin colony. The best time to unobtrusively observe the wildlife and take in the spectacular scenery is to sea kayak here during the breeding season between September to January. Pohatu Marine Reserve showcases great opportunities for spectacular coastal sea kayaking in safe, stable double or single kayaks. Trips are fully guided by their experienced staff.
Go to: **www.pohatu.co.nz**

West Coast of the South Island — Fiordland National Park

Fiordland is another sea kayaker's dream location, a geographic wonder so dramatic it feels like you could be kayaking in the most primitive place on earth. Fiordland is one of the largest national parks in the world, bordered on its eastern flank by the stunning glacial lakes of Manapouri and Te Anau and on the western shores by 14 fiords which give the park its name. Its geography of mountains, valleys, rivers, lakes, waterfalls, fiords and rainforests, its weather and its wildlife including many endangered species, the marine mammals and their unique underwater habitat all conspire to make it the perfect location in which to paddle a kayak.
Go to: **www.fiordlandadventure.co.nz**

Bottom End of the South Island — Otago Peninsula

Dunedin has a clear, blue-green ocean, a score of white-sand beaches sheltered by towering cliffs, and a quiet landlocked harbour sprinkled with small bush-clad islands. The Otago Peninsula is home to a richly diverse population of coastal wildlife, including the northern royal albatross, the yellow-eyed penguin and the rare (and shy) little blue penguin. Expect also to see many wading birds as well as a variety of shags that use the coastal bluffs for nests. New Zealand fur seals are seen quite often in the tidal areas performing tricks too.
Go to: **www.wildearth.co.nz**

Stewart Island

For the truly adventurous, hop over to Stewart Island for a chance to explore Paterson Inlet, bush-fringed sheltered waterways, about 20 uninhabited islands and 2 navigable rivers. Charter launches can also take you to even remoter coastal regions. This company offers flexible itineraries and guided tours.
Go to: **www.rakiura.co.nz**

SAFETY AND SURVIVAL SKILLS

Whether you're canoeing across a flat calm harbour or kayaking the high seas, it's important to be prepared for weather changes. So take some common-sense precautions about safety before you embark on your next waterborne excursion.

Sea kayaking options are as varied as the weather — which is to say that it's still an activity that requires you to consider the elements — unpredictable elements that can turn a simple sea paddle into a frantic battle to stay alive. Safety, knowledge and boat skills are something that the old pioneers practised constantly. They also developed an acute awareness of weather patterns, tides and the changing environment that are still as important today as they were hundreds of years ago.

Staying safe no matter what form of vessel you're riding in means keeping track of the weather. MetService and local area authorities offer important marine weather predictions that all boaties should be aware of both before and during their expedition. Check the MetService forecast online before you depart or check the satellite weather channel forecast if you have SKY TV. Most radio stations also update the weather forecast hourly and nationwide talkback radio such as Newstalk ZB updates the marine forecast too.

With the amount of pleasurecraft in New Zealand waters it's a good idea to be seen, especially when you are very low in the water: wear a bright Day-Glo lifejacket and fix a cycle-type flag pole to help overcome the visibility problem.

Carry a fully charged mobile phone (in a plastic bag) as a backup in an emergency — this has initiated successful rescues in the past. No matter what body of water you are on in New Zealand, take a hand-held GPS on the trip and you'll never get lost. Know and study the region's tide charts before leaving

shore and you'll be in good shape. Also pay considerable attention to heat and dehydration. Make sure you and your companions drink plenty of fluids, even if you don't feel thirsty. Dehydration can quickly lead to heatstroke. Drinking water will aid the cooling-down process and keep you hydrated.

'Slip, slop, slap and wrap' is the Kiwi expression that says it all about sun protection: slip out of the sun, slop on some sunscreen, slap on a hat and wrap on your shades. Always use a good-quality sunscreen and apply it liberally, especially when in open boats. Wear a protective hat and always use quality UV sunglasses to cut down reflective glare. When looking for a sunscreen, choose one that has a SPF 15 rating or higher, that protects against both UVA and UVB rays (broad-spectrum), and is water- and sweat-proof. SPF 15 or higher lip balms applied liberally and often will help guard against burning — and an added benefit of using lip balms is the moisturising effect, preventing chapping and dryness.

Finally, file a trip report with the local coastguard if you are heading out to sea and tell family and friends to raise the alarm if you're not back by a certain time. Wear a lifejacket and be well prepared and you'll surely have the time of your life. For further information on staying afloat and staying alive at sea go to:

■ Kiwi Association of Sea Kayakers:
  www.kask.org.nz
■ MetService:
  www.metservice.co.nz/national
■ New Zealand Recreational
  Canoe Association:
  www.rivers.org.nz
■ Sea Kayak Operators Association of
  New Zealand:
  www.skoanz.org.nz
■ Water Safety New Zealand:
  www.watersafety.org.nz

Surf's Up — Kitesurfing, Surfing, Windsurfing

KITESURFING IN NEW ZEALAND

Kitesurfing (also known as kiteboarding) can be done on almost any beach or harbour location as long as there are large open bodies of water with good launch areas. While the most common launch location is off long flat beaches, kitesurfing can also be practised on lakes, flat low-lying estuaries and wide harbours. The one common denominator for all kitesurfers is that they all need consistent, steady side/onshore winds 10 to 35 knots or higher.

For people trying the sport for the first time it's good to fix in your head the two practical applications you're dealing with that each need to be controlled — one is the board and the other is the kite. If you have had previous experience with snowboarding, wakeboarding or skateboarding, you'll already have a head start on other users. But that's not to say it will be any easier. Some related activities include landboarding (land-based kiting), which is very popular with people taking up kitesurfing as it's a lot more affordable. It's also a great way to pick up the kite skills necessary for getting out on the water.

In this section, rather than highlight where you should go to kitesurf in New Zealand, it's more appropriate to guide you to certain schools that can offer lessons and instruction in the basics and beyond. After all, it's not as though you can just go and hire a kite and board and take off — some adventure sports do need to be cultivated. So whether you're kitesurfing in Ruakaka in Northland (a favourite spot for many locals) or trying out your kite on the storm-lashed coastline of the Catlins in Southland, there are bound to be some other prime spots to let your board loose on in between.

■ Kite Sports — Christchurch

New Zealand has always been a great destination for adrenalin sports, and with its accessible beaches and wind you can be sure of a great kiteboarding experience. One thing you'll find about kitesurfing is that from the moment you pick up your first kite it's a huge amount of fun. However, the most important thing you can do after any lesson is get a kite and

Kitesurfing waves at Mount Maunganui.

practise the techniques you've been taught. All kite sports require the development of good kite-flying technique. So whether you try your hand at land-based kiting on a flat stretch of beach, surfing the waves, or freestyling on tidal flat spots — there are plenty of options for honing your skills. These guys are based in Christchurch and seem to have a good handle on what's needed to get you started in kitesurfing (as well as land-based kiteboarding or snow-based snowkiting). They also supply rentals, lessons, clothing and kite supplies.

Go to: **www.kitesports.co.nz**

New Zealand Distance Record

On 24 October 2009, kitesurfer Louis Tapper sped his way into the record books when he kitesurfed from Devonport to Russell in the Bay of Islands — the same route as the Coastal Classic Yacht Race. His distance of 261km set a new New Zealand distance record — which took 13 hours when he was finally forced to retire due to an outgoing tide and lack of wind just 8km short of the finish line! The 35-year-old IT consultant spent 10 months training for the event and had previously kitesurfed across Cook Strait. His kite of choice was a 13m Cabrinha Crossbow which works well in 8 to 30 knots of wind and is said to be the fastest and most user-friendly kite out there.

Kitesurfing in strong breezes, Auckland.

SAFETY AND SURVIVAL SKILLS

Many problems and dangers encountered while learning kiting can be avoided or minimised by taking professional instruction. Kitesurfing schools provide courses and lessons to teach skills including kite launching, flying, landing, usage of the bar, lines and safety devices.

Power kites can be dangerous. Because of strong forces that can be generated by sudden wind gusts, people can be lofted, carried off, dashed against rocks, harbour walls, terrain or power lines, resulting in what's termed a 'kitemare' (kite + nightmare). Most kiteboarding fatalities are the result of being lofted or dragged out of control, resulting in a collision with hard objects including sand. It is possible to be seriously injured simply by hitting the water surface at speed or from a height. Collisions with windsurfers, other kiteboarders or watercraft are potential hazards, particularly at busy locations.

Jumping and being airborne at inappropriate places (such as shallow water or near fixed or floating objects) can be hazardous. A kitesurfer travels farther offshore than an easy swim, which is the primary reason kitesurfing in directly offshore winds is discouraged. Marine hazards include sharks, jellyfish and dolphins, depending on the location.

Weather planning and awareness is the key to safe kitesurfing. According to a safety adviser for one of the sport's governing bodies, a number of riders have been injured in kitesurfing-related accidents since 2000. Paying attention to the weather and staying within the limits of the rider's ability will provide the safest experience.

SURFING IN NEW ZEALAND

Because this type of activity is considered extremely hard to learn — perhaps the most difficult of all sports in the beginning — surfing requires the participant to work with the ocean environment, each moving against the other at speed. This is why most first-time surfers flounder around like a drowning rat on a sinking ship. Ideally, most first-timers will start off in small surf with waves of about a metre. Luckily, there are beaches on almost everybody's back doorstep in Kiwi-land where you can get started and take the plunge. Riding that first green wave is the bonus.

Long board surfing was first introduced here when the Hawaiian Olympic swimmer and surfer Duke Kahanamoku toured New Zealand in 1915. He gave demonstrations at Muriwai on Auckland's west coast, Lyall Bay in Wellington, and New Brighton Beach in Christchurch, inspiring a few locals who by the 1920s were using solid wooden long boards. However, modern surfing only really gained a foothold in the late 1950s as the surf lifesaving movement grew bigger. Lifesaving rescue equipment in those days included heavy, hollow long boards, up to 4.9m long. Yet it was the arrival of two young American lifeguards in November 1958 that took the surfers of New Zealand by surprise. Surfing in New Zealand changed dramatically when Bing Copeland and Rick Stoner stayed at the Piha Surf Lifesaving Club for about four months, demonstrating the art on their new Californian Malibu boards — shorter, lighter and more manoeuvrable so they could cut across the waves, something not possible on a long board.

In 1963 the first national championships were held at Mt Maunganui and won by Peter Way. Surprisingly, it took until 1976 for New Zealand to host the Amco/Radio Hauraki Pro at North Piha which became the first event of the very first year of the World Professional Surfing Tour. Since then, surfing has been awash with tournaments and annual events that seem to dominate the sport in the country.

In this section, campgrounds or backpacker-style accommodation has been included.

Michael Gardiner, surfer, Raglan 1962/63

SURF BEACHES — NORTH ISLAND

■ Ahipara Beach — West Coast, Northland

Ahipara Beach forms the southernmost point of Ninety Mile Beach. Ahipara is a raw and rugged iconic seaside village next to a slice of surfie paradise. Its main beach is small in length being only 600m at high tide and bookended at either side by rocky outcrops. However, one of New Zealand's world-class left-hand point breaks is to be found just to the south of Shipwreck Bay where at low tide some of the wrecks are still visible. This break is offshore in a southwest wind and is best when a southwest swell wraps around the point. You can take your 4-wheel drive around to get to this surf spot. The bay performs well on all tides and produces big swells. It was featured in the ground-breaking 1966 surf movie *The Endless Summer* and has never looked back since. Ahipara Beach is located 15km southeast of Kaitaia on the west coast of Northland, and has a proud history of Maori settlement, gum digging and sea adventures. The name Ahipara means 'Sacred Fire'.

Where to stay

Ahipara Motor Camp is a spacious, shady campground with camping and backpacker facilities only minutes from Ninety Mile Beach. There is plenty of room for kids to run around, and dogs are welcome. For further information go to: **www.ahiparamotorcamp.co.nz**

■ Awana Bay Beach — East Coast, Great Barrier Island

This is a well-known beach to Great Barrier Island surfers and boogie boarders — so turn up, drop

Choppy seas at Shark Alley, Great Barrier Island

in, and hold on! Awana Bay offers a fairly exposed, deep beach break that has consistently good surf, especially in the southern corner. As with most North Island surf beaches, spring and summer offer optimum conditions. Offshore winds usually blow from the southwest, but northerlies can sometimes turn things topsy-turvy, the best swell direction being from the northeast. It is noted for its good all-year-round surfing conditions and variety of waves, which result from rapidly shifting sandbanks.

Any respectable easterly swell will push up fast-moving, heavy beach breaks on an incoming tide. There are good left-hand breaks at the northern end and strong rips at the southern end that offer the best conditions and a powerful ride when the tide is incoming. They can also be short, hollow and rapid. It is rarely crowded and has to be one of the most scenic beaches on Great Barrier Island. Beware as care is needed when waves peak over 2.5 m. There's little chance of a helping hand if you get in trouble. You can expect sucky, hollow waves on a beach prone to more serious rips. Other excellent surf spots are to be found at Okiwi, Kaitoke Beach and Medlands Beach.

Great Barrier Island lies 90km east of Auckland and a 35-minute flight from the city. SeaLink operate a regular 4.5-hour passenger/car ferry service to and from the island in summer. There are no scheduled bus services on the Barrier, but shuttle buses run to most townships — biking and hitchhiking is

also considered a fair means of getting around. If possible, get a group together and bring your own vehicle over to share the ferry costs.
Go to: **www.sealink.co.nz**

Where to stay

Many surfers use any one of 5 DoC campgrounds or there are a few backpacker lodges to choose from. The nearest town to the surf beaches is Claris which has a health centre, pharmacy, airfield, cafés, restaurants, store and backpackers' lodge.
Go to: **www.doc.govt.nz**

■ Gisborne — East Coast, Bay of Plenty

This part of the East Cape overlooks the blue of Poverty Bay and the white peaks of Young Nicks Head. Gisborne is also the first place in the world to see the sunrise each day, so surfing early in the morning here is a bonus. If you want to escape the popular hangouts in and around Gisborne, head further north up the Cape to some renowned beach breaks at Tolaga Bay, Tokomaru Bay, Waipiro Bay and Hicks Bay.

Makorori is a fairly exposed beach and reef break and produces excellent right and left breaks that build over reefs and sandbars. The best conditions are swells from the south or east at mid to high tide, with the best winds from north-northwest. Ground swells are more common than wind swells, however. North Makorori also has the potential for brilliant surf in easterly swells, but watch out for a heavy undertow. Makorori Point has all the qualities of a perfect surfing hangout too. A right breaks over a shallow reef system setting up a long sweeping ride. Also be prepared for swells from the southeast with waves around 2 to 3m from mid to high tide.

Another well-known gem is Wainui Beach, renowned for one of the world's best breaks, 'The Stock Route'. This lovely 3km crescent of golden, sandy beach—just 6km from Gisborne City—is often portrayed as the archetypical world-class surfer's beach that rolls in consistent surf breaks. This can be a busy beach to surf though. In Gisborne itself is 'The Pipeline', a very, very good break right in town — it doesn't get any handier than this. From Auckland to Gisborne is a distance of 504km, making it a good day's drive.

Where to stay
Showgrounds Park Motor Camp is a tranquil location, handy to Gisborne City, adjacent to a golf course, and close to Midway and Waikanae beaches. Facilities include 10 new cabins, 50 power points, spacious kitchen, dining room, lounge, showers, toilets and laundry. Pets are welcome — even horses! Go to: **www.gisborneshow.co.nz**

■ Lyall Bay — Wellington
It would have been sacrilege to leave Wellington's south coast surf at Lyall Bay out of this line-up. Members of the Maranui Surf Club pioneered long board surfing on 5m boards in this big open bay back in the 1920s. 'The Wall' is known as the prime spot in the bay. A sandbank off the end of the airport breakwater can carry you right to the beach on most good days, but expect it to be insanely crowded. And as only Wellingtonians know, when the howling northerlies arrive it can get very rough out there. Houghton Bay and Island Bay lie to the west and offer nice reef and beach breaks in a strong south ground swell. Lyall Bay is right next to Wellington Airport so you can't miss it.
Go to: **www.lyallbayslsc.org.nz**

Heading up the west coast from Wellington brings you to Titahi Bay where there are excellent beach breaks. Further up the coast, holiday beaches such as Otaki, Foxton and Himatangi can also provide good rolling breaks at high tide with a heavy west or southwest swell.

Where to stay
Capital Gateway Motor Inn is only 7 minutes from Wellington City. They offer 1 and 2-bedroom units, some self-catering, plus their new Campervan Motorhome Park with 27 powered sites and all facilities. In the city you'll be able to find a budget range of accommodation such as backpacker lodges. Go to: **www.capitalgateway.co.nz**

■ Mt Maunganui — East Coast, Bay of Plenty
Known colloquially in New Zealand simply as 'The Mount', the town itself is located on top of a sandbar that connects the mountain to the mainland, an extinct geographical volcanic formation known as a tombolo. Because of this formation, the residents of Mt Maunganui are lucky enough to have both a harbour beach (Pilot Bay) and an ocean beach with great surf within a very short distance of each other.

New Zealand's first artificial reef has recently been installed at The Mount. Construction of the reef was originally hampered by lack of funds and, ironically, too many waves. However, recently the media has reported that local surfers are disappointed with the waves being produced. In addition, the reef has also been blamed for creating rips — some you win, some you lose.

Mt Maunganui is only 10 minutes away from Tauranga over the harbour bridge and each year hosts the Northern Regional Surf Championships. Go to: **www.mountlifeguards.co.nz**

Where to stay
Cosy Corner Holiday Park has 60 powered sites within private hedge-lined rows. Campers, motorhomes and campervans are always welcome. Full facilities are available including wireless internet. They have a greywater dump outlet on site and there is a free sewage dump station nearby. Go to: w**ww.cosycorner.co.nz**

■ Muriwai Beach — West Coast, Auckland
Muriwai has a long history, with long board surfing first demonstrated here way back in 1915. A windswept rugged coastline, 60km of surf beach and rolling dunes of black sand characterise Muriwai, making it one of Auckland's most popular west coast beaches. This is a year-round weekend

Contemplating a surf at sunrise.

surf beach with an exposed beach break that offers very consistent surf, mostly up to 2m, but it can get 'gnarly' with up to 6 to 8m swells. Wind conditions from the east are considered to be the best, with the best swell conditions from the southwest. This black-sand beach has breaks from both left and right, with ground swells just as likely as strong wind swells. Surfing is probably best around high tide conditions and the best location/most popular place to get some peaky surf is in front of the car park, just to the right of the rocks.

This is a very long beach, the entire length being classified as a public road, so you will always find waves no one is surfing on. The beach has easy access and plenty of wave variation. Due to a nearby seal colony, this is an area often inhabited by sharks. Muriwai is located about 35 minutes northwest of Auckland as you head towards Kumeu — keep driving west through the town until you see the Muriwai sign. Go to: **www.muriwaisurfschool.co.nz**

Where to stay
Muriwai Regional Park extends from Maori Bay in the south up Muriwai Beach for 8km. Muriwai Beach Motor Camp is a privately run campground. Go to: **www.muriwaimotorcamp.co.nz**

■ Piha Beach — West Coast, Auckland
Auckland's Piha Beach on the west coast is probably the best known surf beach in the North Island and therefore can get very crowded in summer, especially with hikers and beach lovers. On arrival you'll find stunning views, bush-cloaked valleys and rugged cliff faces. The beach consists of North Piha and South Piha, which are divided by Lion Rock. This is a year-round surf Mecca known for its really bad rips, currents and undertow, yet it offers one of the most powerful beach breaks in the country, when the Tasman Sea on maxed-out days sends in huge swells regularly creating long beautiful rides. Lion Rock is good for both left- and right-hand waves as they backwash off the rocks. North Piha also features good left- and right-hand rippers, with good peaks up nearer the stream mouth at the very northern end.

Piha Beach is a small coastal village located on the west coast of Auckland below the Waitakere Ranges — about 45 minutes' drive from the city. Head out to the protected rainforest in the Waitakeres and look for the sign that will guide you to Piha. Go to: **www.pihaslsc.com**

Where to stay
Although fairly basic, Piha Domain Motor Camp offers hot showers, flush toilets and laundry facilities. To complement these amenities there is a cookhouse with stovetop cooking, microwave and a coin-operated BBQ, plus 4 huts with bunks, table and chairs etc. Go to: **www.pihabeach.co.nz**

■ Raglan — West Coast, Waikato
This is arguably the most famous black-sand surfie destination in New Zealand. Its world-famous breaks are found at 3 points: Manu Bay, Whale Bay, and Indicators. The point breaks throw up fairly consistent surf that offers year-round opportunities to ride some very big barrels. Here it's always good in offshore winds, mainly from the southwest. Manu

Bay is as good a place to start as any and gets you into the feel of the place. It even throws up the longest, most accessible world-renowned left-hand break. It's often the most crowded spot too.

Manu Beach is also able to handle light onshore wind swells and ground swells. The best breaks are all left over a boulder bottom and you'll have to fight to get onto them with the hordes of locals that hog the waves. This bay also featured in the 1966 cult surfing movie *The Endless Summer* and is a highly surfable spot in a variety of winds making it one of the most consistent surf breaks in the country.

NOTE: While Raglan surf can be consistent, the rocky ledges and reefs command great respect and make surfing experience essential. This is not newbie or young 'grommet' surfer territory. It's a 45-minute drive west of Hamilton and a 2-hour drive south of Auckland.

Surf school

Raglan Surf School offers private and group lessons for learners and the more advanced surfer, surfboard and wetsuit rentals, friendly and experienced top surf instructors, school and holiday youth camps, women's surf retreats in association with Surf Dames, and surf packages including lodgings at their base camp in Whale Bay, the Karioi Lodge.
Go to: **www.raglansurfingschool.co.nz**

Where to stay

Raglan Kopua Holiday Park is a big family park situated on a peninsula in the Raglan Harbour, the land that the campground occupies being almost entirely surrounded by water. With vehicle access by a lone road bridge, this virtual island has its own sandy beach, boat ramp and takeaway store, with comfortable powered camping on site.
Go to: **www.raglanholidaypark.co.nz**

▥ Te Arai Beach — East Coast, Northland

Te Arai is situated on the east coast between Pakiri Beach and Mangawhai Heads. It offers uncrowded surf breaks, especially around the rocky outcrops at the southern end, and includes some great fishing and an untouched landscape. Te Arai is a very exposed beach break that has consistent surf conditions. Offshore winds are usually from the west-southwest. Most of the surf here comes from ground swells with a northeast swell giving the ideal angle.

The beach breaks both left and right and while on any summer weekday there are hardly any surfers, weekends can sometimes feel slightly crowded. Nearly every bit of coastline from Auckland to Whangarei has been developed — yet Te Arai remains untouched (for now!), offering a very remote and 'non-urban' character. This is a place to go to truly take in nature — whether surfing, fishing, walking or swimming. From Auckland it's about 110km or around 80 minutes' drive. Follow the sealed, winding country road off State Highway 1 — then, south of Mangawhai, take the turnoff onto Black Swamp Road to Te Arai Point Road to reach the beach.

Where to stay

Mangawhai Forest Camp is a quiet location off Ocean View Road at Te Arai Point with power sites, basic communal kitchen with fridge/freezer as well as communal showers and flush toilets. Dogs are allowed with manager approval only. Phone: (09) 431 4335

▥ Whangamata Bar — East Coast, Coromandel

Surfers have been coming to the surfing Mecca of Whangamata since the early 1960s, which nowadays is considered one of the country's premier surf breaks. The main reason is the 4km-long crescent beach of smooth white sand that curves around from the narrow harbour entrance to the mouth of the Otahu River. It has dozens of good sandbank breaks, big ocean swells and a flat profile making it one of the safest beaches in New Zealand. The Whangamata Bar at the northern end is one of the favoured spots, producing long breaks in northeasterly swells on an incoming tide. If the bar is crowded, which it often is in summer, or the tidal flow is too much, you can simply head down the beach and choose another great spot. Whangamata is only 2 hours or 154km from Auckland by road in a southeasterly direction.

Where to stay

Wentworth Valley Campground is a DoC-managed facility at the south end of Whangamata offering remote-style camping in native bush, with streams and wildlife surrounds. Expect peace and security provided by permanent on-site managers. Facilities include gas BBQ, food preparation and cleaning areas, toilets, hot and cold showers, campervan sites, native bush walks, waterfalls and freshwater swimming.
Go to: **www.whangamata.co.nz/camping.htm**

Catlins — South Coast

Along with a great surfing beach this area really is a very special place in New Zealand. The relatively isolated southeast coast of the South Island is still largely undiscovered in surfing terms. It is also home to the world-famous 180-million-year-old Curio Bay fossil forest, yellow-eyed penguins and the local Hector's dolphin colony — nowhere in New Zealand do you get so much packed into one small place. If you're brave enough to bear the sub-zero temperatures and on average 5°C waters, you'll occasionally get a look in at some of the largest waves in the South Island as well.

Porpoise Bay and Curio Bay

Porpoise Bay is a stunning little exposed beach that throws up a consistent grunty beach break and surf in either wind swell or ground swell conditions. The ideal swell comes from the south, but there are both reef and beach breaks left and right for surfers, with some brilliant exposed peaks that are worth plying the waves for. On a cold winter's day you'll surf with perhaps a handful of other people. The views over the Catlins are just amazing and on a clear day you can even see Stewart Island. The beach is quite long, and the west end is protected from the strong northwest winds, whereas the eastern end is nicely exposed.

Curio Bay is a small settlement mainly visited by tourists who pass through via the Southern Scenic Route. Follow the Southern Scenic Route signs when you leave Invercargill and turn off at Curio Bay, signposted between Fortrose and Papatowai.

Catlins Surf School

This is a safe surf spot to learn to surf in and one of the cleanest, most unspoilt bays in Southland. They supply everything you need for learning to surf from all types of quality rental wetsuits through to accessories. Hot showers and a shop are also nearby. The soft-foam surfboards used for beginners' surfing lessons are stable, safe and easy to learn to surf on. They also rent long boards, short boards, fun boards, SUP (stand up paddle) and boogie boards. Go to: **www.catlins-surf.co.nz**

Where to stay

Curio Bay Campground offers basic facilities including showers, kitchen, sheltered tent, campervan and caravan sites (including powered sites). There is also a small shop providing basic groceries and snacks, plus picnic and BBQ areas. Go to: **www.curiobay.org**

Kaikoura — West Coast, Canterbury

The quality of the waves in and around Kaikoura is put down to the proximity of the Hikurangi Trench which allows swells to come straight out of deep water. Numerous spots catch swells from far up

Surfers at St Kilda Beach, Dunedin.

north to the big deep low-pressure swells of the Roaring Forties. Be prepared for big, powerful and hollow waves and some pleasant surprises. The waves are less consistent in the summer but very consistent in winter. At Kahutara (19km south of Kaikoura) you'll find an excellent set-up, with a right-hand point break at the river mouth. The point can hold good-sized waves in a southerly swell.

The north coast also offers challenging rides off a boulder beach with consistent breaks on moderate swells at 'The Meatworks', located near the railway lines at the Hapuku settlement. At Mangamaunu (16km north of Kaikoura) there is a very sensational right-hand point break that peels along an extensive boulder reef that will tempt you back time and again. In fact, there's a wealth of surprisingly great surf breaks along this scenic South Island coastline, so stop frequently and size up the waves. A popular tourist town famous for its whale watching, Kaikoura is located on the east coast about 2 hours' drive north of Christchurch.

Where to stay
Alpine Pacific Holiday Park is set in a peaceful and picturesque rural setting with stunning mountain views, but still only 400m from town. It offers an excellent selection of accommodation: cabins, motel and en suite units, plus park facilities for powered campervan or tent sites. Amenities include heated pool and spas, wireless internet and high-pressure showers. Go to: **www.alpine-pacific.co.nz**

■ St Clair Beach, Dunedin — West Coast
This coast can deliver the best surfing in the South Island. To survive the severe winds and chilly waters you'll need to be fortified with nerves of steel and a full bodysuit. St Clair is Dunedin's main beach where most surfer dudes hang out. On a really good day the beach can produce hollow waves, with large sandbanks producing consistent beach breaks in swells up to 2m. The right-hand point breaks well when big south swells coincide with high tides and strong winds. St Kilda, just north of St Clair, has heavy beach breaks as well as some deep tubes. Not to put you off, but both these beaches have recorded great white shark activity and this is the only beach in the country that has shark nets in the sea during the summer months.

There are also long beach breaks north of St Clair as well as additional good swells and beach breaks at places such as Allans Beach, Smails Beach and Sandfly Bay. Across the harbour is Aramoana Spit, which is a sandy beach at the mouth of Otago Harbour. The beach is separated from the harbour by the breakwater known as 'The Mole'. The breakwater acts as a staging point for clean breakers to run parallel down its side. Locals nickname the beach 'Tube City', for the amount of hollow breaks that roll in very fast. The best winds here are from the southwest, but the favourite swells are northeasterly that in perfect conditions produce surfable swells to 2.5 m. There are surf clubs at St Clair and St Kilda at the northern end.
 Go to: **www.stclairsurfclub.org.nz**

Where to stay
Leith Valley Touring Park is less than 3km from downtown Dunedin and offers accommodation ranging from motel units through to sites for campervans, motorhomes, RVs, buses and tents in a lovely bush setting with streamside camping sites. Go to: **www.leithvalleytouringpark.co.nz**

SAFETY AND SURVIVAL SKILLS

It's usually inexperienced surfers who get into trouble, especially when they're surfing the west coast beaches where rips, undercurrents and outgoing tides can easily drag people onto rocks or out to sea. The best advice is to wear a wetsuit and stay within your limits and surf with a buddy at all times.

For additional information go to:
www.watersafety.org.nz/goodadvice/beaches.asp

For additional surfing websites go to:
www.beachlive.com
www.surf.co.nz
www.surfbreak.org.nz
www.surf-forecast.com
www.surfline.com
www.surf2surf.com

WINDSURFING

Our best-known windsurfers are the brother-and-sister combo Bruce and Barbara Kendall. Barbara is probably the better known of the siblings having won a gold medal in the 1992 Barcelona Olympics, New Zealand's only gold medal winner of the Games and the first achieved by a New Zealand woman in 40 years. She then followed that up with silver at the 1996 Atlanta Olympics and bronze at the 2000 Sydney Olympics. She has attended five Olympic Games in total. Not to be outdone, Bruce Kendall gained a bronze medal at the 1984 Los Angeles Olympics and a gold at the 1988 Seoul Olympics. Without their success it's highly unlikely the sport today would have achieved such a high profile in this country.

Like kitesurfing, windsurfers are spoilt for choice in New Zealand. Just about anywhere there's a body of water accompanied by a good wind you'll be able to windsurf: beaches, estuaries, harbours, lakes and occasionally rivers. Many surf shops and surf clubs hire out windsurfers, so if you have some rudimentary skills you'll be able to test your mettle on most stretches of water.
Go to **www.windsurfingnz.com**

WINDSURFING CLUBS

NZ National Windsurfing Association:
www.windsurfingnz.com
Auckland Windsurfing Association: **www.awa.org.nz**
Taranaki windsurfing Club:
www.taranakiwaveclassic.com

Windsurfing on Lake Wanaka.

Wellington Windsurfing Association: **www.wwa.org.nz**
Canterbury Windsports Association: **www.cwa.org.nz**
Dunedin Windsurfing Association:
www.watercooled.co.nz
Southern Lakes Windriders Club:
windsurfsue@hotmail.com
Invercargill Windsports Club:
royandleanne@xtra.co.nz

SAFETY AND SURVIVAL SKILLS

For board surfers, windsurfers and kitesurfers it's a good idea to have a fundamental understanding of sea breezes, caused by a thermally induced wind blowing during the day from a cold ocean onto an adjoining warm landmass. The bigger the difference in temperature between the land and the ocean, then the stronger the wind will blow. Remember to study the region's tide charts before leaving shore and you'll be sorted.

Also pay considerable attention to heat and dehydration. Make sure to drink plenty of water, even if you don't feel thirsty.

Dehydration can also lead quickly to heatstroke, which could land you in hospital. Drinking water will aid the cooling-down process and keep you hydrated.

Remember the 'slip, slop, slap and wrap' rule of sun protection: slip out of the sun, slop on some sunscreen (SPF 15 rating or higher), slap on a hat and wrap on your shades.

Always go out on your board with a buddy. And at all times watch out for other surfers and severe rips and undertow.

Wakes & Waves — Water Skiing, Wakeboarding

These two water-based (either saltwater or freshwater) sports have always had a loyal following and as such continue to attract new talent especially on the world's professional circuits. Water skiing has been around for about 80 years or so but wakeboarding is a relative newcomer. While the sports differ in a number of areas, they also have a lot in common in that both are surface water sports in which an individual attached to a motor boat by a cable or a rope is being pulled along in the boat's wake. Moreover, both involve surfing the water with smooth objects fitted to the feet of the individual and both rely on performing tricks. In fact, tricks and stunts are the heart and soul of wakeboarding.

In New Zealand and worldwide, wakeboarding was developed from a combination of water skiing, snowboarding and surfing techniques. It has borrowed the theory that a board, about the size of a snowboard, can ride a wake from the boat in much the same way a surfer rides a wave. It's also a sport which is defined by a blend of cutting-edge concepts and improvements in technology. You'll also notice that wakeboarding as opposed to water skiing usually has a more youthful following. The wakeboarder is typically towed behind a boat at speeds of 25 to 35kph depending on the water conditions, board size, rider's weight, and rider's comfort speed. Find a body of water big enough to plonk a motor boat on and you'll also probably find someone being pulled along behind it with a wakeboard attached to their feet. So unless you have a boat of your own it's best to become a member of a club first. Go to: **www.wake.co.nz**

For New Zealand water skiing and wakeboarding clubs and associations see:
- Auckland Wakeboarding (Waipuna Water Ski Club) — Go to: **www.wake.co.nz/clubs/aucklandwake**
- Elbow Water Ski Club — Go to: **www.elbow.org.nz**
- Karapiro Waterski Club Inc — Go to: **www.skikarapiro.co.nz**
- Otago Water Ski Club — Go to: **www.otagowaterski.org.nz**
- Piarere Water Ski Club — Go to: **www.pwsc.co.nz**
- Rotorua Water Ski Club Inc — Go to: **www.rwsc.co.nz**
- Wairoa Water Ski Club — Go to: **www.wwsc.co.nz**
- Wellington Water Ski Club Inc — Go to: **www.huttcity.com/waterski-club**

Wakeboarding as the sun is setting.

SAFETY AND SURVIVAL SKILLS

It goes without saying that both waterskiing and wakeboarding pose some inherent risks as people are travelling over an uneven surface at high speeds and accidents do happen. Always have a lookout person in your boat and be ready to flag the area in which you are skiing or boarding if someone comes off.

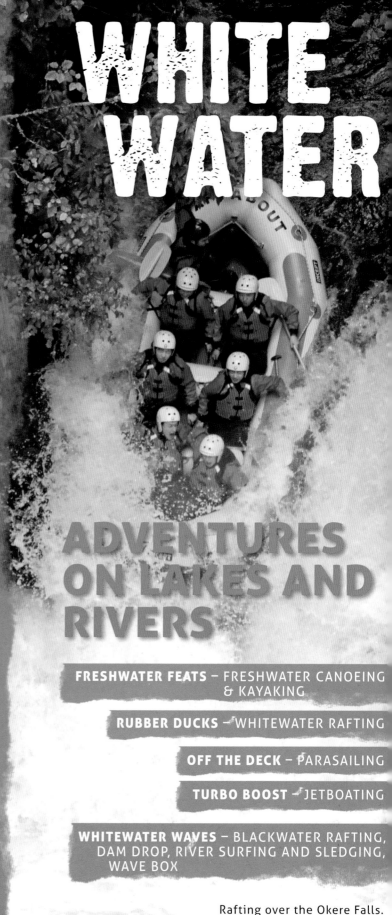

CHAPTER 9

WHITE WATER

ADVENTURES ON LAKES AND RIVERS

From the sedate adventures of wilderness kayaking and canoeing through to such extreme sports as whitewater rafting, jetboating, river surfing and river sledging, the Land of the Long White Cloud serves up some rip-roaring and wet, wet, wet adventures!

Commercial whitewater rafting really took off in New Zealand in the 1980s, as did jetboating — both of which are now recognised adventure tourism industry leaders. Even the once dangerous sport of kayaking has flourished from a little-known, speciality outdoor voyaging escapade in the 1970s to being somewhat of a born-again way to discover the symbiotic nature of land and water. Newer trends emerging include such innovations as river surfing and sledging — exciting activities that push the boundaries in the most adventurous of us.

As you will discover, each waterway possesses its own unique character and there are some rivers and lakes with just one outfitter operating on the water and others with multiple operators, so it's in your best interest to do some research on which one suits your needs and those of your mates and family, as the trips can be anything from Grade 3 float trips to Grade 5 serious whitewater rapids anywhere from 3 hours to 5 days long. It should also be noted that many operators work different sections of rivers depending on the length of the river and the extent of each trip, so do your homework first on the type of trips they undertake. For that reason, up to 3 website choices are offered per entry. So dive into this wet and wild section and learn all about it.

FRESHWATER FEATS – FRESHWATER CANOEING & KAYAKING

RUBBER DUCKS – WHITEWATER RAFTING

OFF THE DECK – PARASAILING

TURBO BOOST – JETBOATING

WHITEWATER WAVES – BLACKWATER RAFTING, DAM DROP, RIVER SURFING AND SLEDGING, WAVE BOX

Rafting over the Okere Falls.

Late evening kayaking on Lake Wakatipu, Queenstown.

Freshwater Feats — Freshwater Canoeing and Kayaking

Without doubt, freshwater kayaking and canoeing have gone mainstream over the last 10 years or so. A sport that was once just for the very adventurous is today a way the whole family can enjoy time together. Both freshwater kayaking and canoeing are pastimes that allow the modern-day explorer to venture into national parks and wild rugged areas that few city dwellers have seen. This is an opportunity to leave all your worldly trappings behind and delve into the thousands of wilderness lakes and streams that dot our wonderful country.

Prior to the opening of our major roads and the introduction of the motor car, pretty much the only way to go from place to place was on horseback or by boat. Lakes and rivers were highway arteries that allowed prospectors, miners, hunters, woodsmen, stakeholders and farmers to venture into the great unknown. Today kayak operators can deliver the kind of outdoor adventure that will leave you with a greater appreciation of New Zealand's unique landscape and the challenges it presented our forebears.

The rivers and lakes listed here are ones that offer a variety of options depending on whether you have your own kayak or canoe or are hiring one for the purpose of the trip. Either way, kayaking with a double paddle or canoeing with a single paddle on the rivers and lakes of New Zealand is one of the best ways to see many of our remote regions and spectacular countryside from a whole different perspective — so put that mobile phone down and get paddling!

LAKES AND RIVERS — NORTH ISLAND

■ Lake Rotoiti — Central North Island

This is a great opportunity to experience an early-morning or afternoon paddle across beautiful Lake Rotoiti where you can enjoy stunning views of the lake as you kayak alongside native bush that reaches down to the water's edge. In just 40 minutes you'll get the chance to enjoy natural thermal pools on the edge of Lake Rotoiti at Manupirua. Sink back into the pools and take pleasure in the peaceful environment which can be experienced via water-only access. You'll enjoy spectacular views from this little-known jewel. This company offer short and full-day excursions, overnights and multi-day trips. Go to: **www.adventurekayaking.co.nz**

■ Lake Taupo — Central North Island

This is a fascinating part of New Zealand to experience by canoe or kayak. Lake Taupo (about the size of Singapore) has itself experienced at

least 26 volcanic eruptions in the last 26,000 years, two of which were possibly some of the largest the world has witnessed in recent geological times. So it comes as no surprise to find it has a rich vein of history. One of the reasons to explore Lake Taupo's beautiful shoreline is to head out to the Maori rock carvings that are over 10m high (possibly the largest of their type in the world) and only accessible by boat or kayak. Paddling out with these eco-adventure specialists will allow you to get up close to the carvings with plenty of time to study their details. You'll hear the story of how they were carved, and also about their cultural significance. This is a half-day kayak trip and no previous experience is needed, so allow around 4.5 hours, which includes a refreshment stop.
Go to: **www.kayakingkiwi.com**

■ Mohaka River — Mokau, Central North Island

One of the few remaining 'wild and scenic' rivers in the North Island not affected by hydro development, the Mohaka offers some of the best introductory wilderness canoeing around. This is a trip for those who want to get away from the day-to-day grind on a nice sedate canoeing experience. The Mokau region also provides stunning views of the only lowland coastal forest left in its natural state. Starting at Te Matai you'll paddle alongside limestone cliffs and through a few small shallow rapids. This quickly turns into willow-lined regenerating farmland with minimal to no rapids (nice and safe). You will paddle past some lowland nikau forest before finishing close to Mokau.
Go to: **www.yetitours.co.nz**

■ Puhoi River — North of Auckland

The Puhoi flows southeast from its source 10km southwest of Warkworth, passing through the town of Puhoi before reaching the coast of Whangaparaoa Bay, 7km north of Orewa. This is a great little river trip in which you can take your own canoe or rent a kayak as it meanders from historic bohemian Puhoi Village to the scenic Wenderholm Regional Park. The river is 8km of flat (no rapids or waterfalls!) tidal water. If you decide to go exploring you can extend the trip up to 10 to 12km. One-way will take about 2 hours. If you are hiring the vessel they pick you up and transport you back to the Puhoi Pub — a great place for lunch and a pint. This company have kayaks or canoes to suit the whole family and cater to almost all ages.
Go to: **www.puhoirivercanoes.co.nz**

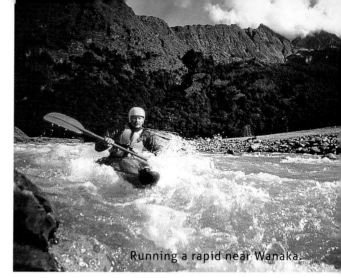
Running a rapid near Wanaka.

■ Rangitikei River — Central North Island

Trips on the Rangitikei River are considered easy to moderate and suitable for ages 7 and above. They start at the end of the whitewater rafting section at River Valley and can last 3 to 4 days, although you can also start progressively further down the river, as each section has its own remarkable scenery. However, while it offers flexibility in trip length the Rangitikei still retains a tremendous wilderness setting and presents numerous small fun rapids (Grades 1 and 2) to keep paddlers working. As the river snakes its way through the deep gorges of the Kaimanawa and Ruahine ranges on its journey to the Tasman Sea, there is clear water for swimming with a good number of trout fishing spots, bush-covered slopes, flat welcoming campsites alongside the river's edge, some short walks to waterfalls along with the amazing 'Rangitikei Boulders'.
Go to: **www.canoesafaris.co.nz**

■ Whanganui River — Central North Island

Among the few remaining places in the world today where there are no roads, no phones, no television and very few other people is the Whanganui River. You can hire canoes or book with outfitters who offer 3 to 5-day guided canoe trips as the river winds its way from the mountains to the Tasman Sea through countless hills and valleys. Lowland forest surrounds the river in its middle and lower reaches, the heart of Whanganui National Park. Once you are on the water below Whakahoro there's no turning back — and no place to buy anything you may have forgotten either! The 145km river journey from Taumarunui to Pipiriki takes on average 5 days to complete by canoe. A shorter 3-day journey from Whakahoro to Pipiriki is also possible. Go to:

www.whanganuiriveradventures.co.nz Although a river journey, the Whanganui is part of DoC's 'Great Walks' network.
Go to: **www.doc.govt.nz**

LAKES AND RIVERS — SOUTH ISLAND

◼ Avon River — Christchurch

This is not exactly an extreme sport but sometimes just a lazy paddle in a canoe down the Avon River in the middle of summer will blow away the cobwebs and whet your appetite for more of the same. A short walk from Cathedral Square and next to the Botanic Gardens is the iconic Antigua Boatsheds. Built in 1882, they are still used for the original purpose of hiring out rowboats, canoes, kayaks and paddleboats. Boat hire hours are from 9am with last boats out at 4pm in winter; and from 9am with last boats out at 4.30pm in summer.
Go to: **www.boatsheds.co.nz**

◼ Clutha, Hawea, Makarora and Matukituki Rivers — Wanaka

The Wanaka region has a superb range of rivers, from the mighty Clutha River (New Zealand's largest-volume river), the Hawea River (medium volume), to the remote and majestic glacial-fed Makarora and Matukituki rivers. Alpine Kayak Guides offer fun, scenic and safe kayaking trips from October through to April. You'll experience the thrill of kayaking from a relaxed introduction to a full-on day of paddling. Their guides will reveal the wonders of this spectacular region and you'll come away with an experience that is altogether unforgettable. The best river is chosen each day to maximise your paddling experience. No previous kayaking experience is required for any of their trips but water confidence is essential. Go to: **www.alpinekayaks.co.nz**

◼ Dart River — Glenorchy

The Dart River — Te Awa Wakatipu in the Maori language — flows through rugged forested country in the southwestern region of the South Island. Partly in Mount Aspiring National Park, it flows southwest and then south for 60km from its headwaters in the Southern Alps and the Dart Glacier, eventually flowing into the northern end of Lake Wakatipu near Glenorchy. A Dart River Funyaks trip combines a jetboat ride, 2-hour canoe trip, wilderness lunch, and 30-minute back-road journey. This excursion allows visitors to truly explore the area with canoes ('funyaks'), allowing access to parts of the river inaccessible by jetboat. After the jetboat ride to the Dart's upper reaches, you'll get safety and paddling instruction before your funyak journey begins. Paddle downstream amid glaciers, rocky peaks and dense rainforests, including exploring the Rockburn Chasm (accessible only by canoe).
Go to: **www.dartriver.co.nz/dartriver/FunYakSafari**

◼ Glacier Lake Kayaking — Aoraki/ Mount Cook National Park

Kayaking is the ultimate way to experience the magnificence of this world-famous national park. At over 750m above sea level you can become part of the environment, paddle beneath towering glaciated mountains and view the majestic glaciers and summit of the mighty Aoraki/Mt Cook. This is your chance to leave the crowds behind and explore the nooks and crannies of the glacier lake surrounded by a variety of wildlife and icebergs — yes, icebergs! All trips are fully guided and the guides have a vast knowledge of the area and its various inhabitants. Their trips suit all levels of kayaker from beginners through to very experienced paddlers. This is the only operator in New Zealand providing a natural glacier outdoor experience using traditional 'sea kayaks' as your means of transportation.
Go to: **www.mtcook.com/glacierkayaking**

◼ Lake Te Anau and Lake Manapouri — Fiordland

Much underrated because of their close proximity to the awe-inspiring fiords, the glacial lakes are a real guided or rental alternative for wilderness kayaking, camping and exploring. It's all national park, so no one lives out there. Lake Te Anau offers 440km of shoreline and numerous uninhabited islands, while Lake Manapouri has 190km of uninhabited shoreline and 34 islands — an accessible wilderness custom-made for kayaking and canoeing. Avail yourself of 1 to 6-day camping/wilderness trips to explore either of these clear, deep lakes edged with sandy beaches, coves and cliffs, dotted with islands, fed by waterfalls and pure mountain streams, and cradled by glaciated valleys of classic Fiordland native bush and sensational mountain scenery.
Go to: **www.fiordlandseakayak.co.nz**

Preparing for a kayaking trip on a glacier lake.

■ Lake Wakatipu — Queenstown

This has to be one of the most scenic of New Zealand's southern lakes, but beware as it can be extremely cold some days and flat water can suddenly turn into whitecaps if the wind is blowing. The majestic mountains that surround the lake will make you feel like you're in Switzerland. At an altitude of 310m, Lake Wakatipu is an inland lake located in the southwest corner of Otago, near its boundary with Southland. With a length of 80km, it is also New Zealand's longest lake and at 291sqkm it's the third largest. There's a variety of coastline to explore by kayak at both the Queenstown end of the lake and at the more remote and wilderness Glenorchy end where the Dart River enters. Go to: **www.queenstownseakayaks.com** or **www.rippledearth.co.nz**

Whitewater NZ

Whitewater NZ — formerly the New Zealand Recreational Canoeing Association (NZRCA) — is the national body representing recreational whitewater canoeing and kayaking in New Zealand. It has over 16 member clubs corresponding to around 800 active members. The Whitewater NZ River Guide contains information on 271 sections in 168 rivers. Go to: **www.rivers.org.nz**

SAFETY AND SURVIVAL SKILLS

Rivers and lakes are a living feature of this land and having a healthy respect for them provides a broader understanding of the environment and perhaps gives one pause to stop and think before taking unnecessary risks. Always wear a lifejacket and have some form of emergency equipment to hand: extra food supplies, whistle, signal devices, towline, compass, duct tape, multi-tool, repair kit, spare paddle, sun cream, sunhat, sunglasses and a warm hat. Go to: www.watersafety.org.nz/goodadvice/rivers.asp

Rubber Ducks — Whitewater Rafting

There is nothing better than getting all excited about a rafting trip, whether it's for 2 hours or 3 very wet days. As the water flows by serenely the guides will go through their drill on what's required should you fall in or how to survive some steep whitewater rapids. The great thing about all rivers is that there are gentle smooth sections where you lazily paddle and look at the scenery or splash your mates and then suddenly the noise of the turbulent rapids get louder, the water starts to move faster, boiling in places, before suddenly you're in a maelstrom of crashing waves that pound the raft, sending spray over the entire crew, and then it's over and the tingling sensation and adrenalin dies down.

Thousands of people every year take rafting trips on some of our sensational world-class rivers. Outfitters here are well equipped for multi-day trips — camping equipment, food, water, wet-weather gear and so on — but it's always wise to check their website for specifics such as waterproof bags (dry bags) for cameras etc. It's also a good idea to research exactly what the rafting operators are offering. For instance, is it a float trip with some narrative on the flora and fauna and indigenous culture or is it an out-and-out rafting adventure trip full of Grade 4 to 5 rapids?

It's always worthwhile taking along a good sense of humour too — especially seeing as you may get drenched. Pack additional warm clothing for overnight trips and be prepared for biting insects and outside loos. You'll also be expected to pitch in and help with chores sometimes, as well as doing your fair share of paddling — so if you're a complainer it probably isn't the sort of trip you should be on. It's also healthy to have an appreciation of the outdoors as you'll more than likely be seeing a good deal of it as you drift between canyons or across wide plains. It's a crazy sport and one where you'll have to roll with the waves no matter what happens, so learn to go with the flow and have fun — it's what river rafting is all about.

RAFTING RIVERS — NORTH ISLAND: GRADE 3 OR BETTER

■ **Kaituna River, Rotorua — Grade 5**
This is considered a short blast of extreme rafting adventure and fun. The Kaituna River is famous for featuring the highest commercially rafted waterfall in the world — at 7m the Okere Falls offers an unparalleled rafting challenge. It also has 14 other rapids, amazing scenery, plus a wealth of regional history and culture. Allow 3 hours. Go to: **www.kaitiaki.co.nz** or **www.wetnwildrafting.co.nz** or **www.raftabout.co.nz**

The joy of rafting some big white water rapids.

Paddling out of a maelstrom of rapids on the West Coast.

■ Mohaka River, Taupo or Napier — Grade 2 To 5

The Mohaka is a superb wilderness rafting trip that can be undertaken in 2 parts. The upper section is Grade 2 to 3 and the lower section is Grade 4 and 5. This is a fantastic trip no matter which option you choose. Select from a 1-day or 2 to 5-day expedition-style trip. Go to: **www.krs.co.nz/rafting/mohaka** or **www.soulsport.co.nz**

■ Motu River, Opotiki or Rotorua — Grade 3 To 4

This is the North Island's last remaining fully navigable wilderness river, and runs through virgin native forest for the entire length of the journey. This is a seriously powerful river by North Island wild river standards. The Motu's 100km course to the sea is a good mix of Grade 3 to 4 rapids with some amazing scenery along the way. Allow a full day. Go to: **www.wildrivers.org.nz**

■ Ngarururo River, Hastings, Napier, Taihape — Grade 2 To 5

This is a truly sensational remote wilderness rafting trip. The Ngarururo River offers top-quality 2 to 7-day rafting, heli-raft and vehicle access options, and delivers totally stunning scenery together with some very impressive rapids. In fact, there are 10 major Grade 4 to 5 rapids plus numerous smaller ones. The Grade 5 rapid is a 12km run taking 3 hours to complete. There are day options through to 7-day rafting trips. Go to: **www.wetnwildrafting.co.nz** or **www.mohakarafting.co.nz**

■ Rangitaiki River, Rotorua — Grade 4

From the buzz of the world-famous Geoff's Joy, a thundering torrent of whitewater, to the spectacular scenery between the rapids, this trip has something for everyone. If you're looking for a full-day adventure with loads of variety, this trip's thrilling rapids and spectacular scenery won't disappoint. This is also a renowned trout fishing river. Allow 6 hours. Go to: **www.riverrats.co.nz** or **www. wetnwildrafting.co.nz** or **www.raftabout.co.nz**

■ Rangitikei River, Taihape — Grade 2 to 5

This is a world-class whitewater adventure with big Grade 5 rapids like Max's Drop, Fulcrum and Foaming. The Rangitikei mingles beautiful scenery with superb whitewater excitement and thrills. All creature comforts await you at trip's end. The Grade 2 lower section from Pukeokahu to Mangaweka offers 3 to 5 days of relaxing family rafting with excellent fishing and spectacular scenery including areas used in the filming of *The Lord of the Rings* movie trilogy. Allow 4 hours or 3 to 5 days. Go to: **www.riverdrifters.co.nz** or **www.soulsport.co.nz**

■ Tongariro River, Turangi — Grade 3

The Tongariro River journey is one of the best rafting adventures in New Zealand. The rapids are Grade 3, which makes this an ideal adventure for expert or first-time rafters alike. In 2.5 hours you'll navigate over 60 rollercoaster rapids with an expert guide at the helm — an exciting full-on rafting experience that you'll never forget. Enjoy this beautiful, scenic and world-famous trout river with its internationally renowned crystal-clear waters. A large part of the top section of the trip can only be accessed by raft or kayak, so you'll see plenty of spectacular unspoilt wilderness. Allow 3 hours. Go to: **www.riverrats.co.nz** or **www.waimaori.com** or **www.raftingnewzealand.com**

■ Wairoa River, Tauranga and Rotorua — Grade 5

This is a full Grade 5 river and is open just 26 days a year (most Sundays during summer), when water is released from the Ruahihi Power Station upstream. This is an ultimate (day trip) rafting adventure that includes some steep and difficult rapids. Some previous experience is an advantage due to the technical nature of this river — meaning it's a technically difficult course of water to negotiate and can be dangerous to the inexperienced. The scenery is outstanding along a rock- and bush-lined gorge that is every bit as good as the rafting experience itself. Allow 6 hours. Go to: **www.riverrats.co.nz** or **www.wetnwildrafting.co.nz** or **www.raftabout.co.nz**

RAFTING RIVERS — SOUTH ISLAND: GRADE 3 OR BETTER

■ Buller River, Westport, Murchison — Grade 3 to 5

This brilliant large-volume river trip will take you through the mighty Buller Gorge. You'll never forget this day of rafting down some breathtaking rapids such as O'Sullivans, Whale Creek, Jetboat Rapids and Ariki Falls as well as the sensational white-knuckle Grade 3 and 4 Earthquake Rapids. Allow for 3 hours, 1 day or multi-day wilderness rafting. Go to: **www.adventuretours.co.nz** or **www.whitewateraction.com**

■ Clarence River, Marlborough — Grade 2 to 3

This classic river journey starts high up at Lake Tennyson on the eastern slopes of the Spenser Mountains in the Lewis Pass area. The Clarence is one of New Zealand's longest and least known rivers as it snakes its way through open tussock lands and 3 towering canyons of twisted rock strata. The swift waters eventually flow through an isolated valley between the Seaward and Inland Kaikoura Ranges, opening out to a braided riverbed before finally rushing to the sea in a rollercoaster climax to the trip. This multi-day adventure starts at historic Molesworth Station as you travel from the mountains to the sea, starting at an altitude of 700m and finishing 215km later at the coast. Go to: **www.clarenceriverrafting.co.nz**

■ Grey River, Greymouth — Grade 3 to 4

This river is described as technical fun and is a secret little gem dear to West Coast rafters. Here you'll raft good-quality Grade 3 to 4 rapids amid super-scenic bush-clad gorges and mind-blowing mountain scenery. After a lot of rain this trip is full on. Allow for a 3 to 4-hour day trip or a multi-day adventure for travellers or families. Go to: **www.hiddenvalleys.co.nz**

■ Hokitika River, Hokitika — Grade 3 to 4

This is another isolated, rugged region that you'll need to helicopter into first and then raft out from. The amazing scenery on this trip will leave you speechless. This is well touted as an exciting river with numerous adventurous rapids and the cleanest water on the planet. Allow for a half-day heli-rafting trip. Go to: **www.piraterafting.com/hokitika.php**

■ Hurunui River, Hanmer Springs — Grade 3

The Hurunui discharges out of Lake Sumner, which guarantees good water levels throughout the summer, and flows through a remote mountain catchment with a number of enjoyable rapids along its length — but most notably the almost continuous whitewater excitement of the Maori Gully stretch. This trip encapsulates the splendour of the Canterbury high country. Allow a full day. Go to: **www.thrillseekerscanyon.co.nz**

Whitewater rafting
at its best.

■ Karamea River, Karamea, Westport — Grade 4 to 5

Helicopter into this rugged, isolated region and raft out through the impressive Kahurangi National Park. Remote and wild with huge awesome rapids combined with spectacular scenery, this is a fantastic adventure trip in its own right. Allow for multi-day wilderness rafting.

Go to: **www.rivers.co.nz/rft-heliraft.htm** or **www.rivers-wild.com/trips/karamea**

■ Kawarau River, Queenstown — Grade 4

Perhaps not as well known as the Shotover, but still worth four hours of anybody's time — make the effort to raft the Kawarau River and you'll be well rewarded. Besides being the closest river to Queenstown itself, the surrounding area is without doubt stunning. Lake Wakatipu drains to the Kawarau River, which flows generally eastwards for about 60km until it reaches Lake Dunstan near Cromwell. The Shotover River enters it from the north. The river passes through the steep Kawarau Gorge during its journey, which makes for plentiful action and excitement. Allow for a 4-hour day trip.

Go to: **www.raft.co.nz** or **www.queenstownrafting.co.nz/kawarau**

■ Landsborough River, Haast or Wanaka — Grade 3 To 5 (depending on flow)

This is another river that offers remote rafting in the Southern Alps. It's considered a truly astounding wilderness rafting trip with spectacular alpine scenery and wonderful scenic camping en route. Access to the Landsborough River is by helicopter only. It's mostly Grade 2 with a section of Grade 3 to 4 at normal flows with a serious new Grade 5 rapid at high flows called Hellfire which can be portaged. If there's one thing you'll learn on the Landsborough, it's that when you're rafting you really don't know you've hit whitewater until you've hit it! Allow for a 3-day rafting trip starting late November to end of March.

Go to: **www.queenstownrafting.co.nz/ landsborough**

■ Perth River and Whataroa River, Whataroa, West Coast — Grade 5

It's no wonder the Perth River is graded high as it's one of the remotest rivers in the Southern Alps. You'll need to chopper in to get you to this isolated, rugged region and raft out again through mind-blowing scenery and exciting rapids. The Perth is snow-fed, in contrast to the milky hues of the

Whataroa, which flows from alpine glaciers in the high country. You may raft a single river as a 1-day wilderness trip or choose both rivers in a weekend or extended itinerary. These rank among the most adventurous trips that you can undertake in New Zealand. Allow for a 1 or 2-day heli-rafting trip. Go to: **www.hiddenvalleys.co.nz/heli-rafting.html**

■ Rangitata River, Geraldine, Christchurch — Grade 5

Fed by the enormous catchment of the upper Rangitata Basin, this Grade 5 river flushes out a massive volume of water as it winds its way down the valley to the Pacific Ocean. The Rangitata is the closest whitewater rafting trip from the city of Christchurch. Allow 3 hours. Go to: **www.rafts.co.nz**

■ Shotover River, Queenstown — Grade 5

Rafting from Deep Creek over peaceful waters at first, you'll head towards the exhilarating rapids of the lower canyon. Adrenalin will swiftly kick in as you paddle Rock Garden, Sharks Fin, Toilet, Pinball and Jaws. This is an 18km trip which culminates in a spectacular ride through the Oxenbridge Tunnel — a 170m chute which is a legacy of the pioneering gold miners. This is the most famous rafting trip on the area's most famous river in the adventure sports Mecca that is Queenstown. Allow for 4 hours or a day trip. Go to: **www.raft.co.nz** or **www.rafting.co.nz**

■ Taieri River, Dunedin — Grade 3

This trip offers a medium to low Grade 3 whitewater trip that wanders through the beautiful native bush and dramatic rock outcrops of the Taieri Gorge. Most trips offer rafters the opportunity to recharge with a refreshing BBQ lunch and time to relax in peace and tranquillity on the banks of this beautiful river. Allow a full day. Go to: **www.wildearth.co.nz**

■ Waiatoto River, Haast — Grade 4 to 5

This is a unique river in a large glaciated valley. Expect incredible alpine scenery including views of Mt Aspiring as well as 1 full day of continuous technical rapids in the middle section. On this premier wilderness multi-day raft trip you'll encounter Grade 4 at normal flows and Grade 5 at high flows. There's a 3-hour flat-water paddle out to the road bridge or a jetboat out option. Allow 1 day (with jetboat out option) or for a 2 or 3-day heli-rafting trip. Go to: **www.hiddenvalleys.co.nz**

■ Whataroa River, Whataroa, West Coast — Grade 4

A Whataroa River trip is one of the finest 1-day whitewater experiences you'll find anywhere. This rafting trip is pure adventure, offering pristine wilderness, superb mountain scenery, steep drops, long scenic reaches, absolutely incredible river canyons and 3 stunning gorges. This is an awe-inspiring journey below some of the highest peaks of the Southern Alps. Allow for a 1-day heli-rafting trip or 2-day hike in, overnight camping and raft out. Go to: **www.rivers-wild.com/trips/whataroa**

GLACIER EXPLORERS — TASMAN GLACIER TERMINAL LAKE

Once in a while along comes a product that is hard to categorise — and Glacier Explorers is just that. Here you have a rigid-based inflatable raft with an outboard motor on a glacial lake, only in New Zealand. This is your chance to get up close and personal with the 27km-long and 600m-deep Tasman Glacier. Your departure is from Mt Cook Village down the Tasman Valley followed by a pleasant 30-minute stroll through the Aoraki/Mount Cook National Park. There you will board the raft for your glacial lake adventure.

NOTE: The guide decides the proximity of boats to the glacier and icebergs on the day as a direct result of glacier/iceberg as well as underwater ice sheet stability and weather conditions. Wear warm clothing, sunscreen, sunhat and sunglasses, long pants and walking shoes. Their rafts carry between 9 and up to 15 passengers.
Go to: **www.glacierexplorers.com**

NEW ZEALAND RAFTING ASSOCIATION

For further information and a list of all North and South Island rafting operators go to the New Zealand Rafting Association website and click on river guides: rivers are listed by region. Go to: **www.nz-rafting.co.nz**

SAFETY AND SURVIVAL SKILLS

Operators will give your group a full safety briefing and they will be carrying all the necessary equipment to ensure your journey is a safe one. However, if you are planning on using your own rafting gear always have emergency equipment to hand: whistle, signal devices, towline, compass, duct tape, multi-tool, repair kit, lifejacket, spare paddle, sunscreen, sunhat, sunglasses and a warm hat. Wear a lifejacket and be well prepared and you'll have the time of your life.

Parasailing is a popular sport in Rotorua.

Off the Deck — Parasailing

Parasailing is a great recreational activity where a person solo or in a tandem harness is towed behind a vehicle (usually a boat) while attached to a specially designed parachute known as a parasail. The boat then drives off, carrying you, or you and partner, into the air. If the boat is powerful enough, 2 or 3 people can parasail behind it at the same time. You have little or no control over the parachute which is connected to the boat by the towrope. The activity is primarily a fun ride, and not to be confused with the sport of paragliding.

With a mild climate, great scenery and magnificent lakes and harbours, the activity of parasailing has grown considerably in New Zealand over the last few years. If you are not in the habit of jumping off ledges, mountains and from planes with a parachute attached, this could be for you. There are commercial parasailing operations located around the country and it can be enjoyed mainly on lakes but is sometimes performed on harbours. Heights usually vary from 120 to 365m, so once you're up there you really are flying with the birds.

■ Big Sky Parasail — Lake Taupo, Central North Island

When in Lake Taupo you should try the fastest elevator ride around. As with all parasailing, this company takes off from a platform at the back of the boat. They will hoist you to either 120m or 245m and include an optional simulated freefall which is when they stop the boat and let you parachute down to the water only to be whisked back up into the sky again. All flights are 8 to 10 minutes long. Big Sky Parasail can fly 2 people at the same time as long as their combined weight does not exceed 190kg. There are no age restrictions.
Go to: **www.bigskyparasail.co.nz**

▓ Kjet — Lake Rotorua, Central North Island

This parasailing venture is based 5 minutes from Rotorua's CBD and operates an 8m boat that seats 12 people and is purpose-built for parasailing. You can take solo or tandem 10-minute flights, but there is a minimum age of 5 years, minimum weight of 50kg and maximum weight of 180kg. As they operate all year round it can get cold out on the lake, so they will provide you with spray jackets and gloves to keep you warm and dry.
Go to: **www.kjetrotorua.co.nz**

▓ Lake Wakatipu — Queenstown, South Island

Of all the harnesses you can strap yourself into in Queenstown this one might just be the best fun. The breathtaking views of the surrounding mountains and the town are just too good to miss as you soar to 180m above Lake Wakatipu. This is hands-free harness flying at its best. The company operate a 12-person boat that has the option of solo, double or triple flights — so it's perfect for families. Minimum weight 35kg and maximum weight 200kg.
Go to: **www.paraflights.co.nz**

▓ Parasail NZ — Paihia, Bay of Islands, Northland

This must be the easiest adventure jaunt you'll ever try. With no age restrictions and little instruction, you'll be flying high in no time. Once you're airborne and the collywobbles have settled down a notch or two it's time to take in the scenery at seagull level. There are 2 options in this location: try out New Zealand's highest ride that elevates you to 365m for about 10 to 12 minutes or shoot the breeze at a mere 245m for 8 to 10 minutes of flight. This is an activity that all the family can enjoy.
Go to: **www.parasail-nz.co.nz**

SAFETY AND SURVIVAL SKILLS

All parasail boat operators are strictly monitored and must abide by rules and regulations in accordance with industry practice. This is a very safe way to enjoy the freedom of flying under a fixed-line parachute. So make sure you've buckled your lifejacket securely and simply let the speed of the boat whisk you skywards.

About to land back on the boat after a successful time aloft.

Turbo Boost — Jetboating

Without the invention of the Hamilton waterjet in the 1950s, the tourism adventure industry we associate with jetboating today would have been impossible. Many South Island rivers were unnavigable by conventional propeller-driven craft until a local Canterbury farmer named William Hamilton invented and perfected the principle of waterjet propulsion. By the 1960s there was an international demand for his propellerless jet, a rudimentary yet very effective high-pressure water pump driven by adapted car engines. The absence of a propeller also allows the boat to have a shallower draught and gives it the ability to spin a full 360 degrees, constituting a tourism attraction in its own right. Nowadays you'll find many New Zealand rivers and lakes home to commercial jetboat tourism operations entertaining visitors with plenty of high-speed action, spills and thrills.

The only way you can try jetboating is with commercial operators. As with other categories such as rafting, there might be some rivers where just one jetboat has the concession or there may be a number of operators running different sections of the same river. It's always advisable to find out beforehand just what you can expect from the trip. In some cases operators offer more than just the thrill-a-minute aspect of the ride, and include additional attractions such as hiking into geothermal areas as well as explaining the cultural and natural history of the region. So hold on tight because this adventure sport has something for everyone!

JETBOATING — NORTH ISLAND

■ Agrojet — Rotorua

Here's your chance to power round a purpose-built watercourse similar to professional courses for 7 minutes at speeds that can reach 100kph in 4.5 seconds. There are 2 passengers per boat and a professional driver. The G-force exerted is similar to a Formula One racing car at full throttle. These 4m state-of-the-art jetboats are built for speed — so once you're strapped in with a 4-point race harness, prepare to be blown away. Yes, it is fast. No, you can't fall out. Yes, it is safe. No, you won't get wet. And NO — you can't drive one yourself!
Go to: **www.agroventures.co.nz**

■ Kaituna River — Te Puke, Bay of Plenty

Expect full speed the whole way up this tight, narrow river into an untouched native gorge. This is a 30-minute thrill ride designed to 'blow out the cobwebs'. The first section is a 12km journey up the Kaituna River — but be warned, drivers on this river have a serious need for speed. Be prepared for a fast and furious blast back downriver, with 360-degree spins always included!
Go to: **www.longridgepark.co.nz**

■ Motu River — Opotiki, Bay of Plenty

This is no ordinary jetboat ride as you travel into the last significant area of untracked native bush in the North Island. The Motu River was also the first in New Zealand to be protected by a water conservation order. While it's still fun and exciting, this tour differs from the many other jetboat joyrides in that it gives people of all ages access into some unique wilderness country which is totally remote, unaltered, and rarely viewed. The commentary concentrates on the ecological and historical values of the river, with the added taste of adventure and excitement. Go to: **www.motujet.co.nz**

■ Upper Waikato River, Awapurua Rapids — Taupo

On this section of the river above Huka Falls, Rapids Jet take you up close to the Aratiatia Power Station and to the base of the Aratiatia Rapids (jetboats are not allowed up there), New Zealand's biggest and longest rapids that spill out daily from the Aratiatia Dam. On the downriver run your jetboat will shoot through the narrowest canyon on the Waikato River. Be ready to surf in the rough stuff, the awesome Nga Awapurua Rapids, which means 'River of Springs'.
Go to: **www.rapidsjet.com**

■ Upper Waikato River, Huka Falls — Taupo

Travel to Huka Falls on a thrilling 30-minute jetboat ride. This is a half-hour of thrills, fun and excitement as you power through a beautiful river environment, lined with native bush, sheer rock cliff face and natural hot springs. For an amazing must-do opportunity they'll combine speed with 360-degree

A jetboat in the middle of a 360-degree spin.

spins, before even reaching the awe-inspiring majesty that is the falls. From the unique vantage point of the jetboat you have the best water-level view of Huka Falls, New Zealand's most visited natural attraction. Go to: **www.hukafallsjet.com**

■ Waikato River — Rotorua

The Waikato is New Zealand's longest river as it meanders 425km from the eastern slopes of Mt Ruapehu before joining the Tongariro River and emptying into Lake Taupo. It then drains Lake Taupo creating the Huka Falls before passing over the Waikato Plains and emptying into the Tasman Sea at Port Waikato. There are many outfits that use this river with a range of put-in points, so check first. One crowd that offer a twist to the jetboat adventure experience combine it with a geothermal hike and incorporate some history on the region. The first portion of your scenic trip delivers the wildlife and scenery of the mighty Waikato River including the magnificent Tutukau Gorge. You'll then get the opportunity to hike an outstanding thermal reserve, Orakei Korako, to see for yourself geysers, silica terraces and pools of boiling mud and water. The return leg is all full-speed thrills and spills with 360-degree spins. Go to: **www.riverjet.co.nz**

■ Whanganui River — Pipiriki, Whanganui

There are a few jetboat operators on the Whanganui River who specialise in taking visitors through the area's spectacular natural scenery, including a visit to the Bridge to Nowhere. Spirit of the River Jet operate on the whole river and offer a jetboat tour with canoe and kayak options in either 1 or 2-person canoes. They can also customise trips to your particular requirements — perhaps a picnic on the riverbank or stop-off in some lovely spot to boil up the billy. There's so much of the Whanganui that's only accessible by water — and jetboats and canoes are the only way to do it! Departures are from Whanganui City. Go to: **www.spiritoftheriver.co.nz**

JETBOATING — SOUTH ISLAND

■ Buller River — Westport, West Coast

Hang on as you power through the primeval subtropical forest of the Lower Buller Gorge within metres of massive rock walls and craggy overhangs, before zipping across shallow shingle riverbeds with mere centimetres of water under your boat's hull! An informative commentary outlines the historic and geological features of this fascinating river such as the hand-hewn Hawks Crag section of the Lower Buller Gorge Highway, which runs alongside the river. As you'll travel 44km, allow 75 minutes on the water. Go to: **www.adventuretours.co.nz**

Racing up the Clutha River
on a jetboat excursion.

■ Clutha River — Wanaka

Relax and enjoy the 15-minute excursion across the lake with unsurpassed mountain views before entering the mighty Clutha River. The Clutha is the second longest river in New Zealand and flows south-southeast for 338km through Central and South Otago to the Pacific. Here, your jetboat will skim across the water and shallow sandbars, powering through the rapids and giant pressure waves of New Zealand's largest-volume river. The Clutha River is known for its scenery, gold-rush era days and swift-flowing turquoise waters. Allow for a 1-hour boat ride.
Go to: **www.lakelandadventures.co.nz**

■ Dart River — Glenorchy

Taking a Dart River Jetboat Safari is perfect for those who wish to experience the exhilaration of the longest jetboat ride in the region offering 3 hours of classic action along the shifting, shallow, braided channels of this magnificent glacier-fed river. You'll discover the beauty that makes up the unforgettable Dart River Valley scenery and learn about the natural heritage of this area dating back millions of years. Your driver will also relay tales and legends of the area's cultural and pioneering legacy. The Jetboat Safari is an exciting way to explore one of the world's most unique protected areas. Allow a 6-hour round trip from Queenstown.
Go to: **www.dartriver.co.nz**

■ Kawarau River — Queenstown

Starting right at the pier in the heart of Queenstown, this trip leaves hourly and provides a memorable jetboat experience as you are transported from alpine resort town glitz into the channels of 2 of New Zealand's most scenic rivers. Your run takes you across the lake under the gaze of the mountains, down the Kawarau River, before turning up the Shotover and then the return ride back to town. The Kawarau run alone is worth the ticket — that and the fact you don't need to be shuttled anywhere by bus. Allow 3 hours. Go to: **www.kjet.co.nz** or **www.goldfieldsjet.co.nz**

■ Rakaia River — Methven, Canterbury

This is one of the largest braided rivers in New Zealand, but one of the least known. A braided river ecosystem is in constant movement, with small shingle bars appearing and disappearing, river channels shifting and water flows varying. The Rakaia River rises in the Southern Alps and travels 150km to the Pacific Ocean. For much of this jetboat journey you'll travel over wide shingle beds. Close to Mt Hutt, however, the river is briefly confined to a narrow canyon known as the Rakaia Gorge. It's the perfect mix of thrill ride and dazzling scenery. Allow 40 minutes for the full gorge trip.
Go to: **www.rivertours.co.nz**

■ Shotover River — Queenstown

World renowned as the ultimate jetboat experience, the Shotover River has been thrilling visitors for over 40 years. Once all the instruction is out of the way, you'll begin your journey at speed through the dramatic Shotover River Canyon. Your jetboat ride takes you through unique, breathtakingly narrow canyons on an adrenalin-inducing, seat-of-your-pants trip. In addition to the blasting-past-rock-walls-at-speed scary bits, there are gentle sections where you'll gain some knowledge on the folklore and history of this gold-mining region. Allow for a 30-minute ride. Go to: **www.shotoverjet.com**

Shotover River, Skippers Canyon — Queenstown

Unlike the old gold miners who once trudged this region, blast your way up the Shotover with the only jetboat to operate in Skippers Canyon. The trip itself is only half the adventure as first you have to negotiate the 4-wheel-drive Skippers Canyon Road for 45 minutes. Carved from schist rock, this trail travels through some of the best scenery in the South Island. The spine-tingling jetboat outing offers the usual 360-degree spins and hair-raising close calls with canyon walls and outcrops and will leave you with teary eyes and big smiles all around. Allow for a 30-minute ride and 3-hour round trip. Go to: **www.skipperscanyonjet.co.nz**

Waiatoto River — Haast

This river trip is New Zealand's only sea-to-mountain jetboat adventure. Unlike some of the big commercial jetboats, this trip averages about 8 people at a time, so it feels a lot more personal. You'll begin on a side channel close to the sea, travelling upstream with lots of stops for chats about the wildlife, geology and history, until you reach the Sharks Tooth — a set of serious rapids and the halfway mark. Your return to the ocean serves up all the speed, spins and obstacles that you'd expect as well as dodging stumps and fallen trees in a rainforest channel. Allow 2.5 hours.

DIRECTIONS: Take the Haast to Jacksons Bay road for 26km to the Waiatoto River Bridge departure point. Go to: **www.riversafaris.co.nz**

Waiau River — Hanmer Springs, North Canterbury

The Waiau River runs from Lake Te Anau to the sea in Te Waewae Bay. This jetboat ride takes you the entire length of Hanmer's spectacular Waiau Gorge following the contours of the steep canyon walls, rocks and cliff faces. Soak up the magnificent scenery, and then hold on tight while you experience the famous Hamilton jet spin. Narrow gorges, braided shallows, whitewater rapids — this river has it all. Allow about 35 minutes.
Go to: **www.thrillseekerscanyon.co.nz**

Waimakariri River — Springfield, Canterbury

This trip starts from Springfield, just over an hour from Christchurch, and takes you on an exciting and fascinating 36km jetboat adventure along the full length of the Waimakariri River Gorge. Although the braided riverbed changes year to year, drivers often switch off the engine at various points to allow you to climb out and go for a short walk to view historic sites that can't be seen from the boat. No roads, no tracks — just the river and the mountains. Allow for either 30 minutes or 60 minutes on the water depending on which trip you take. Go to: **www.alpinejet.co.nz** or **www.jetthrills.com**

Wairaurahiri River — Otautau Via Tuatapere, Southland

Discover New Zealand's last frontier and challenge yourself on one of the most exhilarating jetboat journeys in the land. Travel first across Lake Hauroko to the Wairaurahiri River, all 27km of Grade 3, rock-strewn whitewater rapids that drop 180m to sea level. A short walk over the Wairaurahiri swing bridge into virgin Waitutu Forest is also a must-do. The return upriver gives you time to take in the unique scenery and feel the full force of Grade 3 rapids. Allow 3 to 4 hours on the water. Total distance covered is 83km. Go to: **www.wjet.co.nz**

Wilkin River — Makarora, North of Wanaka

This trip on the Wilkin River is a 3-in-1 combo: scenic flight, 3-hour walk, and jetboat trip back. Start with a 25-minute flight over glaciers, ice, snow, mountain lakes, hanging valleys, vast rainforests and dramatic unspoiled beauty. In the Siberia Valley you begin a 3-hour walk through native beech forest and river valleys on a well-marked track linking the remote Siberia with the wilderness of the Wilkin Valley. Lastly, hop aboard for a thrilling and uniquely scenic 30-minute trip back to your starting point. Allow 4 hours. Go to: **www.wilkinriverjets.co.nz**

SAFETY AND SURVIVAL SKILLS

A 100 per cent safety record for commercial jetboat companies is not something they can guarantee — but given the tens of thousands of passengers annually that go for speed and thrill-seeking rides, there are very few accidents. Every company has to provide full safety instruction briefings and a quality range of safety equipment (including lifejacket) that satisfies a government regulatory body.

Splashdown as cavers experience blackwater rafting.

Whitewater Waves — Blackwater Rafting, Dam Drop, River Surfing and Sledging, Wave Box

BLACKWATER RAFTING

■ Dragons Blackwater Cave Rafting — Greymouth, South Island

Waitomo isn't the only place in Kiwi-land to experience a blackwater adventure — there's blackwater cave rafting to be tried in the South Island just outside of Greymouth as well. At the base, you'll be fitted out with thermal clothes to keep you warm and comfortable — wetsuit, socks and river shoes, helmet and lifejacket — before a 30-minute drive to an easy practice river where they teach you the art of river tubing. You'll then have a 15-minute walk with your tube through the rainforest to the start of the tubing.

This is a beautiful and fun section of river with some gentle rapids. You'll be linked together with other tubers to provide a stable 'snake' of tubes, but you can increase the challenge level by tubing the rapids on your own (dependent on river levels). From the cave entrance your float takes you gently into the darkness beneath a shimmering galaxy of glow-worms in the ceiling. At the end of the float section you'll finish with an optional inner-tube jump. Allow for a 5-hour round trip. Go to: **www.fun-nz.com**

■ Waitomo Caves — North Island

The Legendary Black Water Rafting Company is New Zealand's first and still one of our best blackwater adventure operators. It's also the only tour that takes you through the incomparable Ruakuri Cave. Cave tubing involves the use of an inflated rubber inner tube — the kind you would normally find in a car or truck tyre — as a flotation device to take you downriver. Each blackwater rafting expedition includes 8 to 12 people and 2 expert guides.

Black Labyrinth

On this original and amazing underground cave tubing experience you'll work your way through tight squeezes, take leaps of faith over cascading underground waterfalls, and float serenely downriver as you enjoy the glow-worm show on the vaulted limestone galleries up above. Your journey concludes when you re-emerge into sunlit Waitomo

Surfing the crest of a wave in the river.

forest. You must be 12 or over and weigh a minimum 45kg and all you'll need is swimwear and towel. Wetsuits and footwear are provided, with 12 people per tour maximum. Allow 3 hours.

Black Abyss

Descend spider-like into the black depths of Ruakuri Cave and enjoy a caving adventure tour on an expedition that combines abseiling the breathtaking tomo, climbing, tight rock squeezes, and cave tubing down the river all in one memorable journey. At every stage you'll be accompanied and supported by experienced caving guides. You must be 16 or over and weigh a minimum 45kg and all you'll need is swimwear and towel. Wetsuits and footwear are provided, with 8 people per tour maximum. Allow 5 hours. Go to: **www.waitomo.com/black-water-rafting.aspx**

DAM DROP

■ Taranaki Outdoor Adventure

It's not often you get to throw yourself over the side of a dam, but in Taranaki you can do just that. The challenge, should you choose to accept it, is to kayak a 9m dam drop. This is a one-off pure adrenalin rush! You have the option of using sit-on kayaks that are easy to use or sit-in kayaks, which require a little more nerve. After the Dam Drop there is an option of a scenic Grade 2 river trip — a great way to relax after all the excitement. You are provided with wetsuit, helmet, lifejacket and all the equipment you'll need. Go to: **www.toa.co.nz**

RIVER SURFING AND SLEDGING

■ River Surfing — Queenstown

This adventure utilises Morey and Manta body boards and 5mm full steamer wetsuits. There's no experience required to river surf as experienced guides will teach first-time surfies how to use the board and read the river, including how to surf a standing wave, run rapids and ride whirlpools. Ultimately, you are in the sledge seat and in control. Just bring your own swimwear and a towel. Go to: **www.frogz.co.nz or www.riversurfing.co.nz**

River choices

Several commercial companies now offer both whitewater surfing trips and river sledging trips. In Queenstown, there are 2 different sections of the Kawarau River to descend on — including some serious whitewater portions to get your adrenalin pumping, such as the Grade 4, 8km Chinese Dogleg and the Grade 3, 6km of whitewater on the Roaring Meg section.

■ River Sledging — Rotorua

River sledging is also offered in the North Island on the Upper Kaituna River and Lower Kaituna River near Rotorua. The lower section is known as Awesome Gorge and is a Grade 3 to 4. It's a narrow gorge surrounded by native flora and fauna, providing the peaceful surroundings of some untouched wonders of nature as only found in New Zealand. There's also river sledging on the nearby Wairoa River. Go to: **www.kaitiaki.co.nz**

Kayaking down the 9m
dam drop in Taranaki.

■ Whitewater Sledging —
Queenstown and Rotorua

This wacky activity uses purpose-built, highly
buoyant and manoeuvrable sledges more suitable
for people who are not quite so confident in the
water, as they provide additional buoyancy and
stability when compared to a body board. In other
words, a different kind of experience designed for
people who can swim and want to explore the rapids
but who may not feel confident enough to river surf.
Equipment includes wetsuit, booties, lifejacket,
helmet and fins. Go to: **www.sledgeabout.co.nz**

SAFETY AND SURVIVAL SKILLS

These trips are for fun lovers who are capable
swimmers with at least some level of fitness.
Any water activity contains certain elements
of risk. There has only been one fatal accident
in recent times but it is wise to observe all
the guides' safety instructions, follow your
experienced instructor and keep together as
a group.

WAVE BOX

■ Indoor Surfing — Albany, Auckland

Jarrod Armitage, a keen surfer and entrepreneur, is
a man who dares to dream big dreams. Accordingly,
he has created New Zealand's first artificial surfing
facility — The Wave Box — located in Albany,
Auckland. Three pools, one with 1 wave and the
other two with 3 waves each, present a series of 7
standing waves ranging in size from half a metre
to the highest at 2m, with wave faces specifically
designed for surfing on real surfboards. All are
contained in a 20 x 30sqm area. The waves are
created using large-volume water flows and are
stationary so they don't need as much area as
moving-swell waves.

The facility also houses a café, indoor climbing wall
with a self-belaying climbing system, retail store
and a surf and water safety school. The Wave Box
aims to provide customers with a total adventure
and entertainment experience in a safe environment
and at an affordable price. **www.thewavebox.co.nz**

CHAPTER 10

Round up — Adventures on Edge

PURSUITS COURSES — OUTDOOR RECREATION CENTRES

Anakiwa Outward Bound — **www.outwardbound.co.nz**
Aoraki Polytechnic — **www.aoraki.ac.nz/courses/outdoor**
Berwick Outdoor Experience, Dunedin —
   www.berwickoutdoorexperience.co.nz
Mt Hutt College Outdoor Pursuits Centre —
   www.mthuttcollege.co.nz/cms/opc.html
NZ Outdoor Instructors Association — **www.nzoia.org.nz**
Outward Bound New Zealand —
   www.outwardbound.co.nz
Peel Forest Outdoor Pursuits Centre, Geraldine —
   www.peelforestopc.org.nz
Sir Edmund Hillary Outdoor Pursuits Centre, Turangi —
   www.opc.org.nz
Tai Poutini Polytechnic, Greymouth — **www.tppweb.ac.nz**

GEOGRAPHIC LOCATOR — FIND AN ADVENTURE

NORTH ISLAND

Northland Region
- Ahipara Beach — Surfing
- Awesome NZ — Ocean Adventure Boating
- Beach Bay Hire — Sea Kayaking
- Coastal Kayakers — Sea Kayaking
- Dive NZ — Scuba Diving
- Dolphin Discoveries — Marine Encounters
- Dromgool Horsemanship — Horse Riding
- Fullers Great Sights — Marine Encounters
- Let's Go Ballooning
- Mac Attack — Ocean Adventure Boating
- Mangaraho — Climbing
- NZ Kayak Tours — Sea Kayaking
- NZ Skydive Paihia
- Parasail Paihia
- Poor Knights Divers — Scuba Diving
- Rainbow Warrior Cavalli Islands — Scuba Diving
- *Ranui* — Heritage Sailing
- Skydive Ballistic Blondes — Whangarei
- Skydive Zone — Kerikeri
- Te Arai Beach — Surfing
- Wairere Valley Quad Bike Tours

Auckland Region
- Active Sky Hang-Gliding
- AJ Hackett, Auckland Harbour Bridge — Bungy Jump
- Aqua Air Adventure — Blokarts, Hang-Gliding
- *Arcturus* — Heritage Sailing
- Auckland Adventures — Canyon, Caving, Abseiling
- Auckland Harbour Bridge Climb — Hiking
- Auckland Whale & Dolphin Safari — Marine Encounters
- Awana Beach, Great Barrier Island — Surfing
- Balloon Expedition Company
- Blown Away — Blokarts
- *Breum* — Heritage Sailing
- Canyonz — Canyon, Caving, Abseiling
- Dolphin Explorer — Marine Encounters
- Explore NZ — Americas Cup Yacht Racing
- Fergs Kayaks — Sea Kayaking
- 4 Track Adventures — Quad Biking
- Goat Island Dive — Scuba Diving
- Great Barrier Island — Mountain Biking, Scuba Diving, Sea Kayaking, Surfing
- Mercer Skydiving Centre — Skydiving
- Mission Bay Water Sports — Kayaking, Windsurfing, Kitesurfing
- Mt Eden Quarry — Climbing
- Muriwai Beach and Surf School — Blokarts, Surfing
- NZ Tours and Travel — Kayak Fishing
- Outdoor Discoveries — Sea Kayaking
- Pakiri Beach — Horse Riding
- Piha Beach — Surfing
- Piha Canyoning — Canyon, Caving, Abseiling
- Puhoi River — Freshwater Kayaking
- Raglan Beach — Surfing
- *Ranui* — Heritage Sailing
- Ross Kayaks — Sea Kayaking, Waiheke
- Sea Kayak Auckland — Kayaking
- Sky Jump — Wired Jump
- Skysailing — Gliding
- Sky Walk — Hiking
- Sky Wings — Paragliding & Paramotoring
- *Soren Larsen* — Heritage Sailing
- South Kaipara Horse Treks
- *Spirit of Adventure* — Heritage Sailing
- Wave Box — Indoor Surfing
- Windsurf Auckland — Kayaking, Windsurfing
- Wings and Waves Paragliding & Kitesurfing
- Woodhill Forest — 4-Wheel-Drive Routes, Mountain Biking

Coromandel Region
- Adrift NZ — Sea Kayaking
- Canyonz — Canyon, Caving, Abseiling
- Dive The Coromandel — Scuba Diving
- Sea Kayak Tours — Sea Kayaking
- Whangamata Bar — Surfing

Waikato Region
- Adventure Waikato — Abseiling, Caving, Flying Fox
- Balloons Over Waikato — Balloon Festival
- River Jet — Jetboating
- Skydive Waikato
- The Legendary Blackwater Rafting Company — Caving, Abseiling, Tubing
- Waitomo Combo — Abseil, Rafting, Caving, Climbing
- Wharepapa — Climbing

Rotorua Region
- Agroventures — Rotorua Bungy, Rotorua Swoop, Shweeb Biking, Agrojet, Freefall Extreme
- Kaituna River — Rafting, River Sledging
- Kjet — Parasail
- Lake Rotoiti — Freshwater Kayaking

- NZone Skydive
- Rangitaiki River — Rafting
- Rotorua Bungy
- Rotorua Swoop
- Shweeb — Biking
- Sledgeabout — Sledging
- Zorbing — In A Sphere
- Waikato River — Jetboating
- Whakarewarewa Forest — Hiking, Mountain Biking

Bay of Plenty Region
- Adventure Kayaking
- Butler's Swim With Dolphins — Marine Encounters
- Dive White Island — Scuba Diving
- Dolphin Blue — Marine Encounters
- Dolphin Down Under — Marine Encounters
- Dolphin Seafaris — Marine Encounters
- Game On Activities — Blokarts
- Kaituna River — Jetboating
- Levitate Paragliding
- Longridge Park — Obstacle Course
- Longridge Park Combo — Jetboat, Rafting, Helicopter
- Motu River — Jetboating
- Mt Maunganui — Surfing
- Ngahere Adventures — Horse Riding
- South Sea Vagabond — Marine Encounters
- Thompsons Track — 4-Wheel-Drive Route
- Wairoa River — Rafting

Lake Taupo Region
- Big Sky Parasail
- Freefall Skydive
- Huka Falls Jet — Jetboating
- Lake Taupo — Freshwater Kayaking
- Mohaka River — Rafting
- Ruahine Adventure — Horse Treks
- Rock'N Ropes — Obstacle Course
- Skydive Taupo
- Taupo Bungy
- Taupo Tandem Skydiving
- Upper Waikato River — Jetboating

Ruapehu Region
- Tongariro Alpine Crossing — Hiking
- Tongariro Forest — Mountain Biking
- Tongariro Northern Circuit — Hiking
- Tongariro River — Rafting
- Turoa Skifield — Skiing, Snowboarding
- Whakapapa Skifield — Skiing, Snowboarding

Gisborne/East Coast Region
- Eastender Horse Treks
- Gisborne — Surfing
- Kaitiaki Adventures — River Surfing, Sledging, Rafting

Hawke's Bay Region
- Airplay Paragliding School
- Dive Tatapouri — Scuba Diving
- Early Morning Balloons
- Eskdale Mountain Bike Park
- Lake Waikaremoana — Hiking
- Ngaruroro River — Rafting
- Wilderness Safaris — 4-Wheel-Drive Tours

Manawatu/Whanganui Region
- Lift Off Levin — Balloon Festival
- Mokai Gravity Canyon — Bungy Jump, Flying Fox, Swing
- Mohaka River — Freshwater Canoeing & Kayaking
- Rangitikei River — Freshwater Canoeing & Kayaking, Rafting
- Whanganui River — Freshwater Canoeing, Jetboating

Taranaki Region
- Dam Drop — Kayaking
- Taranaki Outdoor Adventures — Canyon, Caving, Abseiling

Wellington/Wairarapa Region
- Akatarawa Forest, Wellington — 4-Wheel-Drive Route
- Balloons Over Wairarapa — Balloon Festival
- Capital Adventure Tours — 4-Wheel-Drive Tours
- Early Morning Balloons
- Fergs Kayaks — Sea Kayaking
- Karapoti Forest — Mountain Biking
- Lyall Bay, Wellington — Surfing
- Makara Peak Mountain Bike Park
- Titahi Bay — Climbing

SOUTH ISLAND

Nelson/Marlborough Region
- Abel Tasman Combo — Kayaking, Boating, Biking
- Abel Tasman Coastal Track — Hiking
- Abel Tasman Kayaks — Sea Kayaking
- Adventure Paragliding & Kiteboarding
- Clarence River — Rafting
- Cumulus Paragliding
- Dolphin Watch Eco Tours — Marine Encounters
- Go Dive Marlborough — Scuba Diving
- Hang-Gliding NZ
- Live-Life Experiences — Canyon, Caving, Abseiling
- Molesworth Tour Company — 4-Wheel-Drive Tours
- Nelson Paragliding
- Queen Charlotte Track — Hiking, Mountain Biking, Kayaking
- Rainbow Ski Area Skifield — Skiing, Snowboarding
- Simply Wild Combo — Heli-Hiking, Biking, Rafting, Sailing
- Skydive Abel Tasman
- Skywire — Flying Fox
- Sounds Wild Kayaking — Sea Kayaking
- Tasman Sky Adventures — Hang-gliding, Microlighting

West Coast Region
- Adventure Tours — Rafting
- Buller Adventure Tours — Quad Bike Tours
- Buller River — Jetboating, Rafting
- Cape Farewell Horse Treks
- Dragons Cave — Blackwater Rafting
- Fox Glacier — Glacier Hiking, Ice Climbing, Skydiving
- Franz Josef Glacier Guides — Glacier Hiking
- Grey River — Rafting
- Heaphy Track — Hiking
- Hokitika River — Rafting
- Hukawai Glacier Centre — Indoor Ice Climbing
- Karamea River — Rafting

- Mokihinui River — Rafting
- Perth and Whataroa Rivers — Rafting
- River Safaris — Jetboating
- Taipo River — Rafting
- Ultimate Descents Combo — Heli-Rafting
- Whanganui River — Rafting
- Whataroa River — Rafting

Christchurch/Canterbury/ Mackenzie Region

- Adrenalin Forest — Obstacle Course
- Adventure Trail Rides — Quad Bikes
- Alpine Guides — Climbing, Heli-Skiing
- Alpine Jet — Jetboating
- Alpine Recreation — Climbing, Mountaineering
- Alpure Peaks — Snowcat-Skiing
- Akaroa Kayaks — Sea Kayaking
- Aoraki Balloon Safaris
- Avon River — Freshwater Canoeing, Kayaking
- Backtrax Quad Bike Tours
- Clarence Reserve — 4-Wheel-Drive Route
- Dive Kaikoura — Scuba Diving
- Dolphin Encounter — Marine Encounters
- 4x4 New Zealand — 4-Wheel-Drive Tours
- 4x4 Adventures — 4-Wheel-Drive Tours
- *Fox II* — Heritage Sailing
- Glacier Lake — Kayaking, Rafting
- Hassle Free Combo — Coach, Jetboating, 4-Wheel-Drive, Train
- High Country Horse Adventures
- Hurunui River — Rafting
- Hurunui Trails — Horse Riding
- Jet Thrills — Jetboating
- Kaikoura — Surfing
- Kite Sports Christchurch — Kitesurfing, Snowkiting, Board Surfing
- Lake Wakatipu — Parasail
- Mackenzie Alpine Horse Trekking
- Methven Heli-Skiing
- Mt Cook — Heli-Skiing
- Mt Dobson Skifield — Skiing, Snowboarding
- Mt Hutt Skifield — Skiing, Snowboarding
- Mt Lyford — Horse Riding, Skiing
- Nimbus Paragliding
- Ohau Skifield — Skiing, Snowboarding
- Parapro Paragliding
- Pohatu Sea Kayaking
- Porters Skifield — Skiing, Snowboarding
- Port Hills Tracks — Mountain Biking
- Rakaia River — Jetboating
- Rangitata River — Rafting
- Roundhill Skifield — Skiing, Snowboarding
- River Tours — Jetboating
- Sea Kayak Kaikoura
- Ski The Tasman — Glacier Skiing
- Skydive Kaikoura
- Southern Alps Guiding — Climbing, Heli-Skiing, Ski Mountaineering
- Swimming With Dolphins — Marine Encounters
- Thrillseekers Canyon — Bungy, Jetboating
- Timeout Tussock Tours — 4-Wheel-Drive Tours, Horse Riding
- Ultimate Challenge — Obstacle Course

- Whale Watch Kaikoura — Marine Encounters
- Waimakariri River — Jetboating
- Waiau River — Jetboating
- Wilderness Adventures — 4-Wheel-Drive Tours

Lake Wanaka Region

- Aspiring Guides — Climbing, Mountaineering, Ski Touring
- Cardrona Adventure Park — 4-Wheel Driving, Quad Biking
- Cardrona Alpine Resort Skifield — Skiing, Snowboarding
- Clutha, Hawea, Makarora and Matukituki Rivers — Kayaking
- Clutha River — Jetboating
- Deep Canyon — Canyon, Caving, Abseiling
- Hidden River Canyons — Canyon, Caving, Abseiling
- Landsborough River — Rafting
- Nevis Snowmobile Adventure
- Skydive Lake Wanaka
- Snow Park Skifield — Snowboarding
- The Contact Epic — Mountain Biking
- Treble Cone Skifield — Skiing, Snowboarding
- Waiatoto River — Rafting
- Waiorau Snow Farm — Cross-Country Skiing, Dog Sledding
- Wanaka Paragliding
- Wanaka Rock Climbing
- Wilkin River — Jetboating, Hiking, Helicopter Combo

Queenstown Region

- AJ Hackett Bungy, Kawarau Bridge Bungy, Nevis Arc, Nevis Bungy, The Ledge Bungy
- Arrowtown to Macetown — 4-Wheel-Drive Route
- Bob's Peak — Paragliding
- Climbing Queenstown — Rock Climbing
- Coronet Peak Skifield — Skiing, Snowboarding
- Coronet Peak Tandem Paragliding & Hang-gliding
- Dart River — Canoeing, Jetboating
- Extreme Air Hang-Gliding & Paragliding
- Frogz — Water Sledging
- Goldfields Jet — Jetboating
- Harris Mountain Heli-Skiing
- Heli-Ski with Heli-Guides
- Kawarau River — Jetboating, Rafting, River Sledging, River Surfing
- Lake Wakatipu — Kayaking, Parasailing
- Nomad Safaris — 4-Wheel-Drive Tours
- Nzone Skydive
- Pure Glenorchy Overland Tours — 4-Wheel-Drive
- Queenstown Combo — Bungy, 4-Wheel-Drive, Jetboating, Rafting
- Remarkables Skifield — Skiing, Snowboarding
- Routeburn Canyoning — Canyon, Caving, Abseiling
- Shotover Canyon Swing
- Shotover River — Jetboating, Rafting
- Shotover River, Skipper's Canyon — Jetboating
- Skiing Combo — 4 Skifields in One Day
- Skipper's Canyon — 4-Wheel-Drive Route
- Sky Trek — Hang-gliding
- Southern Lakes Heli-Ski
- Sunrise Balloons
- The Rung Way, Via Ferrata — Climbing

Quad biking in Woodhill Forest, Auckland.

- 12 Mile Canyoning — Canyon, Caving, Abseiling
- Wilderness Heli-Ski
- Ziptrek — Flying Fox

Fiordland Region
- Dusky Track — Hiking
- Fiordland Sea Kayaing
- Greenstone-Caples Track — Hiking
- Hollyford Track — Hiking
- Kepler Track — Hiking
- Lake Mavora — 4-Wheel-Drive Route
- Lake Te Anau and Lake Manapouri — Freshwater Kayaking
- Milford Track — Hiking
- Routeburn Track — Hiking
- Tawaki Dive — Scuba Diving
- Wairaurahiri Jet — Jetboating
- Wilderness Safaris — 4-Wheel-Drive Tours

Otago Region
- Maniototo 4WD Safaris
- Nasbey Forest — Mountain Biking
- Nasbey Ice Luge
- Otago Rail Trail — Biking
- Red-Cat — Scenic Biplane
- St Clair Beach, Dunedin — Surfing
- Southern Soaring — Gliding
- Taieri River — Rafting
- Wild Earth — Kayaking

Southland Region
- Porpoise Bay, Catlins — Surfing
- Invercargill Land Sailing — Blokarts
- Rakiura — Kayaking
- Rakiura Track — Hiking
- Tawaki Dive Stewart Island — Scuba Diving
- Wairaurahiri River — Canoeing, Jetboating

DESTINATION BUREAU WEBSITES
Alpine Pacific Tourism — **www.alpinepacifictourism.co.nz**
Central South Island Tourism — **www.southisland.co.nz**
Christchurch and Canterbury Tourism —
      www.christchurchnz.com
Destination Fiordland — **www.fiordland.org.nz**
Destination Lake Taupo — **www.laketauponz.com**
Destination Manawatu — **www.manawatunz.co.nz**
Destination Marlborough —
      www.destinationmarlborough.com
Destination Northland — **www.northlandnz.com**
Destination Queenstown — **www.queenstown-nz.co.nz**
Destination Wairarapa — **www.wairarapanz.com**
Go Wanganui — **www.wanganui.com**
Hawke's Bay Tourism — **www.hawkesbaynz.com**
Lake Wanaka Tourism — **www.lakewanaka.co.nz**
Mackenzie Tourism — **www.mtcooknz.com**
Nature Coast — **www.naturecoast.co.nz**
Nelson/Tasman Tourism — **www.nelsonnz.com**
New Zealand Tourism — **www.newzealand.com**
Positively Wellington Tourism — **www.wellingtonnz.com**
Stewart Island Promotion Association —
      www.stewartisland.co.nz
Tourism Auckland — **www.aucklandnz.com**
Tourism Bay of Plenty — **www.bayofplenty.co.nz**
Tourism Central Otago — **www.centralotagonz.com**
Tourism Coromandel — **www.thecoromandel.com**
Tourism Dunedin — **www.dunedinnz.com**
Tourism Eastland — **www.gisbornenz.com**
Tourism Waikato — **www.waikatonz.co.nz**
Tourism Waitaki — **www.tourismwaitaki.co.nz**
Destination Rotorua Tourism Marketing —
      www.rotoruanz.com
Tourism West Coast — **www.west-coast.co.nz**
Venture Southland — **www.southlandnz.com**
Venture Taranaki — **www.taranakinz.org**
Visit Ruapehu — **www.visitruapehu.com**

Admiring the view,
Tongariro Crossing.

PICTURE CREDITS

The photography featured in this book is used with the permission of the companies and copyright holders listed below:

Abel Tasman Kayaks, page 139
Agroventures, Rotorua, page 22, 27, 48, 70
AJ Hackett Bungy, pages 19, 20, 21, 24, 25, 29 (twice)
Aqua Air Adventures, page 49
Auckland Bridge Climb, page 95
AWOL Adventures, page 84, 85
Andrew Balme, page 112
Blown Away, Takanini, Auckland, page 68
Shane Boocock, pages 4, 13, 77, 137, 144, 163
Ben Bruno, page 113
Buller River Adventures, page 158
Calluman, page 12
Cardrona Alpine Resort, page 102
CAT Tours, page 54
Chris McLennan, page 10, 60, 99
Christchurch & Canterbury Tourism, page 120, 156
Climbing Queenstown, page 92
Clutha River Jet, Wanaka, page 166
Contract Epic, page 50, 66
Coronet Peak, page 105
Coronet Peak Tandems, page 43, 45
Deep Canyon, Wanaka, page 86
Destination Marlborough, page 65, 80
Destination Rotorua, page 134 (bottom)
Destination Queenstown, page 30 (bottom), 47, 119
Destination Wairarapa, page 61
Dive Kaikoura, page 129

Dive Tutukaka, page 128
Explore NZ, page 123, 124, 131, 132
4-Track Adventures, Auckland, page 174
Fox Glacier Guiding, page 111
Freefall Skydive, Taupo, page 33 (bottom)
Mike Gardiner, page 143
Games On Activities, Tauranga, page 69
Happy Valley Adventures, page 115
Harris Mountain Heli-ski, page 107
Hawkes Bay Tourism, page 117
Andy Heap, page 40, 41
Miles Holden, page 97, 101
Kawarau Jet, Lake Rotorua, page 162
Lake Wanaka Tourism, page 94, 150, 154
Jeep 4WD Adventure Park, page 52
Mackenzie Alpine Horse Trekking, page 116
Bryce Martin (www.rockclimb.co.nz), page 91
Mokai Gravity Canyon, page 26
Nevis Snowmobile Adventure, page 110
Nimbus Paragliding, page 46
Nomad Safaris, page 57
NZone, page 32, 33 (top), 34
NZ River Jet, Wanganui River, page 165
O'Brian Watersports, page 151
Ohau Skifield, page 104
Over the Top Helicopters, page 109
Planet Bike MTB, Rotorua, page 62
Raftabout & Sledgeabout, Rotorua, page 152
Rangitata Rafts, Canterbury , page 160
Rippled Earth Kayaking, page 153
River Rats Kaituna, back cover
Roundhill Skifield, page 103
Serious Fun, River Surfing, page 168
Shotover Jet, Queenstown, page 17
Ski Marketing Network, page 106

Skippers Canyon Jet, page 53
Skydive Kaikoura, page 35
Skydive Lake Wanaka, front cover
Skydive Wanaka, page 36
Skyjump, page 28
Skywalk, page 96
Skywire, page 30 (top)
Karl Soulos. page 121
Southern Alps Guiding, page 108
Sunrise Balloons, page 38, 39
Taranaki Outdoor Adventures, page 169 (twice)
Taupo Bungy, page 16, 23
Terry Wong, page 6, 125
TIME Unlimited Tours, page 135
Tourism Bay of Plenty, page 14, 141, 146
Tourism Central Otago, page 11
Tourism Coromandel, page 136
Tourism Dunedin, page 147
Ultimate Descents, page 18
Up, Up and Away Balloons, page 9
Venture Southland, page 67, 72
Waitomo Adventures, page 71, 88, 89, 167
Wet'n'Wild Rafting, Rotorua, page 157
Walking Legends, page 79
Whale Watch Kaikoura, page 134 (top)
Wings and Waves, page 44, 142
www.cycle-photos.com, page 63
www.nelsonnz.com, page 76
www.mtruapehu.com, page 176

Feedback is always welcome. If you have experienced sensational
trips in New Zealand that are not included in this book,
please feel free to email the author at:
explorersretreat@ihug.co.nz.

First published in 2010 by New Holland Publishers (NZ) Ltd
Auckland • Sydney • London • Cape Town

www.newhollandpublishers.co.nz

218 Lake Road, Northcote, Auckland 0627, New Zealand
Unit 1, 66 Gibbes Street, Chatswood, NSW 2067, Australia
86–88 Edgware Road, London W2 2EA, United Kingdom
80 McKenzie Street, Cape Town 8001, South Africa

Copyright © 2010 in text: Shane Boocock
Copyright © 2010 in photography: As individually credited
on page 175
Copyright © 2010 New Holland Publishers (NZ) Ltd
Shane Boocock has asserted his right to be identified as the
author of this work.

Publishing manager: Christine Thomson
Editor: Mike Wagg
Design: Nick Turzynski, redinc., Auckland

Front cover photo: Tandem skydiving over Lake Wanaka.
Back cover photo: Over the edge, on the Kaituna River in the
   Bay of Plenty.

10 9 8 7 6 5 4 3 2 1

Colour reproduction by Pica Digital Pte Ltd, Singapore.
Printed in China at Everbest Printing Co, on paper sourced from
sustainable forests.

National Library of New Zealand Cataloguing-in-Publication Data

Boocock, Shane.
The New Zealand adventure guide / Shane Boocock.
Includes index.
ISBN 978-1-86966-277-6
1. Outdoor recreation—New Zealand—Guidebooks.
2. Extreme sports—New Zealand—Guidebooks.
3. New Zealand—Guidebooks. I. Title.
796.0993—dc 22

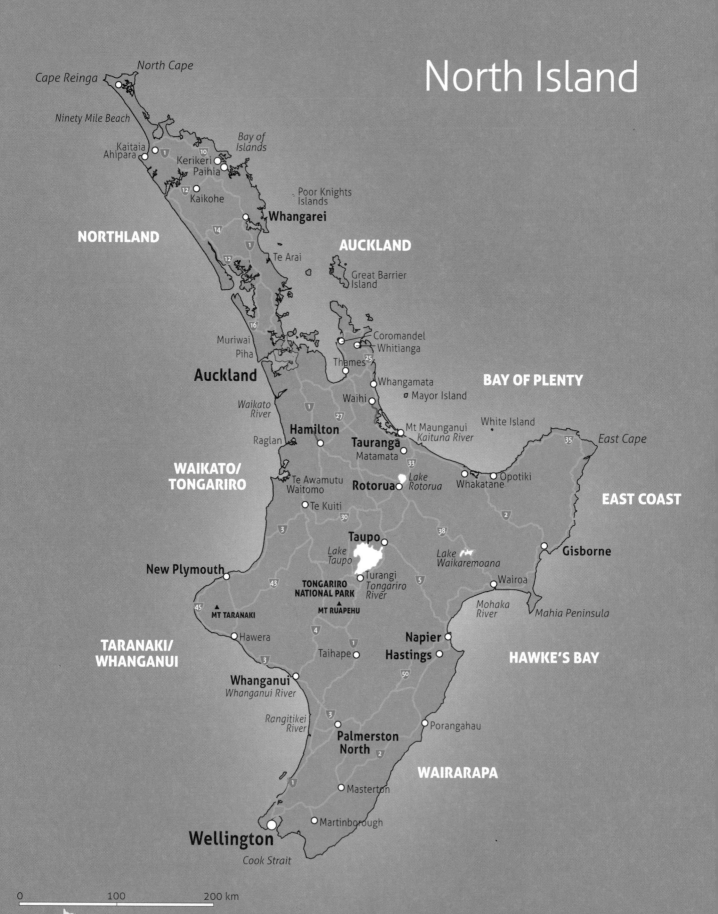